ALIGNING YOUR **CURRICULUM** TO THE **COMMON CORE** STATE STANDARDS

Dedicated to my mom, Genevieve Crawford,
who helped me become the person I am and made
sure I did what I needed to do, by hook or by crook.
I love you and miss you.

ALIGNING YOUR **CURRICULUM** TO THE **COMMON CORE** STATE STANDARDS

JOE CRAWFORD

FOREWORD BY KAREN YOUNG

CORWIN
A SAGE Company

FOR INFORMATION:

Corwin
A SAGE Company
2455 Teller Road
Thousand Oaks, California 91320
(800) 233-9936
Fax: (800) 417-2466
www.corwin.com

SAGE Ltd.
1 Oliver's Yard
55 City Road
London EC1Y 1SP
United Kingdom

SAGE India Pvt. Ltd.
B 1/I 1 Mohan Cooperative
Industrial Area
Mathura Road, New Delhi 110 044
India

SAGE Asia-Pacific Pte. Ltd.
33 Pekin Street #02-01
Far East Square
Singapore 048763

Acquisitions Editor: Arnis Burvikovs
Associate Editor: Desirée Bartlett
Editorial Assistant: Kimberly Greenberg
Project Editor: Veronica Stapleton
Copy Editor: Dan Gordon
Typesetter: C&M Digitals (P) Ltd.
Proofreader: Dennis W. Webb
Indexer: Kathleen Paparchontis
Cover Designer: Scott Van Atta
Permissions Editor: Karen Ehrmann

Printed in the United States of America

A catalog record of this book is available from the Library of Congress.

This book is printed on acid-free paper.

11 12 13 14 15 10 9 8 7 6 5 4 3 2 1

Contents

See Joe Crawford's website **(www.partners4results.org/demo)** for more information and resources.

Foreword

I have had the privilege of designing the speaker lineup for and hosting more than 200 national conferences. I select the books we feature at those conferences and read many of them. Committed educators in schools and districts look to us to help guide them to consultants and publications that can help them reach their goals, and some of my most delightful moments happen when we discover talented people who can positively impact teaching and learning. Over 10 years ago, I saw Joe Crawford in action for the first time, and it was a delightful moment.

Like you, I have heard speakers who changed my perspective in meaningful ways, and I have endured sessions that felt like someone had dropped the clock into cold molasses as time and my skin simultaneously began crawling. I have interacted with Joe in many contexts: as a listener, a participant, a colleague, and a reader. The time has always passed quickly. His spoken and written words help me improve my work. In my own library, I have a treasured set of books I call the Skin Horse collection. In *The Velveteen Rabbit,* the Skin Horse had most of his hair loved off and he was loose in the joints and a bit shabby because a child had loved him for a long, long time. That's what a valuable resource book looks like over time; it becomes real. My Skin Horse books have wrinkled bindings, dog-eared pages, notes in the margins, highlighted passages, and coffee stains. But as the Skin Horse said, "These things don't matter at all, because once you are Real you can't be ugly except to people who don't understand." Long before I finished the last page of this book, I knew I was placing it in my Skin Horse collection. This book helps me see the process for effective implementation of the Common Core State Standards more clearly, and I will use it many times.

Joe is excellent at designing road maps that make the complex and overwhelming understandable and accessible. In this process manual, he outlines a step-by-step guide that will truly empower local educators to engage in the work ahead with implementation of the Common Core State Standards. It takes a lot of experience to know what to do and what not to do when tackling a massive task. Joe's 36 years of doing this work well and guiding others to do this work well comes through on every page. This book is an essential read for all local teams who strive to turn the Common Core State Standards into a *learnable* curriculum.

Joe is a generous man. He has given educators a remarkable gift: a useful set of tools they can use to create the curriculum and instruction support our learners need on their journey to career and college readiness. Use this as a guide. Joe's writing will give you many delightful moments.

Karen Young
Founder and president of A+ Educators
Founder, former president of Learning 24/7

Preface

What Is the Purpose of This Book? The purpose of this book is to give the reader a better understanding of the issues revolving around implementing the Common Core State Standards (CCSS), to offer the possibility of using the CCSS as the basis for a new national curriculum model, and to provide a step-by-step process to develop, refine, and use that curriculum model at the local level to improve student performance.

The Common Core State Standards (CCSS) are here! Whether you receive that news with gratitude or trepidation, the reality is that public education must find a way to implement them. So the question becomes, now what do we *do* with them? While many have clamored for some kind of national document that outlines learning expectations for all students, whether those students live in New York City, Arkansas, Illinois, Alaska, or wherever, many have been equally vociferous in opposing any kind of national standards or curriculum that will deprive local educators and local education units of the academic freedom to decide what their students will learn in the local public school experience. All that being said, we now have those national standards to be applied in almost all of our states. The majority of states have adopted these CCSS and further adoptions are sure to be completed in the near future. Therefore now is the time to plan at the national level for implementing these CCSS. Educators need a chance to begin the conversation and the planning needed to do that implementation work.

As I pondered this national-scale endeavor, I could not help but remember an incident in my life that has driven me ever since it happened. Please bear with me for a moment as I retell that story. I have always been fascinated with and in love with water. I finally bought a home on a small inland lake and soon found a small, used Butterfly sailboat. Having never sailed, but having looked through books on the subject and talked to several amateur sailors, I was really eager but afraid to try it. My best friend, Bill, told me he knew how to sail and would be glad to teach me. He came over, we rigged the boat, and off we went. After capsizing the boat several times and struggling to get it back on course, we figured it out and had a great day sailing around the lake, tacking, coming about, and so on.

As we packed away the sail for the night, I asked Bill where and when he had learned to sail. He said that day was his first day sailing, but he knew we could figure it out together. The lesson has never left me; educators cannot study and get into "analysis paralysis" and study these new CCSS to death. Experience has taught public educators a great deal about standards-based learning, so let's just go do it. That is exactly what this book will help the reader know how to do—implement the CCSS.

As a first step to implementing these CCSS, education should look to previously successful standards work. The research and practice of taking large, complex curriculum expectations and "refining" those expectations into teachable, learnable amounts by building Power Standards is crystal clear. Doug Reeves, Larry Ainsworth, and others have shown educators how to build these realistic, learnable documents, and research has shown this approach improves student performance. It is the purpose of this book to apply that successful model of identifying those most critical skills in the new Common Core State Standards (CCSS) to build more learnable curriculum expectations in the form of local CCSS.

This book outlines the process and the issues involved in doing that work. We will use those proven strategies developed and used in the past to address state standards and apply those successful strategies to the CCSS, modify those strategies as needed, and learn to do the implementation work better. Educators must be like the students in a standards-based model—learn it, try it, get feedback, try it again. We will learn from this action research, and we can learn from each other, if we are willing to listen and learn. We can do this; come on, let's go sailing!

While this book is not intended to be a discussion of the rightness or wrongness, good or evil, or quality of those national standards, I do believe the CCSS are a great natural next step to improving student performance. Education must define the standards that students are expected to master, and then do the design and implementation work to operationalize those standards. While not everybody agrees with the national standards or national curriculum model idea, it is important to explore these issues and seek common ground. What will we *do* with the CCSS? What issues do the CCSS create? What issues do they address? What's a local district to do in order to move forward with those CCSS?

It is important to understand some of the realities of the CCSS as we work to implement them. The first and perhaps most important thing to realize is that the CCSS have been or will be adopted by all 50 states, sooner or later, in some form or format. The form and format of those CCSS may be somewhat changed or tweaked as they move through the process of adoption and implementation in all 50 states, but I believe we have to move forward on the assumption that these CCSS are here to stay and will be a major driver in public education for years to come.

While the CCSS have been or will be adopted by all 50 states sooner or later, the assessment system to measure student mastery of those standards has not been developed but will, hopefully, be in effect in 2014. We still have to move forward on this huge task for designing curriculum and instruction to address these new national core standards. The assessments will be here in 2014, and those assessments will require some changes and adjustments to curriculum materials, and so on, but we will address those improvement issues when they present themselves. While states have the option to adopt or not adopt these CCSS, the reality is a national assessment system based on these CCSS will be in effect in 2014, and we simply must prepare for that assessment system. That is, perhaps, the most compelling reason to begin this work now.

What is the logic of the chapters in this book? This book will take the instructional leader through a logical sequence of tasks that need to be completed in order to successfully build local curriculum documents that reflect the CCSS and serve as documents to define curriculum expectations. Instructional leaders need to understand the national standards before they can implement them. In order to implement the national standards, instructional leaders will need to define and create local CCSS aligned with the CCSS that make the material to be covered more organized and manageable. In order to successfully teach the skills outlined in the local CCSS, instructional leaders will need to develop and implement common formative assessments that will offer teachers feedback as to what students have mastered and how to modify their instruction to improve learning.

What makes this book unique? First and foremost, these CCSS are such a new issue that very little research or past practice in implementing these CCSS exists. This book will take what education has learned from previous successful curriculum and assessment initiatives and apply that learning and experience to the CCSS. The book will take the reader through a discussion with specific steps for what local leaders can and should do to implement this latest innovation in education in order to best improve student learning and performance.

This book will give the reader

1. a plan for using the CCSS as the basis for design of local curriculum documents that clearly define the skill to be learned, and when that skill will be learned;
2. a better understanding of the issues revolving around implementing the CCSS;
3. the possibility of using the CCSS as the basis for a new national curriculum model; and
4. a step-by-step process to develop, refine, and use that new curriculum model at the local level to improve student performance.

In order to outline this work for the reader, I will rely on the work and research of the great masters, Larry Lezotte, Doug Reeves, Larry Ainsworth, Mike Schmoker, Rick Stiggins, and others. I will then combine my experience in actually doing the work of aligning curriculum to these CCSS at the local level with my own 36 years in public education and 10 years of national consulting experience to give the reader a step-by-step guide to doing this work. This book is designed as a process manual to help the reader go from Point A (CCSS) to Point B (Power Standards and instructional objectives) as the basis for a new national curriculum model. This is a "brave new world" for educators, but education has learned much on the journey to standards-based learning, and this book will help the reader apply those previous lessons to our new task, implementing the CCSS.

We will also revisit the need for the creation of a curriculum and assessment *system* that defines what is to be learned and when it is to be learned and how it is to be assessed so that systems thinking can be applied to that system. Remember, you cannot apply systems thinking if you don't have a system in place.

That is the purpose of this book—to help all educators think about and effectively implement the new CCSS. I believe that will require a new national curriculum model that helps provide learning for all while taking advantage of the culture, technology, and norms present in this new learning environment. Schools cannot continue to do what they have always done and expect a different result.

Beginning the conversation. Also, in this new environment driven by national standards, it is imperative to realize that the teachers and administrators of this national education system, as a national learning community, have much to learn and share with each other. Public education must work together to apply this implementation model, learn from each other's experiences and issues, and then share with and learn from each other—not shout others down.

That message of cooperation and sharing with each other is one of the most important messages of this book. Let's learn together and work together to create a new national model that responds to the needs of our students and to our own needs as professional educators. We all became educators because of our love of and commitment to the students, so let's work together to improve what we do. The new model presented in this book is intended to be a starting place to begin the conversation and to allow all of us to exchange ideas and learn from each other.

How can you use this book? This book is designed as a step-by-step process manual with explanations of those specific steps as the book goes through them. Readers should first review the overall process advocated in this book and then make judgments on the political, financial, and leadership issues present in their own districts. Do all the steps advocated apply directly to the reader's situation? Is the reader's knowledge of and experience with a particular phase of the process such that the particular step can be omitted or amended? All of these questions and others can be answered by readers as they work through this process.

This book is all about a process and addressing the issues that come up during that implementation process. Like most processes, it can be done with a variety of tools and methods, and this author will share with you both the approach (the process) and tools I use and have used. To help make sure the reader is able to fully participate in both the process and the tools that I have used, a demonstration website has been set up at https://www.partners4results.org/demo. The reader may go to that website and do all of the work that I describe in this book.

A sample K–12 curriculum based on the CCSS in the format discussed in this book is also on the Website and may be used by the reader as an example of this new curriculum model. This website is interactive and allows for visitors to post comments, share observations, and so on. It is my hope that this will be a place where educators can participate at no charge in a real-time, meaningful conversation about and around the CCSS and a new national curriculum model.

Some terms should be clarified:

- **Power Standards** refers to those curriculum expectations developed by Larry Ainsworth and Doug Reeves that identify the most critical, most important learnings that all students must know and be able to do—a kind of "safety net" curriculum explained in more detail later in this book.
- **Local CCSS** represent the application of those principles contained in Power Standards directly to the CCSS, thus creating local curriculum expectations aligned to and derived from the CCSS.
- **The new curriculum model** proposed in this book applies the focus of the Power Standards concept and applies it to the CCSS, defining both what standard is to be learned and when that standard is to be learned. This curriculum model is more appropriately called local CCSS rather than Power Standards because while the local CCSS are built on the work and research of Doug Reeves and Larry Ainsworth, these new local CCSS are a different entity with a different focus and slightly different developmental process.
- **Standards-based curriculum** refers to the curriculum defining the standard to be mastered rather than the content to be used.

Go through the book, examine the processes and suggested approaches, and implement those processes within your own situation. Share what you are learning and doing, both locally and through the website above. This book begins the conversation, and the reader should feel welcome to participate in this reform initiative and conversation.

In order to ensure that I am a good consumer of my own product, please feel free to contact me with any issues, concerns, or problems you may have along the way. This book really is about creating a discussion among educators about ways to improve services to students and to implement the CCSS. Feel free to share your thoughts, ideas, need for clarification, and so on with me at joe@partners4results.org. I will respond as I am able. Feel free to leave your phone number, and I will call you. Come on, let's go sailing together!

Acknowledgments

First and foremost, it is essential to acknowledge the work and dedication of the school districts and their staffs who have actually done much of the curriculum work in this book. These districts used the processes outlined in this book to develop their own local CCSS and instructional objectives and are willing to share their work with the reader to help move us forward in this very important work. My special thanks go out to these Illinois school districts:

- Bradford Community Unit School District 1
- Bureau Valley School District 340
- Community Consolidated School District 168
- Country Club Hills School District 160
- Mundelein High School District 120
- Geneseo School District 228
- Sandwich Community Unit School District 430
- Wethersfield Community Unit School District 230

I share their work here with their permission and really appreciate both their work and their willingness to share. Thank you.

In looking at any work on curriculum alignment and systemic reform, the work and inspiration of Larry Lezotte, Doug Reeves, Mike Schmoker, and Rick Stiggins has to be acknowledged. They are the pioneers, the keepers of the vision, and the giants on whose shoulders I try to stand.

Special thanks to the editor, Arnis Burvikovs, for his support and hard work in getting my best work out of me. And thanks to the entire Corwin team—they are awesome.

Thanks to the team of people at partners4results who work tirelessly and creatively to bring my curriculum and assessment ideas to life on the Internet and in the districts we are partnering with in this exciting journey.

Thanks again to Dr. Jody Ware, who continues to expand my horizons and keep me on my toes to keep this entire process usable, accurate, and doable. Her leadership is exceptional, and her friendship is invaluable.

Thanks to Karen Young, who continues to inspire and encourage me in this journey. She is much more than a CEO of a staff development company; she is a true leader trying to improve teaching and learning in America. She is awesome.

About the Author

Joe Crawford spent 36 years in public education at the high school, junior high, middle school, and district level as an English teacher, assistant principal, principal, and assistant superintendent focusing on improving student performance. He has been recognized by the Illinois State Board of Education in the Those Who Excel program and by the Carnegie Foundation with a National Systemic Change Award. Additionally, he was principal of a twice-recognized National Blue Ribbon School of Excellence and met two presidents as part of that recognition. He was also chosen by the Illinois State Board of Education and the Milken Family Foundation as a National Distinguished Educator. He has also been active in Total Quality Management and continuous improvement, and his work reflects the tenets of these industry-standard approaches to improvement. While he was doing this work, his district received a Silver Award from the Baldrige Foundation.

Following the work of Larry Lezotte, Doug Reeves, Mike Schmoker, and others, Crawford works with local districts to apply this invaluable work and research in the real world of public schools and kids—making the transition from research to reality possible and even pleasant. He works with teachers and districts to build capacity and to create a common sense of mission through shared ownership of solutions. By involving those who will implement decisions in the actual decision-making process, he helps create a sense of buy-in and a much deeper understanding of state standards and the improvement process, leading to sustainable, long-term improvement in student performance. He is the author of *Using Power Standards to Build an Aligned Curriculum: A Process Manual,* and numerous articles.

partners4results Software Availability

In doing work as complex and demanding as this, it is almost impossible to do so without using electronic technology to store, score, analyze, and warehouse all this information. There are several software packages out there that readers may be using and/or considering to do this work. It was very difficult to write this book without referencing the software that is being used to specifically address this process, and I did the best I could; however, it is, in my judgment, imperative to share this software and its capabilities with the reader so the reader may better understand the power and potential of this process.

Throughout this book, in the discussion of the processes and forms, there is reference to the partners4results software package that can be used to do this work. To ensure a level playing field and to better demonstrate these processes, the reader is encouraged to go to www.partners4results.org/demo. When prompted, please complete the sign-in process. Once you sign in, you will be able to navigate the website and actually see and do the work described in this book.

This website has video to show you how to navigate the site appropriately. This will give you firsthand experience in using this software and the Internet to construct local CCSS and instructional objectives and the electronic format for doing so. You will also be able to see the curriculum-mapping component, the publishing capabilities, and the assessment alignment capabilities of the software, giving you firsthand experience with the software discussed in the book. There are also help icons and e-mail capabilities available on this site to answer questions.

I hope this helps you better understand this work and this process without being blatantly commercial about it, but I could think of no other way to share this with the reader. I just read Patrick Lencioni's *Getting Naked,* and he had these same concerns with his work and his company. He turned his book into a fable and "changed the names to protect the innocent," but my writing skills precluded that approach; I hope my more direct approach offends nobody.

1 Overview of CCSS and Associated Leadership Issues

CHAPTER EXPECTATIONS

This chapter is a discussion of what standards are, the new Common Core State Standards (CCSS), and the issues present in those documents and their implementation. There is also be a brief outline of the process of creating local CCSS (Power Standards) and instructional objectives with sample local CCSS and instructional objectives and how CCSS are a real game changer in that development process. The chapter will close with a discussion of system thinking as it applies to curriculum, instruction, and assessments.

ACTION STEPS

Steps to consider and address in doing this phase of the work:

- Leadership Challenges in Implementing CCSS
  - Make sure everyone understands a standards-based curriculum.
  - Establish a belief in and sense of urgency around the new CCSS.
  - Understand the staff development issues involved.
  - Build local consensus.

   - Familiarize yourself with standards, curriculum alignment, and content alignment issues.
   - Break down professional learning into manageable chunks.
   - Align assessments to the CCSS.
- What Are Standards?
   - Develop and use a standards-based curriculum.
   - Align the curriculum.
   - Think of content as a means to a performance end.
- Staff Development Issues
   - As a leader, design, implement, and monitor the process of standards implementation to ensure a common interpretation and implementation.
   - Ensure that all teachers follow a district model to implement and use the academic standards in instruction and assessments.
   - As a district leader, ensure that appropriate staff development is provided.
   - Build understanding of the CCSS.
   - Develop local understanding that a standards-based approach to education is the core issue that must be addressed and then adjust that standards-based approach to the CCSS.
- Defining and Creating Local CCSS
   - Understand local CCSS (Power Standards).
   - Use what has already been developed as a basis for moving forward.
   - Determine how to develop quarterly instructional objectives based on the local CCSS to ensure scaffolding.
   - Ensure that all teachers of a given subject teach and assess the same skills at approximately the same time during the academic year.
- Systems Thinking
   - Define a curriculum, instruction, and assessment system.
   - Determine learning expectations, clearly define those learning expectations, and assign specific learning expectations to grade levels, courses, and academic terms.
   - Develop a system of common, formative assessments based on those intended learnings to be given during the year to measure progress toward the end-of-year expectations.
   - Use an assessment system, share those results, and hold discussions to identify the reasons for variance in student performance and share instructional strategies to improve.
   - Monitor the process to see if the teachers are following the curriculum expectations and ensuring that they are doing so.

LEADERSHIP CHALLENGES IN IMPLEMENTING CCSS

For any initiative as massive and complex as the new CCSS, the challenges for leadership are significant and worthy of consideration. As I have done this curriculum alignment work over the years and just recently begun to really focus this alignment work on the new CCSS, I've noticed several areas that particularly impact leadership and must be addressed by leadership. This process manual will help the reader do that work, but I thought it best to briefly list those challenges with a quick explanation of them in this chapter, whereas more complete discussions will be held throughout the book.

Following are the major leadership challenges associated with this effort:

Make sure everyone understands a standards-based curriculum. While standards have been around for years, not all districts have spent the time and resources to ensure that the teachers really understand standards and faithfully implement a standards-based instruction cycle. This has to be addressed locally and is discussed below.

Establish a belief in and sense of urgency around the new CCSS. Many educators have been through so many initiatives—state, federal, and local—over the years that they have adopted a somewhat jaded "this too shall pass" attitude toward almost any new initiative. We will deal with this throughout the book and in the actual development and implementation of the work processes this book proposes.

Understand the staff development issues involved. Staff development issues in this implementation process are huge. Not only does leadership have to ensure that all in the professional learning community understand and accept the CCSS but that their understanding must span and be articulated among and within grade levels as all the educators strive to implement the CCSS in the same manner at the appropriate level. This issue will be addressed specifically in the design of the work process.

Build local consensus. Building local consensus on the exact meaning of the academic expectations outlined in the CCSS is critical to doing this work. I just spent three days doing this work in a district. Here are some of the questions I heard while I was walking among the teachers doing the work: What does this mean? How will they measure that? How can we get all of this done? What will happen if we identify the wrong CCSS to emphasize? Again, the actual work process itself will address these issues, and these issues will be specifically addressed through the process itself.

Familiarize yourself with standards, curriculum alignment, and content alignment issues. Some of the new CCSS set learning expectations that are not aligned with current state assessment systems. For example, while probability does not really enter the CCSS until sixth grade, some state assessments put great emphasis on that skill in third grade. What should teachers do in the design of curriculum expectations? This is a particularly thorny issue and will be discussed in the appropriate sections of this book, but this is really a local decision. I do, however, encourage teachers to address those skills they know are on the state assessments.

Break down professional learning into manageable chunks. The sheer amount of and complexity of the CCSS is intimidating to many teachers, learning all of those expectations in all of the grade levels is seen as impossible, and many teachers seem unwilling to expend that much effort on an almost undoable task. The professional learning has to be broken down into more manageable amounts. I believe the work advocated and the forms proposed in this book will help address this issue.

Align assessments to the CCSS. Since the CCSS have already been released, what about the assessment system? Will we ask people to do the curriculum alignment work with no knowledge of the assessment system? Many teachers feel they have been "bitten" by unfair, unaligned assessment systems in the past, and they have serious reservations about doing the curriculum alignment work when the assessment system is yet to be developed. This issue is really one where leadership must work with staff to build credibility and confidence and show them the only alternative we really have; move ahead with the curriculum alignment work and then adjust when and if the assessment system is deployed. We simply cannot wait until the assessment system is deployed to begin this work. Leadership must convince the staff that the national assessment is to be in use by 2014, and we cannot wait to see that assessment before doing this critical work.

This is, of course, not an exhaustive list of leadership issues, but it does show the major leadership issues that will need to be addressed. This book will address these at the appropriate time.

WHAT ARE STANDARDS?

Develop and Use a Standards-based Curriculum

The CCSS are here and are in the process of being adopted by all or most of the states. With the local and national politics that are swirling around this complex and long-awaited issue, I will not attempt to outline the current state of that adoption process as that can and will change from day to day. Suffice it to say that the CCSS have been adopted and will continue to be adopted and revised as that adoption process moves forward. That approval process functions as it will and as it should function, completely beyond the control or purview of this author and this book. American democracy will deal with these academic performance standards and all new issues in its own way and edit, change, and amend as the democratic and political processes demand.

The more important issue is that first and foremost this new national initiative is a set of national academic performance *standards*, not a national curriculum in the traditional sense of the word, but a set of national academic performance standards, or a description of the skills that we want all students to know and be able to do. While it seems almost repetitive to discuss standards and what they are, I am always amazed at the lack of awareness on the part of so many about what standards really are and are not. In the traditional curriculum environment, districts that have or had curriculum documents that really drove instruction created curriculum documents that addressed the content to be covered, the chapters in the book to be covered, or presented actual sample lessons to demonstrate for teachers how to teach certain content. That traditional definition of *curriculum* is what, I believe, has so hotly fueled the debate on a national curriculum, but we will discuss this issue in more detail later in this chapter and throughout the book.

In the new era of a standards-based curriculum, content must be a means to a performance end; regardless of the content that is used, the root issue is the student performance or standard that the teacher is trying to get the student to learn. For example, the CCSS for English/Language Arts in sixth grade (RL.6.2.) expects students will "determine a theme or central idea of a text and how it is conveyed through particular details; provide a summary of the text distinct from personal opinions or judgments."

Content Versus Standards

An academic performance standard is a description of skills that we want students to know and be able to do, not a description of content to be mastered. As a young teacher, I taught Julius Caesar, way before anyone was even talking about standards. It was pretty straight forward; we started in Act 1 and worked our way through the entire play, scene by scene and act by act. I wanted the students to understand and retell the story of Antony and Brutus and all the other characters; all of this was covered in a final exam asking students to retell what happened, identify certain things, and interpret the play. That is the way it

(Continued)

(Continued)

was done and in many cases is still done in American classrooms. While I may have accidentally touched on these CCSS shown below, these were not intentionally designed into the lesson, and that is the problem.

- RL.6.1. Cite the evidence in the text that most strongly supports a specific analysis of what the text says explicitly as well as inferences drawn from the text.

  RL.6.2. Analyze in detail the development and refinement of a theme or central idea in a text, including how it emerges and how it is shaped and refined by specific details.

  RL.6.3. Analyze how complex characters, including those with conflicting motivations or divided loyalties, develop over the course of a text, interact with other characters, and advance the plot or develop the theme.

With standards, America is now defining the skills, not the content, students are expected to learn.

As we continue to draw the distinction of a standards-based curriculum, it is important to point out several noteworthy characteristics:

- Content is not addressed. There is no concern for the content to be used; there are suggested books and readings in the CCSS, but the standard itself is a performance, not specific content.
- It defines the skill(s) that is/are expected to be mastered.
- The verbs clearly define the level of Bloom's Taxonomy at which the students will be expected to perform—determine, provide a summary, and so forth.
- There is no attempt to prescribe an instructional strategy.

Align the Curriculum

This is a huge instructional shift for teachers; the issue is no longer the content or the chapter of the book to be taught, but rather the skill the student is expected to know and be able to do. In the example of my teaching strategies, I simply "taught" *Julius Caesar,* and then assessed the students to see if they "knew" the content I had just taught. I used my own assessment and my own grading criteria (though I was forced to use the building grading scale, which has absolutely nothing to do with assessing or reporting on skill acquisition or demonstration) to determine who passed and who failed. I then recorded those results and moved on to the next curriculum piece to be taught.

Had someone asked me what skills or standards I was teaching, I am sure I could have rattled off a very impressive list of skills I was hoping the kids were learning—drawing inference from what the characters said, predicting events, evaluating motivation, and so on—but I was not, nor were any other teachers, teaching any kind of common academic standard(s), even though we were all teaching sophomore English. We were all teaching content and whatever skills followed in mastering that content that we judged important for whatever reasons. I may have been really enthralled with drawing inference from what the characters said or didn't say, but that was my thing and other teachers may or may not have shared that passion.

In this traditional curriculum, this was/is acceptable and even a source of perceived strength by some. This approach to curriculum as content allows teachers to insert their own personality and beliefs and "special interests" into their instruction and helps create that passion for teaching that many educators have and that really generates buy-in and engagement from the students, something we certainly don't want to lose. This is a critical point that is very important and needs to be explored at length and will be discussed in greater detail later in this chapter and in this book.

I "taught" whatever academic skills (standards) I taught, and assessed those skills in my own manner but I used the school grading scale as some kind of assurance of "academic integrity." The things my students were really learning, however, other than content, had no intended or predesigned relation to what students in other classes were learning. As they said in the 1960s, "You do your thing, and I'll do mine, and if, by chance, we find each other, that's beautiful." That was, and in many cases still is, the model of curriculum implementation used in many schools.

Not to pick on English as a department, even though I was an English teacher, but there is frequently a somewhat more deliberate alignment in some of the science and math courses both in past and present practice, because teachers use the chapters in the student textbook to designate the expected learnings. But again, teachers in science and math are still free to skip sections or even chapters and to spend more time on certain areas they deem more important and less time on other parts of the book. Couple all of this with the perceived press teachers feel to "cover" the entire book, and we see why there is little, if any, alignment in the current state of curriculum as a content-driven process. It is not unusual at all to hear teachers bemoan that they had to skip chapters or sections to make sure they finished the year where they "are supposed to," wherever that is.

Such random acts of curriculum alignment through mandating the same content without addressing the skills to be mastered and when those skills are to be mastered is the crux of the problem. Using curriculum alignment to ensure that the same content is taught without ensuring that the same skills are learned further exacerbates the core problem; we need to define and assign a place in the curriculum where specific skills are to be mastered. Teachers can teach the same content, but if the specific skills to be mastered are not identified and assessed, there is no guarantee of real curriculum alignment.

Think of Content as a Means to a Performance End

Just because you and I both taught *Julius Caesar,* there is almost certainly no formal or predetermined way that ensures the performance standards learned in our classes were even remotely related. Whether we like to admit it or not, the same holds true for math and science; just because two teachers taught Chapter 5 or genetics or whatever, there is generally no formal or predetermined process to ensure that students in both classes learned the same performance standards—content, yes, academic standards, no.

STAFF DEVELOPMENT ISSUES

We must ask ourselves, as a system, how much actual concentrated time have we as a district or professional learning community spent on ensuring that the standards are the basis for all instruction and assessments in our district? How much time have we spent in ensuring that teachers understand the current academic standards and are prepared and required to use those academic standards as the basis for lesson and assessment design? This is a system responsibility, not an individual teacher responsibility.

While teachers do have some professional obligation to learn the standards and assessment system, it is a system responsibility to ensure that all teachers follow a district model to implement and use the academic standards in instruction and assessments. Nobody in the district really wants or should want every teacher in the district interpreting the standards in his or her own way. Leadership must design, implement, and monitor the process of standards implementation to ensure a common interpretation and implementation.

As a leader, design, implement, and monitor the process of standards implementation to ensure a common interpretation and implementation

While working with a district that was into its fourth year of Academic Warning based on the No Child Left Behind Act, I asked the faculty how their understanding of the standards was going and noticed a blank look on most faces, so I asked, "How many of you have read the standards that your students are expected to master?" Only a single hand went up. I went on to ask how familiar they were with the standards and the assessment system and, again, blank looks. The point is not to belittle or hold anyone up to scorn, but the reality is, many districts have really not invested heavily in the standards movement and don't understand the fundamental critical attribute of a standard; it is a performance, not content or an activity. District leadership must ensure that appropriate staff development is provided.

While some would argue that the preceding case is a real anomaly and not at all typical of most schools in America, my experiences tell me differently. When speaking, I frequently give the curriculum audit contained in Resource B, and it is far more often the case that almost every member of the audience shares that they and their district have spent very little, if any, time coming to know and understand the state standards and the state assessment system, much less the new CCSS.

Build Understanding of the CCSS

While the individual standards may change slightly, I do not believe we can expect major, earth-shaking changes along the way. A sixth-grade standard will probably not be moved to second grade, or vice versa. The instructional process is different in a standards-based environment, so let us all begin the work of transition of the existing curriculum, instruction, and assessment system from its current state, whatever that might be, to a standards-based curriculum, instruction, and assessment system. Once public education is designed around and for standards, the "tweaking" to address whatever minor changes happen to those standards along the way will be a nonissue that can be readily addressed at the local level.

The current version of the CCSS is about 490 pages long, an impressive but intimidating document to most educators. So as Doug Reeves has pointed out and I continue to espouse, we have to find a way to "power" these down into a learnable amount for all students to master. The entire issue of local

CCSS (Power Standards) as an approach to determining a learnable, critical curriculum is more completely addressed in my first book, *Using Power Standards to Build an Aligned Curriculum: A Process Manual,* and will be summarized later in this chapter, but suffice it to say, it is imperative that some kind of process be designed to help teachers understand the new CCSS *and* to identify and come to consensus on those most critical, most important learnings that all students must master in the 175-day school year we now have available.

Once educators have identified those standards and designed them into a learnable amount, it is the responsibility and opportunity of the system to ensure learning for all, and it can be done. We cannot get into "analysis paralysis" and spend all of our time arguing about these new CCSS—what they mean, how to implement them, and so on. These are the new "laws of the land," and it is our responsibility to move forward and make the best of them that we can.

Use What Has Already Been Developed As a Basis for Moving Forward

Additionally, districts that have done significant curriculum alignment working with the state standards, as many districts have, should not abandon that work and start over from scratch. Use what has already been developed and is in use as a basis for moving forward into the transition to CCSS. Where are there similarities between the current curriculum and assessment work and the new CCSS? Where can this work be used as the foundation for what will need to be done to complete the transition to CCSS and enable the entire staff to effectively implement these new standards?

The new CCSS are different from current state standards, to be sure, but they are not so different that there can't be transfer from one to the other. The things teachers learned and used in the initial work with state standards can have a significant impact on the work that lies ahead and can serve as a nice transition into this new activity.

Some districts really have not done much work with existing state standards and using those state standards to build an aligned curriculum, instruction, and assessment system. Consequently, they are feeling really lost and overwhelmed by the transition to CCSS. There is now a clean slate, and the district can quickly ready itself to begin this process and participate in all the excitement and learning that lies ahead.

Under these new CCSS, the curriculum problems in Illinois are about the same problems someone will be dealing with in Arkansas and every other state. There is a lot to do and a lot to learn, but we're in this with lots of people from all over this great country, and in true American fashion, we will use our "Yankee ingenuity" to design and implement an answer. Enjoy the ride.

As discussed earlier, the root issue remains the transition to a standards-based curriculum. Helping teachers first understand that standards-based approach to education is the real, core issue that must be addressed and then adjusted to the new CCSS.

DEFINING AND CREATING LOCAL CCSS

The entire process of creating the local CCSS described above is based on the work of Doug Reeves and Larry Ainsworth. The process then goes on to not only build these end-of-year expectations but to develop quarterly learning expectations. This book addresses the process of creating those local CCSS based on the Power Standards work of Reeves and Ainsworth and then goes on to develop quarterly instructional objectives to further define and specify the what and the when of expected learnings. This process can be followed with or without specific software. The issue is the process; having software helps, but it is not mandatory. As when I did this work the first several times, there are ways to use Microsoft Word, or other word-processing programs and e-mail programs, to communicate. The major issue here is the curriculum, instruction, and assessment alignment process that is to be followed—that is key. You absolutely must do the necessary work to ensure alignment.

This book shares and makes available to the reader, the software package created by partners4results to facilitate this work. While the software is helpful, the critical issue remains following a specific process to synthesize these new local CCSS and instructional objectives developed from the CCSS into a learnable, manageable document that drives instruction, assessment, and student performance. The instructional leader needs to identify and use a step-by-step process as outlined in this book to lead his or her staff through this process—beginning with the CCSS and then synthesizing and identifying the most critical skills to be learned, deciding when those skills are to be learned, and assigning those skills a specific place in the learning experience is the key issue. While the instructional leader can use Word or about any other word-processing program to do the work, the partners4results software (visit www.partners4results.org/demo) facilitates this work and sharing process.

Power Standards are an attempt to (a) look at all of the things that we *could* teach our students, if we only had the time, resources, and so on and (b) to refine that overpowering list down to a critical but learnable amount.

Of all those possible learnings, we must decide which learnings are so important, so critical, and so necessary for future learning, that we must identify those learnings and build our entire curriculum, instruction, and assessment system around mastery of those learnings. Even once we do that, it is still hard work, but it is now doable work.

Understand Local CCSS (Power Standards)

Larry Ainsworth created the concept of Power Standards, and that concept has been refined, universalized, and generally operationalized through the years by Doug Reeves and his work. They always assign three critical attributes to Power Standards:

1. Endurance: Will the standard provide students with knowledge and skills beyond a single test date?
2. Leverage: Will the standard provide knowledge and skills that are of value in multiple disciplines?
3. Readiness for the next level of learning: Will the standard provide students with essential knowledge and skills that are necessary for their success in the next grade level? (Ainsworth, 2003a)

Power Standards are end-of-year learning targets that very specifically define the expected end-of-year learnings for that grade level, subject, or course. These Power Standards represent the most critical, most essential learnings, based on the state standards (now based on the CCSS) as determined by the local educators. As teachers do this work of looking at the CCSS in their entirety and then synthesizing all of the information contained in the CCSS into a new, more compact, learnable format, the Power Standard, that is, intellectual work at the highest level of Bloom's Taxonomy. This is very complex, difficult work for everyone involved—that is, evaluating and synthesizing a new product from existing work.

Creating Power Standards is really difficult, energy-consuming work that greatly improves local educators' knowledge and understanding of these critical, essential learnings and the expectations in the CCSS. The work itself, though complex and difficult, prepares teachers to better articulate those important learnings and better help students achieve those standards. Suggested forms used in doing this work are in Resource B.

In this model of curriculum development, as shown in the sample local CCSS below, the local CCSS contain the lead-in line, "By the end of grade level/course, the student will . . .," followed by a number of elements or "bullets" that typically address specific domains of the CCSS. These elements define the end-of-year learning expectations associated with those specific domains of the CCSS (in the last column).

The local CCSS presented below is shown as an example of local work, not an exemplar of perfect work. This is the first draft, and will certainly improve with the application of the Plan, Do, Check, Act cycle (explained in the forms in Resource B and throughout this book), but the local educators have taken the first step in the journey to an aligned curriculum, and that is to be applauded.

How to Read These Samples

In this proposed model, there is a lead-in line, "By the end of whatever course, the student will . . .," followed by several elements. To read this chart, the first column is the element number, followed by the specific end-of-year learning expectation, and the final column is the domain of the CCSS used in developing this element.

Table 1.1 Expected Progress by the End of Algebra 1

By the end of Algebra 1, the student will . . .		
Power Standard Element	**Local CCSS**	**Common Core Domain**
1	Interpret the structure of expressions with new emphasis on quadratic and exponential expressions	Seeing structure in expressions
2	Extend arithmetic to polynomial functions	Arithmetic with polynomials and rational expressions
3	Create equations that show relationships between numbers	Creating equations
4	Show numeracy with whole numbers and all real-number operations	Quantities
5	Define, identify, and use irrational numbers	The real number system
6	Understand solving equations and inequalities as a reasoning process and interpret solutions within the context of the problem	Reasoning with equations and inequalities

(Continued)

Table 1.1 (Continued)

By the end of Algebra 1, the student will . . .		
Power Standard Element	**Local CCSS**	**Common Core Domain**
7	Understand the concept of a function and use function notation and interpret functions that arise in certain contexts	Interpreting functions
8	Extend knowledge of equations and relationships to functions, and build new functions from existing ones	Building functions
9	Construct and compare linear, exponential, and quadratic models (functions) and interpret the parameters within a given context	Linear, quadratic, and exponential models
10	Summarize, represent, and interpret data on single and multiple categories and interpret linear models	Interpreting categorical and quantitative data

Used with permission.

What Are Instructional Objectives?

These local CCSS and the accompanying instructional objectives represent a kind of contract between the student and the teacher that these are the skills that will be stressed and for which the student will be held accountable.

The local CCSS are in no way intended as some kind of replacement for or condemnation of the CCSS but rather as a prioritizing of those skills into a learnable amount based on the criteria in Table 1.1. (This work is also facilitated by the software and may been seen and used at www.partners4results.org/demo by clicking on Power Standards Maintenance, selecting a grade level and subject, and following the directions.)

As alluded to earlier in this chapter, the next step in this curriculum model is the development of the instructional objectives. But to facilitate this conversation, let's take a quick look at how instructional objectives are defined and used in this model. If the local CCSS represent the critical end-of-year learnings for a specific grade level or course, then the instructional objectives deliberately scaffold those requisite skills that need to be learned and suggest the order in which those skills need to be mastered during the year in order to master the local CCSS.

If students are to learn these local CCSS by the end of the year, what skills do students need to learn during the year, and in what order/ sequence can we arrange that learning to maximize student learning? The first column tells the academic term, in this case, the quarter, when the instructional objective is to be learned. The second column is the number of the instructional objective that is the approximate order in which it is to be learned (O1.1 means first quarter, first instructional objective, O1.2 means first quarter, second instructional objective, and so on). The third column is the specific language of the learning expectation followed by the numbers of the specific CCSS used to develop this instructional objective in parentheses. The last column references the local CCSS element to which it is tied. The chart below represents the skills identified and their assignment to an academic term as determined by the professional staff to maximize student learning.

To save space, only first-quarter instructional objectives are shown here, but the charts in Chapter 4 will give more specific and complete examples of this work for an entire academic year.

Table 1.2 Algebra 1 Instructional Objectives (End-of-First-Quarter Expectations)[a]

Term	IO Number	Instructional Objective From Common Core State Standards (CCSS)	LCCSS Element
1	O1.1	Perform unit conversions (9–12.N-Q.1, 9–12.N-Q.2, 9–12.N-Q.3)	4
1	O1.2	Apply significant digits to calculations (9–12.N-Q.1, 9–12.N-Q.2, 9–12.N-Q.3)	4
1	O1.3	Simplify expressions by performing order of operations (9–12.A-SSE.1, 9–12.A-SSE.1a, 9–12.A-SSE.1b, 9–12.A-SSE.2, 9–12.A-SSE.3, 9–12.A-SSE.3a, 9–12.A-SSE.3b, 9–12.A-SSE.3c)	1
1	O1.4	Build expressions from a set of written instructions (9–12.A-SSE.1, 9–12.A-SSE.1a, 9–12.A-SSE.1b, 9–12.A-SSE.2, 9–12.A-SSE.3, 9–12.A-SSE.3a, 9–12.A-SSE.3b, 9–12.A-SSE.3c)	1

(Continued)

Table 1.2 (Continued)

Term	IO Number	Instructional Objective From Common Core State Standards (CCSS)	LCCSS Element
1	O1.5	Create equations and inequalities in 1 variable and use them to solve problems (9–12.A-CED.1, 9–12.A-CED.2, 9–12.A-CED.3, 9–12.A-CED.4)	3
1	O1.6	Create equations in 2 or more variables to represent relationships between quantities (9–12.A-CED.1, 9–12.A-CED.2, 9–12.A-CED.3, 9–12.A-CED.4)	3
1	O1.7	Solve linear equations and inequalities, explaining each step in the solving process (9–12.A-REI.4, 9–12.A-REI.4a, 9–12.A-REI.4b, 9–12.A-REI.6, 9–12.A-REI.7, 9–12.A-REI.1, 9–12.A-REI.10, 9–12.A-REI.11, 9–12.A-REI.12, 9–12.A-REI.2, 9–12.A-REI.3)	6
1	O1.8	Rearrange formulas to highlight a quantity of interest (9–12.A-CED.1, 9–12.A-CED.2, 9–12.A-CED.3, 9–12.A-CED.4)	3

a. IO = instructional objective; LCCSS = local Common Core State Standards; 9–12 = Grades 9–12; N-Q.1 = Item 1 in the Quantities subset of Numbers section for high school students in the Common Core State Standards; A-SSE.1 = Item 1 in Seeing Structure in Expressions in the Algebra section; A-CED.1 = Item 1 in Creating Equations; REI.1 = Item 1 in Reasoning With Equations and Inequalities.

Used with permission.

By looking at the local CCSS in terms of requisite learnings that go into mastery of that local CCSS, and then deliberately sequencing or scaffolding those learnings, we address a critical component of student learning: How do students best master content? The instructional objectives presented above are based on the local CCSS shared earlier in this chapter. Again, these instructional objectives are a first draft and will go through the Plan, Do, Check, Act cycle discussed throughout this book. The numbers in parentheses following each instructional objective indicates the exact CCSS being addressed in this particular instructional objective. This clearly establishes the direct link between the instructional objective, which will be the exact skill being taught to the learner, and the new CCSS.

For example and to clarify, let's look at the local CCSS for Algebra I shown above and look very specifically how this logic follows. Here is the first element of the 10 elements in this local CCSS, for Algebra I:

Table 1.3

1	Interpret the structure of expressions with new emphasis on quadratic and exponential expressions	Seeing structure in expressions

Used with permission.

This represents an end-of-year target for the Seeing Structure in Expressions domain of the CCSS. The instructional objectives designed to accomplish these expectations are as follows:

Table 1.4[a]

1	O1.3	Simplify expressions by performing order of operations (9–12.A-SSE.1, 9–12.A-SSE.1a, 9–12.A-SSE.1b, 9–12.A-SSE.2, 9–12.A-SSE.3, 9–12.A-SSE.3a, 9–12.A-SSE.3b, 9–12.A-SSE.3c)	1
1	O1.4	Build expressions from a set of written instructions (9–12.A-SSE.1, 9–12.A-SSE.1a, 9–12.A-SSE.1b, 9–12.A-SSE.2, 9–12.A-SSE.3, 9–12.A-SSE.3a, 9–12.A-SSE.3b, 9–12.A-SSE.3c)	1
3	O3.5	Interpret the parts of an expression (exponential & polynomial) such as, terms, factors and coefficients (9–12.A-SSE.1, 9–12.A-SSE.1a, 9–12.A-SSE.1b, 9–12.A-SSE.2, 9–12.A-SSE.3, 9–12.A-SSE.3a, 9–12.A-SSE.3b, 9–12.A-SSE.3c)	1
3	O3.6	Add, subtract, and multiply polynomials (9–12.A-SSE.1, 9–12.A-SSE.1a, 9–12.A-SSE.1b, 9–12.A-SSE.2, 9–12.A-SSE.3, 9–12.A-SSE.3a, 9–12.A-SSE.3b, 9–12.A-SSE.3c)	1

(Continued)

Table 1.4 (Continued)

4	O4.2	Factor quadratic equations and use to find zeros (9–12.A-SSE.1, 9–12.A-SSE.1a, 9–12.A-SSE.1b, 9–12.A-SSE.2, 9–12.A-SSE.3, 9–12.A-SSE.3a, 9–12.A-SSE.3b, 9–12.A-SSE.3c)	1
4	O4.4	Complete the square on a quadratic function, find the function's maximum or minimum, and sketch an approximate graph (9–12.A-SSE.1, 9–12.A-SSE.1a, 9–12.A-SSE.1b, 9–12.A-SSE.2, 9–12.A-SSE.3, 9–12.A-SSE.3a, 9–12.A-SSE.3b, 9–12.A-SSE.3c)	1

a. 9–12 = Grades 9–12; A-SSE.1 = first item in Seeing Structure in Expressions in the Algebra section.

The readers will see in this example that there are six total instructional objectives for this element of the local CCSS: two for first quarter, two for third quarter, and two for fourth quarter. This is the scaffolding that these teachers felt would best accomplish the expected end-of-year learning that is expected.

These instructional objectives are designed around the internal academic divisions used by the local district, usually quarters, trimesters, or whatever. These instructional objectives subdivide, if you will, the end-of-year learning expectation into quarterly instructional targets, thus designating *what* is to be learned and *when* it is to be learned. The first, foremost purpose of this scaffolding is to maximize student learning. In the example above and in examples later in the book, the instructional objectives scaffold the learning to improve student performance; first the student should learn this, and then this, and so on.

As part of the development process for the instructional objectives, the discussion guide that follows is used to ensure consistency within the instructional objectives. Again, spaces have been deleted for ease of publishing. This form is in Resource B.

Quarterly Instructional Objectives

Critical Attributes: CCSS

1. Are the quarterly instructional objectives written in student- and parent-friendly language?
2. Are the quarterly instructional objectives aligned to the local CCSS?

3. Are all the skills contained in the local CCSS covered (somewhere) in the quarterly instructional objectives?
4. Do all of the quarterly instructional objectives reflect on grade-level standards as defined in the CCSS?
5. Do the quarterly instructional objectives give our colleagues the kind of specific direction needed to guide their instruction?
6. Do the quarterly instructional objectives represent a natural progression of skill acquisition that will maximize student learning?
7. Are the quarterly instructional objectives specific enough to facilitate the development of common, formative assessment items?

The numbering system used indicates the quarter in which the skill is expected to be learned (1, 2, 3, 4), and the second number indicates the approximate order the skills will be learned during that quarter. Since this is the first draft of these Power Standards and instructional objectives, the teachers will implement this instructional schedule this first year, gather quarterly feedback on how well these worked, and redesign these for the coming year. Again, the plan, Do, Check, Act cycle is built right into the process. Sample forms for gathering such feedback are contained in *Using Power Standards to Build an Aligned Curriculum* (Crawford, 2011) and in Resource B.

Why Are Instructional Objectives So Important?

The second and almost equally important purpose of scaffolding is to help ensure that teachers will be teaching and assessing the same skills at approximately the same time during the academic year. When the same skills are taught and assessed at the same time by all the teachers in a grade level or course, there is now a reason for common, formative assessments based on those expected learnings. There is now a reason for teachers to use that real-time data to see if students are mastering the intended curriculum and making adequate progress toward the end-of-year targets (local CCSS). There is now a reason for teachers to sit down and in a collegial manner to discuss differences in student performance between and within teachers' classes.

All the teachers taught the same skills, gave the same assessments, and used the same criteria to score those assessments, so we can now ask and answer really important questions. Are there differences between and among classes in student performance? Did some classes/courses perform better on specific skills (instructional objectives) than other classes? Now that we have all taught the same skills and given the same assessment, we have reason to discuss our results. In the current system, if the teachers haven't taught the same skill at the same time, it is impossible to compare strategies in real time, discuss improvement ideas, identify practices that work and don't work, and so on.

SYSTEM THINKING

Now that the district has done the work of creating local CCSS (Power Standards) and assigning those learnings to specific times within the academic program (instructional objectives), the district now has the beginnings of a curriculum, instruction, and assessment system. The adoption of a set of national standards, even though those standards are not perfect nor ever will be, gives local districts and even America a perfect opportunity to really create an American system of the curriculum, instruction, and assessment piece of education. We can create a curriculum, instruction, and assessment system designed around these CCSS and then engage in a national conversation about continuously improving that system. First there must be a system. Then, and only then, can system thinking be applied.

We in education in some kind of deference to business and industry always talk about system thinking, and try to apply that system thinking to what we do. Since the emphasis of this book is on curriculum, instruction, and assessment, this conversation will focus on the current state of the curriculum, instruction, and assessment systems, or lack thereof, and the application of system thinking to that specific part of education. So when I talk about the system below, I am talking about the district and its system, or lack thereof, of curriculum, instruction, and assessment: How does the system respond or fail to respond to these issues?

Think about the current curriculum, instruction, and assessment system for a moment in the light of the reality of many, if not most, districts here in America. If a system has not *identified* the skills it expects its students to know and be able to do, if a system does not know when those specific skills are expected to be *mastered*, if a system does not know how that mastery will be *assessed*, is there really a system in place? Industry has pretty much determined what is to be done, and when it is to be done; everything has a time and a place. There is a system in place, so system thinking can be applied to that system.

Define a Curriculum, Instruction, and Assessment System

- Identify skills to be mastered.
- Identify when those skills are to be mastered.
- Monitor to ensure these skills are being learned when expected.
- Measure to see if these skills are being learned.
- Use the same measurement tools to measure student performance.
- Share those student performance results with teachers.
- Provide time and resources to discuss results to improve inputs (instruction, etc.).
- Hold members accountable for reaching district expectations.
- Provide for regular, ongoing continuous improvement.

In our current environment, most educational entities are not sure or have not determined what the skills are to be mastered, much less when the specific skills are to be mastered and how that mastery will be measured. That being said, how can system thinking, or really any kind of organizational improvement structure, be used? Student performance in math may not be acceptable, but if the system has not designated what those skills are and when those math skills are to be learned and how that learning is to be measured, there is little the educators can do to improve.

The system must clearly define its end-of-year learning expectations by grade level and course. Those end-of-year learning expectations are then scaffolded throughout the year to ensure that the structure of the curriculum itself maximizes students' ability to learn. The district then puts into place a system to monitor the implementation of this intended curriculum and a system to measure student progress toward mastery of this intended curriculum. Absent such a system, there can be no reform. You have to have a system before you can reform a system.

The district's first responsibility is to determine those learning expectations, clearly define those learning expectations, and assign specific learning expectations to grade levels, courses, and academic terms; now the district knows what is supposed to be learned and when it is to be learned. Now the district can look at student performance and identify what skills students can and can't do and determine where in the academic experience that skill should have been learned. Once such a curriculum, instruction, and assessment system is in place, there is a basis for system thinking; there is a system of curriculum and assessment in place. That curriculum, instruction, and assessment system must be part of a continuous improvement cycle to ensure its continuous improvement, but absent a system, you can't have system improvement. If there is no system, there can be no system improvement.

Think about that in relation to the current system of curriculum, instruction, and assessment in your district. Is there a true system in place in your district that clearly defines the learning expectations and assigns those learning expectations to specific grade levels and courses? Do you then have a formal process to monitor instruction to ensure those expectations are being implemented? Do you then have an assessment system that measures, with common, formative assessments, to see if those learning expectations are being accomplished? Does the system provide time and structure for teachers to compare results and discuss successful strategies?

What About Using National Assessments as Formative Assessments?

If we are going to expect teachers to sequence the learning, then we must develop a system of common, formative assessments based on those intended learnings to be given during the year to measure progress toward the end-of-year expectations. The teachers have all just taught these skills, now the district must administer an assessment to measure student performance on that assessment and use a common scoring process for everyone who took the assessments. The same skills have been taught, so how did our students do on these assessments? What can we learn from these results to improve learning?

As stated earlier in my concerns about alleged formative national assessments, it is very difficult for a group of teachers to sit down and discuss their student performance on AIMSweb, NWEA (Northwest Evaluation Association), or whatever and discuss their classroom or course's student performance on such a test. No disrespect intended to these national assessments, they have value and present valid, reliable data, but they do not necessarily represent specific skills the teachers really just taught.

Certainly those assessments assess skills, but not necessarily the skills that were just taught. Nor do these national assessments necessarily assess these skills at the level of Bloom's Taxonomy at which the skills were taught. That is why I continue to advocate for local formative assessments that are specifically based on skills aligned to the CCSS and taught by all teachers. Once we get teachers to identify, teach, and assess the same skills at the same time, we have the beginnings of a system, and we will discuss those implications later in this chapter. Of course all the teachers are teaching reading or math, but not necessarily the specific skills at the specific cognitive level that the national assessment is assessing the skill.

Additionally, by identifying instructional objectives and tying every single item on the local common, formative assessments to individual instructional objectives, the locally developed common, formative assessments now tell teachers not just which students passed or failed a test but far more important, which students did demonstrate and which students did not demonstrate mastery of specific instructional objectives—those skills that the teacher just taught.

Now teachers can design reteaching activities based on demonstrated, specific skill deficits—not design reteaching based on who passed or failed the overall assessments but on who failed to demonstrate mastery of specific skills. Who cannot reduce fractions? Who cannot simplify equations? Who cannot classify and order real numbers?

Also remember that what happens with an assessment after it is scored is what makes an assessment formative; if student performance on these assessments drives actions to improve instruction and learning, then it is formative. This gives teachers the opportunity and structure to use assessments to improve student learning. (For an example of reports used in this process, please go to www.partners4results.org/demo, click on Power Standards Maintenance, and sample reports to see a sample report of this nature.)

What About Accountability?

Without a system of curriculum, instruction, and assessment, the district or building can have random acts of innovation, but without the system designating when a skill is to be learned and how that learning will be measured (and holding those responsible for that essential learning accountable), there is little that can really be done in any kind of systematic way.

By *accountable,* I don't mean fire or discipline; I mean using an assessment system, sharing those results, and holding discussions to identify the reasons for variance in student performance and sharing instructional strategies to improve. Also, the principal and other leaders must get out there and monitor the process to see if the teachers are following the curriculum expectations and ensuring that they are doing so.

When an issue as important as identifying the essential learnings that are expected and when and how those learnings will be delivered and measured has not been mandated, then teaching and learning are not center stage for a district's expectations. How can districts expect anything but what they have? Please note I do use the word *mandate;* such important tasks should not be an option. Would the Air Force leave the process and specifications for installation of an airplane engine to personal choice? Neither can educators continue to view learning expectations so loosely. What will be learned? When will it be learned? How will it be measured?

System Thinking Explained

While speaking about a curriculum, instruction, and assessment system, I will frequently explain to the audience that my current system of diet, nutrition, and exercise is perfect! My current diet, exercise, and nutrition program really is perfect to achieve my current results–my current weight, waist size, health, and so on. If I want to change my current results, I have to change my current system or at least create a system. Whatever I am currently doing produces the results it produces. If I want to change my results, I must change my system. The same goes for the educational system.

What About Using the Data?

A critical piece of this new system is providing time and resources to use the data to evaluate and design better instruction in the classroom. If there are significant differences between classroom performance (and there surely will be), what accounts for that difference? Different grouping realities? Different instructional strategies? Different classroom activities? No one will know for sure unless the district first generates the data to measure the differences and then provides the time and structure for teachers to deal with that data and plan to improve student performance.

In almost every district I work in, the most common complaint is always time—we don't have the time to do these things. There are no planned times with set agendas to discuss student performance issues. We have time to plan the Halloween party, argue about dress codes and tardy policies, and hear lectures on blood-borne pathogens and new insurance requirements, but never the time to talk about the heart and soul of why we are here—student performance.

Whenever I get into this discussion about time, I always remind the group that high-performing schools do not have 28 hours in their day, nor do they work from 6 a.m. until 8 p.m. We all pretty much work the same workday, but we all choose to organize our time within that day differently. There is no way to discuss all the options for time management in all the districts in the country, but suffice it to say, the time within the workday is something that every district can and must look at in its efforts to drive improvement.

What About Monitoring?

As discussed above, not only must there be a clear set of learning expectations in place, implementation of those learning expectations must be monitored, and I don't mean monitored by collecting lesson plans; I mean truly monitoring to ensure the intended curriculum is being implemented as mandated. Principals cannot and do not monitor curriculum implementation from the office. The only way to know if the intended curriculum is being implemented is to go to the classrooms and see.

If implementing the intended curriculum is a system value, as it must be, then the system must monitor that curriculum implementation to make sure it is happening. This is not said out of mistrust of teachers or as some kind of power play to keep the teacher's "nose to the grindstone" but rather a simple system expectation—we inspect what we expect.

There are several models of classroom walk-throughs on the market, and these 2- to 4-minute walk-throughs, focused on gathering data rather than judgments, can be ideal. They can give a picture to the entire staff of the current state of implementation of the intended curriculum, instructional practices, student engagement, and a wide variety of other classroom practices. By monitoring these leading, rather than trailing, indicators of student performance, we can have discussions about improving current practice before the state assessments.

Since these classroom visits are so brief and intended to gather data rather than make judgments and do not contain teacher names or other identifiers, it is realistic to expect administrators to do many walk-throughs (50 to 200) per month, sharing the data with the entire staff. For example, in my 100 classroom walk-throughs, 68 classrooms had the instructional objective posted, or it was obvious to the students. In 53 of those classrooms, the instruction was aligned to the instructional objective. In 62 of those classrooms, the instructional strategy was lecture, and so on. Now the professional learning community has something to talk about.

Lesson Plans to Monitor?

Many years ago, when I first became a principal, I had a staff of about 50 teachers, and I followed past practice and collected lesson plans every Friday afternoon. The thinking was that collecting lesson plans allowed me to read and return them to the teachers for implementation on Monday morning. What a great plan, and we've always done it that way, so I continued the practice. Like all solutions, it created problems. First, it gave me about 120 or so pages of reading to do over the weekend (really a bad idea), and I had to "chase down" those who failed to turn the plans in on Friday. It kept my secretary and me very busy. As fate would have it, I stayed there long enough and pushed enough curriculum reform that the staff began to legitimately doubt the validity of collecting lesson plans as a way to meaningfully monitor curriculum. Eventually, the lesson plans were peppered with notes: "You don't really read these, do you?" "This is a waste of your time and my time." And so on. As the notes began, I answered them with some cute witticism or smart remark that only made the game more fun for the teachers (remember, just like the kids outnumber the teachers 30 to one, the teachers outnumbered me 50 to one) and more difficult for me. If I missed a note from a teacher, the celebration was instantaneous and spontaneous; everybody but me thought it hilarious and a further demonstration of the futility of my curriculum monitoring efforts. Eventually, I had to concede that they were right, and I really learned more about curriculum from my walk-throughs than by collecting lesson plans, and we all lived happily ever after.

Whatever teaching and learning constructs are identified in the walk-through model can become the data points used to monitor the implementation of the intended curriculum, and that data can and should be shared with the entire faculty as feedback on their efforts to improve student performance. The model of walk-through that a district selects will determine the data points measured and the method of inputting and reporting that data, but the reality is there are lots of systems out there requiring everything from PDAs or handheld devices and software packages all the way down to paper and pencil models that can be implemented for little cost.

However, if implementing the intended curriculum, or anything else, is important to the district, the district will monitor it somehow. If monitoring to ensure that the intended curriculum is implemented is *not* a value to the district, that speaks volumes to everyone about the values of that district. *Classroom Walkthroughs to Improve Teaching and Learning* by Donald Kachur, Judith Stout, and Claudia Edwards (2010) gives a great overview of the many walk-through models out there.

SYSTEM THINKING SUMMARIZED

In order to have a curriculum, instruction, and assessment system, the district must first have a curriculum document that clearly defines *what* will be learned and *when* it will be learned, and those expectations must be shared with everyone—students, parents, teachers, the entire educational community (discussed in Chapter 4).

A common set of formative assessments that set common criteria for demonstrating mastery of that intended curriculum—the same skills are learned at approximately the same time and mastery of those skills is demonstrated on common assessments scored with the same measurement instruments using the same criteria (discussed in Chapter 3).

A formal system is in place to monitor the delivery of the intended curriculum. The accomplishment of the absolute core value of the system—what is learned and when it is learned—cannot be left to chance or good wishes. The core value must be monitored and reported back to the entire professional learning community to ensure faithful adherence to the group goals (discussed in Chapter 1).

A formal process and time are provided for the professional learning community to process all the data gathered from such common, formative assessments. Now that teachers are teaching the same skills, giving the same assessments, and scoring those assessments on the same scale, time must be provided to compare results of those assessments and discuss what led to the difference in those results (discussed in Chapter 4).

This book will continue to define and provide help in operationalizing such curriculum documents as are needed in such a curriculum, instruction, and assessment system, but the development of that system is not part of this book. However, absent the creation and universal use of these curriculum, instruction, and assessment documents and practices, the establishment of a true system is impossible.

PROCESS SUMMARY

At this stage of the process, the reader is gathering information and making decisions on the current state of curriculum in his or her district and coming to understand the new CCSS and Power Standards and instructional objectives. Understanding those issues as early decisions are made is critical. These CCSS are so new that there is no possible way to present a perfect, well-defined process and solution to implementation issues at the national level. We must begin somewhere and move forward together, learning along the way from and with each other.

This entire process is also about the local district creating a system of curriculum, instruction, and assessments; there simply must be a system in place before system thinking can be applied. A system entails specific expectations and time frames and monitoring and corrective action to continuously improve. The guidelines are presented, and the local district must commit to creation of such a system.

PROCESS CHECKLIST

Make sure you have addressed or at least considered each of these tasks and used this in the design of your work.

- ❐ Do the faculty and entire professional learning community really understand what standards are?
- ❐ Do the faculty and entire professional learning community understand standards-based lessons and the design of those lessons?
- ❐ Have I created an environment and sense of importance and acceptance for the CCSS? Do people believe we are serious about this work?
- ❐ Does the process I am designing provide the time and resources to build local consensus on the exact meaning of the academic expectations outlined in the CCSS?

(Continued)

(Continued)

- ❒ How familiar is the professional learning community with the new CCSS?
- ❒ Am I comfortable with and prepared to deal with the reality that some of the new CCSS learning expectations are not aligned with current state assessment systems?
- ❒ Am I prepared to discuss the reality that the CCSS have already been released but the assessment system has not?
- ❒ Am I comfortable with expecting people to do the curriculum alignment work with no knowledge of the assessment system?
- ❒ Do we have local people on staff to help with this understanding?
- ❒ Have we set aside adequate time for the staff development issues we need to address?
- ❒ Am I comfortable with melding this new CCSS alignment work with current or past curriculum work?
- ❒ Do I or someone in a leadership position in the district completely understand the concepts of Power Standards and instructional objectives?
- ❒ Do I understand and am I prepared to create a curriculum, instruction, and assessment system?

2 Curriculum Issues and a National Curriculum Model

CHAPTER EXPECTATIONS

The concept of a curriculum and what it is and what it should be is explored, and a new model for a national curriculum built on the Common Core State Standards (CCSS) will be offered and explained. Those well-versed in curriculum design or not interested in such a national model may wish to skip this chapter, but the chapter does offer food for thought and challenges currently held beliefs. While I advocate for a national curriculum model, I realize that such work must begin at the local level and slowly evolve into a national model.

ACTION STEPS

Steps to consider and address in doing this phase of the work:

- Answer the Question, "What Is a Curriculum?"
  - Consider your options for defining curriculum.
  - Explore and understand the proposed new model for a national curriculum.

  - Determine if the proposed curriculum model fits your purpose or if it needs to be modified in some way.
  - Ensure that you, as the instructional leader, are comfortable with and can justify the model of curriculum to be used.
- Come to Consensus on Defining a Curriculum
  - Establish expectations for the curriculum document.
  - Determine what your curriculum will include.
  - Determine what your curriculum will not include.
- Determine Where Resources Will Be Located
  - Determine the use and placement of curriculum mapping.
  - Determine the role of lesson plans.
  - Identify additional instructional resources, if any, to be made available and part of this project.
  - Determine how all of these resources will be stored, edited, and shared.
- Assemble CCSS Documents for Doing the Alignment Work
  - Identify those documents that will be needed in this process.
  - Determine method of sharing (electronically or in print) and make arrangements accordingly.
  - Identify and make available any state documents that may be needed (i.e., assessment frameworks, etc.).
- Decide If You Need Outside, Expert Support to Do This Work
  - Identify local on-staff personnel, if any, to lead this work, or seek outside help.
  - Determine if any help is available through a state or local agency.
- Determine Staff Development Needs for Transition to Standards-Based Curriculum
  - Determine current level of staff knowledge of and comfort with standards-based learning and the CCSS.
  - Provide adequate time, support, and resources.
- Determine if You and Your District Can Be Comfortable With a Nonprescriptive Curriculum That Emphasizes Certain Parts of the CCSS
  - Learn the proposed curriculum system yourself, and then make sure the political environment can support such curriculum design.
- Build Acceptance Within the Staff for a Curriculum That Will Set the *What* and the *When* but Not the *How* of Instruction
  - Ensure that your staff understands the components of this new system and is comfortable with/can accept such direction.
  - Ensure that local staff expertise is used, where possible, in the design and structure of this new system.

- Address the Issue of How to Best Monitor This New Curriculum to Ensure Faithful Implementation
    - o Determine if a classroom walk-through model of some kind is appropriate to monitor the faithful implementation of the model.
    - o Determine that if you will not use a classroom walk-through model, what formal process will be used?
- Commit to Moving Forward With Common, Formative Assessments
    - o Do so in a realistic time frame, allowing the staff to use the CCSS and quarterly instructional objectives to refine and improve that work.
    - o Do not necessarily move for full implementation the first year but in years to come.

WHAT IS A CURRICULUM?

As the CCSS move forward, there is an increasing call for a new national curriculum model to address the CCSS. As noted in *Education Week*, a partnership between the Gates Foundation and Pearson has announced spending $20 million for just such a project (Gewertz, 2011b). Additionally, again in *Education Week*, there are articles opposing any type of shared curriculum, arguing "that shared curriculum and tests will stifle innovation, threaten local and state control of education decisions, and standardize learning for students with diverse needs" (Gewertz, 2011a).

Consider Your Options for Defining Curriculum

To expedite this conversation, I believe we must come to consensus on what is contained in a curriculum.

- A list of chapters in the book to be covered?
- A list of the pieces of literature, grammar units, and writing projects students are expected to complete?
- A list of the units or historical events that are to be covered—for example, the Civil War through World War II?
- A list of topics to be studied?
- Sample lessons plans for teacher consideration?
- Mandatory lesson plans to be presented by all?
- A day-by-day listing of lesson plans and mandatory classroom activities that all are expected to adhere to and present?
- Pacing guides?

I have seen and worked in schools and districts that employ every one of these models. In my somewhat limited experience (having been in and/or worked with about a hundred schools), I have seen everything from the chapters in the book assigned to weeks and/or months of the school year to absolutely no curriculum documents at all, and everything in between.

While almost nobody would argue the point that there should be no curriculum documents that drive and/or define instruction, it is first and foremost essential that these documents be defined. These documents must be realistic and respect the competence, science, and art of classroom instruction and the role of the classroom teacher in designing that instruction to meet the needs of students.

If the reader really has trouble accepting my observations here, and many people do, please feel free to apply the questions above to your own district and colleagues. Ask yourself first, then your colleagues, these very same questions, to define a curriculum and see what you find out. Do you even have a curriculum? How do you and your colleagues define a curriculum? If you don't have a curriculum and you are going to create one, then it is important that you agree on a definition of what you will create before you create it. After you have considered the questions above either with yourself or your colleagues, the next section of this chapter will describe the proposed new national curriculum model this book espouses. The Curriculum Audit in Resource B may be of help here.

For use of discussion in this book, a *curriculum* is defined as a document, readily available to and understandable by the entire educational community, that clearly outlines standards-based learning expectations for the year and for the academic terms within that year. It specifically addresses both what must be learned and when it must be learned. These skills will be deliberately scaffolded to maximize student learning, and this curriculum will be the basis for all instruction and assessments within the district. This curriculum addresses the what and the when, but not the how. Nor does it contain resources, suggested activities, or assessments; those documents are contained elsewhere, perhaps in a true curriculum map.

A NEW MODEL FOR A NATIONAL CURRICULUM

I am proposing a new national curriculum model here as a place to begin a national conversation now that we have national learning standards, and I am asking readers to participate in the development and use of this new model in their local districts. While we are far from a national curriculum model at this point, I am suggesting a model that instructional leaders can apply at the local level and share with others and contribute to the national learning on this topic. Whether the reader agrees with the CCSS or a national model for curriculum, there is much to be learned from each other as we move forward with the CCSS.

This proposed model presents a vision of public education defining specific skills and assigning a specific place in the educational experience where that learning is to take place. While we know how students learn and the variability of student learning, it must be reiterated that these are placeholders where the skill is expected to be learned. Everything we know about special learning needs and issues will have to be applied to this process, but that is work to be done.

As I ponder the question of the ultimate purpose of this book—to define and help educators understand how the new CCSS are a real game changer in American public education—it is in the design of a new curriculum model that I see the greatest potential to be a real game changer. After years of no national academic performance standards and then several years of 50 or so different sets of academic performance standards, we now have a uniform, national set of common standards, complete with a common design, format, and set of expectations.

That is the most fundamentally important difference between then and now. We no longer have to try to design curriculum models around 50 different sets of standards with different designs, structures, and expectations. We have a common set of standards to work with, and the design of curriculum now has a driving force that defines the parameters around which we must work and around which we can have a national dialogue. Now we can design a curriculum around a common set of expectations and begin the process of implementing that curriculum, getting feedback, and improving that curriculum.

Survival in the City

I read a newspaper article about an elementary school in a very economically challenged nearby community that had posted some pretty incredible student performance results on recent state tests, so I made an appointment to see the principal to discuss his success. While meeting with the principal and leadership team, he showed me their pacing guides–180 days of lesson plans for every subject taught in every grade. First grade alone was around 2,000 pages of mandated lesson plans, activities, and so on that he assured me were followed

(Continued)

(Continued)

religiously by the entire building. I was stunned that such a prescriptive approach to lesson design was showing such impressive results. While walking me out, I had to ask again about the curriculum model being used, and this time he had a very different answer. He said there were people in the meeting with the leadership team that we had just left who did not answer to him. He went on to say that he and the staff had worked to identify the most critical, important learnings and those drove instruction. Supervision of the required curriculum was in form only, but it kept "them" (central office architects of the curriculum pacing guides) off of his back. While creativity has to be used, it is being used to get around system requirements that don't work–the critical, core learnings must be identified and drive instruction to improve student performance.

New National Model Defined

Any curriculum, whether it is local or national, should fit the following criteria:

- Based on and aligned to the CCSS
- Standards based, not content based
- Be a learnable, not teachable curriculum
- Nonprescriptive
- Address the what and the when of student learning
- Encourage creativity and use of alternative learning sources
- Result in common, formative assessments

Let's look at these criteria one by one and begin a discussion. It is my hope that these criteria can become the basis for a real, meaningful discussion of ways to create a national model of curriculum. In order to create a sustainable and workable national curriculum model, we educators must work together to discuss, disagree about, and improve that model. This definition and resulting documents are intended as a starting place, a place from which we can work together to improve this initial work.

Based on the CCSS. The real potential here is to create not only uniform academic expectations but to present those expectations in a similar format that is aligned to the CCSS. The CCSS has established a naming, sorting convention to arrange the skills by subject and grade level and by domains within the subject/grade level. These domains must be addressed, and the CCSS naming conventions must be carried forward into the new curriculum model to demonstrate that exact correlation to the CCSS and allow discussions across states and even the nation on these issues.

This will also facilitate conversations between and among teachers, parents, students, and everyone else in the educational community. For example, in our fourth-grade math example in Chapter 4, it is imperative that the domains used in the CCSS—Operations and Algebraic Thinking, Numbers and Operations in Base 10, Numbers and Operations–Fractions, Measurement and Data, and Geometry—be an integral part of the new curriculum model. This must carry through all the grade levels and all the subjects and strands used throughout the CCSS. These naming conventions must also follow through in the assessments and reporting conventions used as part of the curriculum-instruction-assessment loop. In the sample local CCSS shown in Chapter 1, every element of the local CCSS is tied to one of the domains, and perhaps several of the clusters, or standards in the CCSS. Since this proposed model also ties every instructional objective to a local CCSS element, every instructional objective will be derived from the CCSS domains.

As explained later in this book, every assessment item in this new system will be tied to an instructional objective, which is tied to a local CCSS element, which is tied to a CCSS domain, thereby showing that correlation between the CCSS and local instruction and assessment. And as suggested above, local assessment results will be tied directly to the instructional objectives—creating, using, and demonstrating a curriculum alignment never really possible with so many separate state standards. The potential for an engaged, productive national conversation on curriculum, instruction, and assessments is incredible.

Standards based, not content based. Any new curriculum needs to address standards, *not* content. As discussed earlier, the expectation will be student mastery of specific skills (RL.6.1: Cite the evidence in the text that most strongly supports a specific analysis of what the text says explicitly as well as inferences drawn from the text, and/or RL.6.2: Analyze in detail the development and refinement of a theme or central idea in a text, etc.) and not content based—that is, the content of *Julius Caesar.*

Such curriculum documents must be based on the CCSS, which are standards, and then broken down and synthesized into scaffolded learning building blocks that address the way students learn best, as shown in the local CCSS and instructional objectives model shared earlier in Chapter 1. In the model being proposed, based on the work of Doug Reeves and Larry Ainsworth in particular, the professional learning community or a task force of teachers will take the CCSS through a process of being interpreted into grade-level or course-specific local CCSS (end-of-year learning targets) and quarterly instructional objectives (academic quarter or trimester or whatever learning targets).

But the core issue here is that these learning targets, both end-of-year and quarterly, will be written as standards, *not* as content, to be mastered.

The issue of content used as a means to a performance end must be a critical attribute of this new model: students must learn to cite the evidence in the text that most strongly supports a specific analysis of what the text says explicitly as well as inferences drawn from the text (RL.6.1), not just master the content of *Julius Caesar* or any other piece of literature. Such a specific, standards-based model, to be shared throughout this book, will develop end-of-year academic performance standards and quarterly academic performance standards that are standards based, not content based. This curriculum model will clearly outline for everyone in the educational community what skills will be learned and when those skills will be learned.

This model of curriculum will leave the content, where possible, to the discretion of the classroom teacher. While a social studies class that studies the Civil War must, of course, use the Civil War as its content, the curriculum will address what skills students will be able to apply to the content of the Civil War and at what level of Bloom's Taxonomy that work is to be done.

This particular piece of the definition of a curriculum opens up an entire new horizon for the twenty-first century and its learners. We can now expect our students to learn either skills or standards; the content that the teachers, or the students, use can be almost anything, from Internet material to electronic media to community resources to textbooks and so on. The creativity of the teacher, as well as the location of the school, its culture, resources, and surroundings, are all available in the quest to engage today's learners in today's learning for tomorrow.

Many people are so stuck in the old model of curriculum, driven by content and textbooks, that this standards-based design seems incredibly foreign to them, so it is a system responsibility to help our learning community come to understand and successfully implement this curriculum model and produce content-free, standards-driven curriculum. In this model, we develop the end-of-year academic performance standard and the quarterly standards-based learnings that most effectively lead to that end-of-year target and allow/encourage teachers to use whatever content/resources to engage the students to maximize learning. While the textbook is still a viable resource, it is not the only resource, and the textbook chapters may be used out of order; that is, the chapters may be covered in some other order than chapter 1 through chapter 20.

Teachers in New York City have an entirely different set of community resources than teachers in Little Rock, Arkansas, and this model allows each group to use its own resources. Both groups of teachers, however, have the same resources available to them on the Internet, so there are commonalities that can be shared, and those sharing possibilities will be discussed throughout this book. But, again, the critical issue here is that the curriculum is standards based not content based; in fact, wherever practical, content is deliberately avoided in the curriculum itself.

Oh No, I Had No Idea

In one district where I worked, we had spent a lot of time developing the Power Standards and instructional objectives for a very contentious group for what was considered a very important core course. The day of rollout was finally upon us, and we shared the new Power Standards and instructional objectives with the group. After distributing the documents to the group, I asked if there were any questions. After about 20 seconds, one of the members of the group who had developed the work said, "I'm sorry! I can't do this. It simply can't be done." Somewhat shocked and really caught off guard, I just had to know what was wrong with it. Hadn't we sequenced the skills to maximize student learning? Yes! Hadn't we created a learnable amount of material? Yes. Hadn't we involved everyone in the development of the work? Yes. Why, then, couldn't we implement this work? "It starts in Chapter 7 of the book," was the reply. After a few moments of stunned silence by the entire group (as a former English teacher, I still didn't even get the concern), the group responded, talked her into it, and we moved on, but it did demonstrate for me how deeply held, almost subconsciously, our belief in and use of textbooks is held.

This also creates an entirely new opportunity for curriculum mapping. In the current model, classroom activities are mapped and shared by teachers. In this new curriculum model, teachers can certainly use a curriculum map, but the mapping will be somewhat backward, and all mapping will revolve around suggesting specific instructional/learning activities, resources, and academic vocabulary to the specific instructional objectives. For example, when a teacher finds or uses a resource that is especially effective in helping students learn a particular instructional objective, that teacher will simply map that strategy to that instructional objective and that strategy can be saved for future use and shared as needed. (For example, please go to www.partners4results.org/demo, go to Power Standards Maintenance; then select Curriculum Map.)

Be a learnable not teachable curriculum. We have all seen or been victimized by curricula that are simply far too much and far too complicated for our students to learn in the allotted time. Frequently referred to as the "teach the whole book" syndrome, such unrealistic expectations are frequently the order of business. As the political process developed the state standards, we frequently saw totally unrealistic expectations for the amount of learning to take place. Such curriculum overload is not a rare occurrence, and it is essential that we follow the work and teachings of Larry Ainsworth and Doug Reeves by powering these learnings into the most essential, most critical skills that our students can learn in the allotted time. We have only 175 days or so of instruction, less the confusion and excitement of Halloween, Thanksgiving, Christmas, spring break, and so on, and add to that athletics, homecoming, prom, and the like at the high school level, so we must be sure to define a learnable amount of skills for our students to learn.

We can certainly teach the whole book, but our students certainly can't learn the whole book in the allotted time, so we, as professional educators, must find a way to limit the amount into a learnable rather than teachable amount. The skills that end up in the curriculum must represent that learnable amount and must be sequenced to maximize student learning. Remember, I really did teach my dog to whistle; the only problem is that he didn't learn it. Let's make sure we don't just teach our kids—they have to learn. To help change the focus from teaching to learning, I now try to frame discussions in terms of what students must learn rather than what we must teach; it is all about learning, not teaching.

Nonprescriptive. As discussed earlier, this new curriculum model must, whenever and wherever possible, deliberately and intentionally avoid prescribing teacher instructional activities. This curriculum will define and sequence skills that students must know and be able to do. How to get students to mastery of those skills is the science and art of teaching. To prescribe specific learning activities at the national level (and I believe even at the local level) is pure folly: suggestions, yes—mandates, no. In our diverse, multicultural, multidimensional society, it is totally impossible to design classroom lesson plans that are applicable in every situation in every classroom in America.

It will be the role of curriculum mapping and the creation of a national dialogue around ways to best maximize student learning on particular instructional objectives that will be an additional part of this model. We need to create ways to help educators have a dialogue around specific classroom activities that improve student learning. When more of us are teaching the same skills (standards) at the same time, there will be more reason and opportunities for such professional dialogues. Professional dialogues around improving student learning of specific skills (standards) have much more potential to drive true, meaningful change than arbitrarily prescribing classroom practice.

Address the *what* and the *when* of student learning. This new curriculum model must clearly identify not only the specific academic performance skill but also when that academic performance skill is to be learned. In our current unaligned system, we are frequently not sure when a skill should have been learned, so how do we improve a learning system if we don't know when a skill is to be learned?

For the sake of clarity, when I say *learned*, I mean *mastered*, which is why the instructional objectives have to be so carefully scaffolded to ensure mastery. During the course of instruction, lots of skills will be introduced, reviewed, revisited, and reinforced in the process of instruction; but in this system, the skill in the instructional objective to be learned is the skill to be mastered. This is also why the instructional objectives are limited to a learnable amount during the academic term. This model is not looking for the specific day when a student will master an instructional objective, but rather this model assigns a learnable number of instructional objectives to a nine-week period and assigns an approximate order in which they will be learned. We will now expect teachers to do their best to implement this new curriculum. Then we will gather feedback from those same teachers on what parts of the curriculum worked and how to do things better and refine the curriculum as needed.

By deliberately and intentionally scaffolding the learning, the curriculum ensures that the same skills are being taught in approximately the same time frame by all the teachers in that grade level or course. While the curriculum does not dictate the content or the instructional approach, it does ensure that the skills are being taught at about the same time by all the teachers.

This encourages and enables the use of common, formative assessments—those assessments administered by all teachers in the grade level/course at the same time and graded on the same scale to gauge student progress toward learning the intended curriculum so instruction may be altered. These common, formative assessments will be designed around what was actually taught by all the teachers. For example, all the teachers just taught simplifying fractions and converting to decimals, now those same teachers can administer the same assessment of those skills and see how *our* kids did. Having all teachers teach the same skills (simplifying fractions and converting to decimals), gives us a cause and a reason for a common, formative assessment *and* a professional conversation about differences within and between classes—to determine how well our students learned the skills and whether there were instructional approaches that were used that worked better than other instructional strategies.

In this example, since content and methodology were not prescribed, those teachers can now look at their results and see which students learned simplifying fractions and which students learned converting to decimals. Were there significant differences in learning between or within classrooms? How do we account for those differences? Did one instructional methodology or resource prove particularly effective? Ineffective? Did the assessment itself work? Now teachers can engage in true professional learning community conversations about student performance because the teachers have all taught the same skill and used the same assessments to measure mastery.

In the system being advocated, such assessment reports include item analysis (how each student did overall and item by item), instructional objective analysis (which students did and did not master which instructional objectives), and comparison of instructional objective mastery (by classroom, grade level, and district). Such reports in real time facilitate the professional learning community conversations that are key to improving student performance. (For sample reports, please go to www.partners4results.org/demo, click on Assessment Maintenance and sample reports.)

In my experiences and practice, this is where the national predeveloped assessments can miss the mark. Teachers are busy teaching what it is that they teach, whether that is content or skills, or some combination of both. In the current system, what skills they are teaching frequently vary significantly from classroom to classroom, even when there are attempts to coordinate content. Then along comes one of those locally mandated, standardized national formative assessments that test a completely different set of skills or content than what was being taught by the teacher. Or equally frustrating, the national assessment assesses the skill at a different level of Bloom's Taxonomy than the skill was taught by the teacher. Teachers are busy teaching "this," and they are mandated to give a test that assesses "that."

There is no question of the motivation to use these national assessments during the school year; the national assessments are used to help monitor student progress toward mastery of the intended curriculum. But can the national assessments really do that? Since teachers don't see these tests in advance, and since their instruction is not deliberately aligned to the skills being assessed on that assessment, is there any wonder that teachers bemoan "another test"? We have them busy teaching "this" and now we are busy testing "that." Without specifically and deliberately aligning the formative assessment administered to the skills that all of the teachers have taught, there can be no correlation drawn from assessment results and instructional strategies. This proposed model ensures that assessment/instruction alignment is deliberately and intentionally planned and executed to create the alignment of the curriculum and assessment system.

Encourage creativity and use of alternative learning sources. Since this new curriculum does not prescribe activities but only defines learning expectations, the whole world of resources is open to the classroom teacher. By defining the *what* and *when* of student learning, but not the how of instruction, this new curriculum allows and encourages creativity and alternative materials to maximize student learning. The curriculum itself is not necessarily the place where learning materials and instructional activities belong. The curriculum being discussed defines the what and when of learning. The curriculum map and other resources that encourage a national dialogue on instructional strategies and resources are where materials, strategies, and ideas belong. While no instructional material or approach is mandated in this new curriculum model, the results of common, formative assessments can certainly identify materials or instructional strategies and approaches that work.

As I read the criticisms and concerns that swirl around the American public education system, it is an almost constant criticism that we are not using the new technologies that are so readily available to us. Education is frequently accused of being a nineteenth-century dinosaur trying to meet the needs of the twenty-first-century learner, and we are generally out of touch with our new generation of learners. I hate to admit it, but much of what is currently going on is exactly like the critics call it—out of step.

By redefining curriculum as a set of skills to be learned along the way, we can free teachers and students to find and use new technologies and technology approaches to learn and express the learning of those skills. Technology, when viewed from this perspective, can be part of the answer to our problem rather than part of the problem as we try to force our technology-enabled students through our technology-barren curriculum and learning experiences. I really do see the approach advocated here opening all kinds of doors and opportunities for change and improvement here and in the future.

Result in common, formative assessments: This new curriculum absolutely must result in the development and use of common, formative assessments. Not common tests, but common, formative assessments as defined above—assessments given by all teachers and used to inform instruction. One of the most deeply held beliefs I have struggled with through years of administrative leadership and consulting is the fundamental understanding and use of assessments as formative assessments. I have been able to get teachers to use common assessments, but for them to really understand the use of these assessments to inform instruction, to be the basis for reteaching and retesting is a quantum, very difficult leap for many educators.

Remember, in our new standards-based environment, learning the standard is the issue. Not how quickly you learn the standard, but whether you learn the standard. In our new environment, you learn the standard, try the standard, get feedback, and try it again.

To retest or not to retest? While working as an administrator, we were in the early stages of developing Power Standards and a standard-based curriculum. As the group struggled with limiting the amount to be learned and the concept of teaching the standard, assessing the standard, reteaching to address weaknesses, and reassessing, one of the teachers really flared and demanded if we were going to allow students to be retested and improve their score. Sensing the tension in the room, I suggested we hold that conversation for a later time. A year later that same question came up and the same teacher who had flared a year before, calmly stated, "Of course we will; that's what standards-based instruction is all about." The point of this example? Allow your people to "grow into" these new expectations and experiences.

As John Hattie (2009) points out in *Visible Learning,* the effects of formative assessment are equal to 90% of a standard deviation, while socioeconomic status (SES) accounts for 50% of a standard deviation. By a factor of almost 2 to 1, formative assessments, when properly used, outweigh SES. The proper use of formative assessments is something educators can control—SES is not. What does it mean to use formative assessments properly?

Doug Reeves tells us in *Making Standards Work* (1996–1998) that how we use an assessment is what makes it a formative assessment—what we do with the assessment *after* it is given. In the traditional model of teach, test, grade, and move on, there is no formative assessment; it really does not matter if the assessment is a common assessment (given by all teachers). Even though it is a common assessment, it is not a formative assessment and will not impact learning like formative assessments can and do impact learning unless the results inform instruction. Larry Ainsworth and Donald Viegut's (2006) *Common Formative Assessments* is a great resource for better understanding this work.

Also, helping teachers understand and implement these common formative assessments is a system responsibility and must be a matter of deliberate staff development and expectations that this work be done. As I have seen more than once, districts can develop common assessments and make sure all teachers use them. But the district must develop and implement a process for the use of those assessment results by and with the teachers.

This process of using the data to drive instruction must help teachers understand how to use assessment results to inform instruction and improve student performance. This process must be deliberately designed and built in or it will not happen; nor will it happen if time and resources are not built in. It takes more than noble plans to change the world; the system must make sure to provide its teachers with the knowledge, skills, time, and processes to implement such new learnings.

Those are the criteria for the new curriculum model, but let's make sure we all understand this is not the final, definitive definition or final critical attributes of this new curriculum model. There are lots of people out there with lots more to contribute to this new model, and we must provide an opportunity and a venue for that conversation. I do not claim to have all the answers, but knowledge and experiences give me a perspective to initially frame this conversation. It is now an opportunity for you, the reader, to consider the ideas presented here and to respond to or expand upon those ideas and contribute to the body of knowledge on this topic. This conversation like all conversations among professionals should remain civil at all times. To participate in that conversation, please go to www.partners4results.org/ccss, click on Definition of Curriculum, follow the directions, and post comments as you see fit.

PROCESS SUMMARY

The main issue at this point in the process is building your own as well as others' understanding of curriculum issues and the district's expectations for the coming work. Readers must be sure that they are comfortable with a definition of curriculum; further, it must be ensured that the district expectations for curriculum development are aligned to their expectations. This agreement must also be shared with and consensus built on with the group to do the work and implement the curriculum documents. The entire professional learning community must understand and accept the definitions and processes to be used and the final curriculum documents that are expected.

While the definitions suggested in this chapter may not be completely aligned to either the local leader's definitions or the group's definitions, consensus and agreement must be sought and secured in advance to make sure expectations are established and met. This is another example of beginning with the end in mind.

PROCESS CHECKLIST

Make sure you have addressed or at least considered each of these tasks and used this in the design of your work.

- ❒ Come to consensus on defining a curriculum and establishing expectations for the curriculum document. What will it include? Not include?
- ❒ If not in the curriculum itself, where will resources (curriculum map, lesson plans, instructional resources, etc.) be located? How will they be shared?
- ❒ Will curriculum mapping be part of this project?
- ❒ This new curriculum will be based on and aligned to the CCSS. What documents do you need to make sure that alignment happens?
- ❒ Do you need outside, expert support to do this work?
- ❒ This new curriculum will be standards based, not content based, so what kinds of staff development do you need to provide? Make sure you provide the time, support, and resources.
- ❒ This curriculum must represent a learnable not a teachable amount of learning. Are you comfortable with that concept and able to discuss/defend that position?
- ❒ Are you comfortable with a curriculum that is nonprescriptive, or do you need to build in prescribed activities and mandates for activities?
- ❒ The curriculum will address the what and the when of student learning, so you must be prepared to help teachers work through that and plan accordingly.
- ❒ Are there resources in place or available that will allow for the monitoring of those curriculum expectations to ensure faithful implementation?
- ❒ Are you comfortable with encouraging creativity and use of alternative learning sources?
- ❒ If two teachers use profoundly different materials to teach the same skills, is that acceptable to you and the district?

Are you and the district prepared to move forward with common, formative assessments? Maybe not the first year of implementation, but in years to come?

3 The Development and Use of Local CCSS, Quarterly Instructional Objectives, and Common Formative Assessments

CHAPTER EXPECTATIONS

This chapter outlines the specific steps in the process of building local (Power Standards), instructional objectives, and common formative assessments, all based on the Common Core State Standards (CCSS). A critical issue in this process—carrying the naming conventions and resulting structure of the CCSS across all levels of this new curriculum, instruction, and assessment system—is also explained. This chapter also shares some sample custom bubble sheets and discusses the issues involved in the use of bubble sheets and local assessments in general.

ACTION STEPS

Steps to consider and address in doing this phase of the work:

- Build Local CCSS
  - Directly connect each element of the local CCSS to a domain of the CCSS.
  - Ensure that all domains of the CCSS are addressed in the local CCSS.
  - Vertically articulate local CCSS.
  - Ensure that the progression of skills from grade level to grade level is appropriate.
  - Ensure that the academic rigor of the CCSS is reflected in the local CCSS.
  - Ensure that the verbs in the local CCSS and quarterly instructional objectives directly align to the verbs in the CCSS.
  - Ensure that the local CCSS represent a learnable amount of skills.
- Design Quarterly Instructional Objectives
  - Vertically articulate quarterly instructional objectives.
  - Ensure that the skills in the quarterly instructional objectives represent a logical progression of skill acquisition that flows from term to term.
  - Ensure that every quarterly instructional objective is tied to an element of the local CCSS.
  - Ensure that every quarterly instructional objective will support the development of assessment items to measure student mastery.
- Develop Common, Formative Assessments
  - Ensure that staff completely understands formative assessments and their use in the reteaching loop of a standards-based system.
  - Ensure that assessment items are aligned to the quarterly instructional objectives.
  - Address grade-level and age-appropriate answer sheet issues.
  - Encourage use of higher-level skills, rubrics, and performance assessments.
  - Ensure that staff understands and supports common assessments.
  - Ensure that staff understands and can use data from formative assessments to inform instruction.
  - Provide the time and structure for staff to process the data from these formative assessments and learn to use the data to improve student performance.

  - Identify local exemplary practice and existing practitioners in using formative assessments.
  - Use your current staff members who are already doing this work.
  - Identify current practitioners and allow them a leadership role in moving forward, where and when possible.
- Address Issues in Creating Common Formative Assessments
  - Build a system of support.
  - Provide lots of support and expertise as needed.
  - Address the problems with using premade national assessments.
  - Allow those internal people who wish for the opportunity to move ahead and develop their own local assessments the opportunity to do so.
- Design Local Assessments
  - Ensure that all local assessment items are directly tied to instructional objectives.
  - Ensure that the verb used in the instructional objective is reflected in the assessment items developed.
  - Provide the time and support to develop these assessments.
  - Where possible, use your local leadership who show a particular flair for this work to be leaders in this process.
  - Address the issues of hand scoring and reporting versus machine scoring and reporting and ensure that the system is in place to support your decision.
  - Address the issues of publication, storing, editing, and administering these assessments.

BUILD LOCAL CCSS

Understand the CCSS. As discussed in Chapter 2, the first and most important step in aligning the local curriculum documents to the CCSS is to build local understanding and consensus on the CCSS and their structure and content. The entire task force needs to be brought together to share a group conversation about the CCSS and the document's organizational structure. In working with state standards, this process was far more nebulous because of the 50 different structures of the 50 sets of state standards and the huge variance of materials available to support those curriculum alignment projects. All 50 states will be using the same documents, so the process of building understanding of the CCSS themselves will be far more similar in this initiative than in the myriad state development issues.

The nation has created these CCSS; now the nation's educators must come to understand them in order to implement them. While this may sound like the obvious place to begin and not really worthy of consideration in this or any other book, our experiences in implementing the 50 different sets of state academic standards tell us differently. Perhaps because of the reality of 50 different sets of standards and their complexities or whatever, universal teacher knowledge of and ability to use state standards never reached the level needed for universal implementation. Now that there is only one set of national standards, we can better work together to learn from each other and develop a model of implementation that ensures universal understanding by the teachers, the real implementers of these new CCSS.

One District's Approach

While I was working with a district that had already done considerable work in creating a curriculum based on the state standards, the district realized the need for the change to the CCSS. To accomplish this transition to the CCSS, the group first printed its existing curriculum documents for each member of the team and then went through the new CCSS and looked for similarities in the two documents. Once they identified the similarities, group members then went through and noted differences. They also looked at the state assessment system to better understand the assessments where their students would have to demonstrate mastery. Using all of this information, they were then able to move forward and create their own local CCSS and resulting quarterly instructional objectives. The need to create understanding of the CCSS while honoring and using their previous work was most helpful in moving the group forward.

To give the reader a broad overview, the structure and organization of the CCSS are worthy of mention here. However, in my work, I have found it most productive to get the task force doing the work into grade-level or department groups, explain the fundamental organizational pattern of the CCSS—that is, the domains, clusters, and standards—and then guide the groups through the process of building the local CCSS.

To make sure the reader understands that process, the following information from the CCSS (CCSS Initiative, 2010, Mathematics Standards, p. 4) is presented here.

- The standards set grade-specific standards but do not define the intervention methods or materials necessary to support students who are well below or well above grade-level expectations.

- Organizationally, and across grade levels, the standards are organized using the following method:
  - o *Content standards* define what students should understand and be able to do.
  - o *Clusters* are groups of related standards.
  - o *Domains* are larger groups that progress across grades.

These two statements will be key to the design of our local CCSS in that they will set the parameters for the work and ensure continuity between and within grade level and course design. This standard design format used in the CCSS will help teachers ensure uniformity in the design of the resulting local CCSS and instructional objectives across grade levels. By using that same language and organizational pattern across grade levels and specific courses, the resulting local CCSS and instructional objectives can reflect that same continuity. This is the key design difference in the new CCSS-based curriculum documents: the nomenclature and design will follow through all levels of the resulting curriculum documents.

Design local CCSS. As each grade level/department begins the design phase of this project, I always take it first to the appropriate grade level or department—first grade to first-grade CCSS, and so on. Once they get to the appropriate grade level, the next step is to select one of the domains contained in that grade-level or department set of the CCSS. Once the domain is selected, the group looks at and becomes familiar with the clusters within that domain. Finally, the group turns its attention to the actual standards themselves.

To better understand this process, here is a chart from the CCSS.

Table 3.1

Domain	Cluster	Standard
Geometry	Draw and identify lines and angles, and classify shapes by properties of their lines and angles.	Draw points, lines, line segments, rays, angles (right, acute, obtuse), and perpendicular and parallel lines. Identify these in two-dimensional figures.
Geometry	Draw and identify lines and angles, and classify shapes by properties of their lines and angles.	Classify two-dimensional figures based on the presence or absence of parallel or perpendicular lines, or the presence or absence of angles of a specified size. Recognize right triangles as a category, and identify right triangles.

(Continued)

Table 3.1 (Continued)

Domain	Cluster	Standard
Geometry	Draw and identify lines and angles, and classify shapes by properties of their lines and angles.	Recognize a line of symmetry for a two-dimensional figure as a line across the figure such that the figure can be folded along the line into matching parts. Identify line-symmetric figures and draw lines of symmetry.
Measurement and Data	Geometric measurement: Understand concepts of angle and measure angles.	Recognize angles as geometric shapes that are formed wherever two rays share a common endpoint, and understand concepts of angle measurement.
Measurement and Data	Geometric measurement: Understand concepts of angle and measure angles.	An angle is measured with reference to a circle with its center at the common endpoint of the rays, by considering the fraction of the circular arc between the points where the rays intersect the circle. An angle that turns through 1/360 of a circle is called a "1-degree angle" and can be used to measure angles.

Used with permission.

The reader can see that the Math CCSS go from domain, to cluster, to standards, each level with an increasing level of complexity and/or specificity. The task before the grade-level/department group is now to turn all of this verbiage into a coherent, learnable amount that meets the criteria for a Power Standard—endurance, leverage, and readiness for the next level—that we discussed in Chapter 1.

In this model of curriculum, each grade level or course local CCSS has the lead-in line, "By the end of third-grade math, the student will . . ." and then there are several bulleted elements that specifically describe the end-of-year learning expectation. The design group must now look at each domain and select the clusters and specific standards that will be included in that specific element of the local CCSS. Remember, the local CCSS represent a learnable amount of the most critical, most important skills that learners must know and be able to do. Listed in Table 3.2 is this work as it applies to third-grade math.

While Table 3.2 shows each domain used in developing the individual elements of the local CCSS, it is also important that the group identify and use the CCSS themselves in developing the elements. This allows the specificity of expectations to be better defined both in the local CCSS, above, and in the quarterly instructional objectives, which we'll discuss shortly. Please look at CCSS Table 3.3 on page 54, which is part of the software package at www.partners4results.org/demo. It also shows the specific standards used in developing each element. Note that because this chart is computer generated, the header for the far right column consists of codes designated and used by the software to link the information and may therefore seem nonsensical.

Table 3.2

By the end of Grade 3 Math, the student will . . .		
Power Standard Element	**Local CCSS**	**Common Core Domain**
1	Represent and solve problems involving multiplication and division	Operations and algebraic thinking
2	Multiply and divide within 100	Operations and algebraic thinking
3	Solve problems involving the four operations, and identify and explain patterns in arithmetic	Operations and algebraic thinking
4	Use place-value understanding and properties of operations to perform multidigit arithmetic	Number and operations in base 10
5	Develop understanding of fractions as numbers	Number and operations-fractions
6	Solve problems involving measurement and estimation of intervals of time, liquid volumes, and masses of objects	Measurement and data
7	Represent and interpret data	Measurement and data
8	Geometric measurement: Understand concepts of area and relate area to multiplication and to addition	Measurement and data
9	Geometric measurement: Recognize perimeter as an attribute of plane figures and distinguish between linear and area measures	Measurement and data
10	Reason with shapes and their attributes	Geometry

Used with permission.

Table 3.3

Domain	CCSS	Element ID	Power Standard Element	Power Standard Key	Power Standard Element Key	PS CCSSI STRAND DOMAIN ID
Operations and algebraic thinking	3.OA.1 - 3.OA.2 - 3.OA.3	1.OA	Represent and solve problems involving multiplication and divisions.	4	101	OA
Operations and algebraic thinking	3.OA.7	3.OA	Multiply and divide within 100.	4	103	OA
Operations and algebraic thinking	3.OA.8 - 3.OA.9	4.OA	Solve problems involving the four operations, and identify and explain patterns in arithmetic.	4	104	OA
Number and operations in base 10	3.NBT.1 - 3.NBT.2 - 3.NBT.3	5.NBT	Use place value understanding and properties of operations to perform multidigit arithmetic.	4	105	NBT
Number and operations-fractions	3.NF.1 - 3.NF.2 - 3.NF.3 - 3.NF.3a - 3.NF.3b - 3.NF.3c - 3.NF.3d	6.NF	Develop understanding of fractions as numbers.	4	107	NF
Measurement and data	3.MD.1 - 3.MD.2	7.MD	Solve problems involving measurement and estimation of intervals of time, liquid volumes, and masses of objects.	4	108	MD

Domain	CCSS	Element ID	Power Standard Element	Power Standard Key	Power Standard Element Key	PS CCSSI STRAND DOMAIN ID
Measurement and data	3.MD.3 - 3.MD.4	8.MD	Represent and interpret data.	4	306	MD
Measurement and data	3.MD.6 - 3.MD.7	9.MD	Geometric measurement: Understand concepts of area and relate area to multiplication and to addition.	4	308	MD
Measurement and data	3.MD.8	10.MD	Geometric measurement: Recognize perimeter as an attribute of plane figures and distinguish between linear and area measures.	4	309	MD
Geometry	3.G.1 - 3.G.2	11.G	Reason with shapes and their attributes.	4	310	G

Used with permission.

The domains used in the CCSS are directly tied to the individual elements in the local CCSS; these local CCSS elements are in turn used to develop the quarterly instructional objectives, which are the basis for every assessment item used in the common formative assessments. All of this deliberate alignment allows a demonstrable connection between the CCSS and local curriculum, instruction, and assessments.

This process is then followed by every grade-level and/or course-specific group to develop local CCSS or end-of-year expectations. This process, in my experience, usually takes about a day of staff development, but in one day, the district is able to have a complete set of end-of-year learning expectations, aligned to the CCSS, for every grade level/course in the district—pretty amazing.

Vertical articulation of the local CCSS. Once the end-of-year learning expectations are set, it is time to vertically articulate those between grade levels and courses. It is imperative that the new learning expectations be articulated to ensure they meet the following criteria:

- **Logical, appropriate transition of skills between grade levels.** Spend the time to ensure that the end-of-year learning targets represent a smooth transition of skills between grade levels. Make sure the skills identified in third grade represent a consistent increase between the skills in second grade and fourth grade. Avoid any huge leaps or baby steps between grade levels.
- **Domains should be expressed equally and adequately from year to year.** Spend the time to ensure that the domains chosen and their emphases represent a logical and sequential transition between grade levels. Ensure that the use of domains is consistent and educationally appropriate.
- **Skills represent a learnable amount of the most critical, most important skills.** Remember, we don't want to teach our dog to whistle. The expectations must represent a learnable amount to ensure that teachers have the time for the reteaching loop as needed.
- **The level of rigor is appropriate and reflects the expectations in the CCSS.** Take the time to ensure that expectations are aligned to the expectations in the CCSS and have not been made too difficult or too easy.
- **Ensure that the verbs used in the local CCSS are aligned to the verbs in the CCSS.** Remember, the verb describes the cognitive level at which the skill is to be performed, so we must ensure that our locally developed standards match those in the CCSS.

This is accomplished by having grade-level and/or course-specific meetings when the group discusses the issues above and makes appropriate adjustments. I always have "grade-up meetings" first (K with 1st, 2nd with 3rd, etc.). Once these meetings are held (usually less than an hour), we have "grade-down meetings" (2nd with 1st, 4th with 3rd, etc.). This allows for the articulation to be described again, and allows the group to finalize the local CCSS. They have been developed, reviewed, and articulated, so it is time to move to the next step—quarterly instructional objectives.

Design Quarterly Instructional Objectives

Understand quarterly instructional objectives. As the group transitions from the local CCSS to the quarterly instructional objectives, it is essential that it understands the concept of instructional objectives. Remember from Chapter 1, these instructional objectives scaffold the expected learnings to maximize student learning and to ensure that classrooms are focusing on the same skills at the same time of the year to facilitate the creation of common, formative assessments.

The group will now look at each element in the local CCSS and scaffold the learning throughout the year to ensure that students will master the skills represented in the local CCSS. If we look at the third-grade math local CCSS here, we see there are 10 elements. The group now begins to scaffold the skills by academic quarters to ensure mastery of the end-of-year skill.

Design quarterly instructional objectives. Remember, each element of the local CCSS is aligned to the domains and standards in the CCSS. Therefore, as the elements of the local CCSS are scaffolded into quarterly learning goals (instructional objectives), those quarterly learning goals will be reflected in the standards in the CCSS. To better illustrate this point, let's look at the first-quarter instructional objectives developed for the local CCSS used previously.

Please be reminded that the first column tells the academic term, in this case, the quarter, when the instructional objective is to be learned. The second column is the number of the instructional objective—that is, the approximate order in which it is to be learned (O 1.1 means first quarter, first IO; O1.2 means first quarter, second IO, etc.). The third column is the specific language of the learning expectation followed by the numbers of the specific CCSS used to develop this instrumental objective in parentheses. The last column references the local CCSS element to which it is tied.

This process is followed by each grade level and course for each academic term within the school year (usually quarters, but also trimesters or whatever). This develops the scaffolded learnings that will be needed to achieve the end-of-year learning expectations, the local CCSS standard. During this process, it is essential to remind the group of the critical attributes of the instructional objectives (Chapter 1) to ensure that the instructional objectives meet those criteria and can be used in the next step, the development of the common formative assessments.

Table 3.4 Instructional Objectives (End-of-Term Expectations)[a]

By the end of Grade 3 Mathematics, the student will . . .			
TTerm	**IO Number**	**Instructional Objective (CCSS)**	**LCCSS Element**
1	1.1	Identify thousand's place and know its value (3.NBT.1, 3.NBT.2, 3.NBT.3)	4
1	1.2	Identify ten thousand's place and know its value (3.NBT.1, 3.NBT.2, 3.NBT.3)	4
1	1.3	Subtract across zeros (3.NBT.1, 3.NBT.2, 3. NBT.3)	4
1	1.4	Subtract 4-digit numbers with and without regrouping (3.NBT.1, 3.NBT.2, 3.NBT.3)	4
1	1.5	Identify hundred thousand's place and know its value (3.NBT.1, 3.NBT.2, 3.NBT.3)	4
1	1.6	Say and write numbers correctly in word and standard form (3.NBT.1, 3.NBT.2, 3.NBT.3)	4
1	1.7	Compare numbers using greater-than, less-than, or equal-to of whole numbers and money values (3.NBT.1, 3.NBT.2, 3.NBT.3)	4
1	1.8	Find the unknown number in a whole number problem (3.NBT.1, 3.NBT.2, 3.NBT.3)	4
1	1.9	Subtract 4-digit dollar amounts (3.NBT.1, 3.NBT.2, 3.NBT.3)	4
1	1.10	Add 3-digit numbers with and without regrouping (3.NBT.1, 3.NBT.2, 3.NBT.3)	4
1	1.11	Add 4-digit numbers with and without regrouping (3.NBT.1, 3.NBT.2, 3.NBT.3)	4
1	1.12	Estimate addition problems by rounding up to 5 digits and use estimation to validate answers (check answers) (3.NBT.1, 3.NBT.2, 3.NBT.3)	4
1	1.13	Find unknown numbers in whole-number addition (3.NBT.1, 3.NBT.2, 3.NBT.3)	4

TTerm	IO Number	Instructional Objective (CCSS)	LCCSS Element
1	1.14	Add accurately 4-digit dollar amounts (3.NBT.1, 3.NBT.2, 3.NBT.3)	4
1	1.15	Subtract 3-digit numbers with and without regrouping (3.NBT.1, 3.NBT.2, 3.NBT.3)	4
1	1.16	Estimate subtraction problems by rounding up to 5 digits (3.NBT.1, 3.NBT.2, 3.NBT.3)	4
1	1.17	Add accurately 3- and 4-digit numbers in column addition (3.NBT.1, 3.NBT.2, 3.NBT.3)	4
1	1.18	Compare numbers using even and odd (3.NBT.1, 3.NBT.2, 3.NBT.3)	4

a. 3.NBT.1 = Grade 3, Item 1 in Number and Operations in Base 10 for Grade 3 in the CCSS.

Used with permission.

By deliberately examining the actual standards (those learning expectations derived from the clusters and domains in the CCSS) themselves in this development process, it helps the group see specific examples of the learning expectations contained in the CCSS. As the group develops the instructional objectives, frequently encourage it to look at the standards portion of the CCSS to get a direction in developing the specific language for the instructional objectives. This step is very helpful and eases much of the stress the group is feeling.

Articulating quarterly instructional objectives. Once each grade level or course develops its instructional objectives, it will follow a similar, but slightly different process to articulate instructional objectives. This articulation process is done internally within the grade level/course doing the development work on these learning expectations. But it is worth the time to ask the group to go back through the instructional objectives it has developed and address the criteria used for the local CCSS. Again, we want to ensure a logical progression of skills, and so on. Linking the instructional objective to an element in the local CCSS demonstrates the connection to the local CCSS.

Once this work is done, usually involving two more days of staff development work, the district has a curriculum that is aligned to the CCSS and fully articulated between and among grade levels. Think about that—three days of staff development work, and the district has brought its staff together to agree on an aligned, articulated curriculum based on the CCSS. Now it is time to move to the next level, the common formative assessments.

How Do the Teachers Receive This Work? Listed below are several unedited remarks gathered after the three days of training required to do this work. Here is what this group said about this work and its value.

I feel the strengths of this effort are . . .

- Increased knowledge of standards, common and shared goal and am able to change as needed
- Direction and agreement
- Making consistency of the curriculum in each grade level
- More direction for teachers, alignment to standards
- Improving the education the students will get by focusing on what is important
- A sense of direction–it is great to know what to focus instruction on
- Meeting with teachers in my grade level and across grade levels–I like that I understand it because I did it!
- The collaboration of the team for kindergarten and first grade, as well as just meeting with our own class team
- I'm more confident going into the next school year

These are pretty representative of the kinds of feedback regularly received from teachers who have done this work–the process works, and they appreciate the involvement and direction.

Due to the complexity of all of this change on a system, districts will frequently opt to try the local CCSS and instructional objectives for a semester or two, get feedback from the teachers, and revise and revamp those curriculum documents before taking on the assessment piece, and that is fine. Take your time and do it right.

As with every curriculum effort, this process includes a continuous Plan, Do, Check, Act cycle. Several years ago while working with a district, a science teacher was submitting his first-quarter instructional objectives, and I couldn't help but notice he had 14 instructional objectives for the first quarter. Being younger then, I noted to him that 14 seemed like quite a few. He flared and asked me when was the last time I taught biology? I quickly apologized and accepted his wrath. The following year, after trying the curriculum for a year and going through the continuous improvement loop, I was there when he turned in his seven instructional objectives for the first quarter; this time I was smart enough to keep my mouth shut. The point is that people learn from doing, and that instructional leadership must accept that this system requires time and dedication to get better; make sure you provide the time and the support to let this happen.

Develop Common Formative Assessments

Common assessments. Common formative assessments are, first and foremost, common—that is, given by all teachers of the same grade level or course at approximately the same time, scored using the same criteria, and reported using the same format. Let's talk about that for a bit. Believe it or not, common assessments, even in so foundational a course as Algebra I or Freshman English or even third grade, are relatively unheard of in my experiences and work with many districts. There has been and continues to be in many districts a belief that course content, assessments, and grading are primarily a teacher prerogative.

Whether it is called academic freedom, individual choice, subject matter expertise, or whatever, in many systems, the content, assessments, grading, and almost any other part of a grade level or course are totally a matter of individual teacher choice. While the same basic textbook may be required, its use and the amount of it to be covered are rarely mandated, and individual teacher choice prevails in almost all curriculum and instruction decision making. This generally is accepted as the normal order of business in education. And as has been discussed in numerous other places by numerous other authors, doing what we have always done has got us what we always get—huge disparities in student performance and all of the problems inherent is such a system.

Since education's mission has changed to compulsory attendance *and* learning for all, we have to come to consensus on new tools to deliver new results required by that new mission—compulsory learning for all. The most fundamental of those tools is the common curriculum expectations described and explained in the first two chapters of this book and throughout the literature on curriculum alignment. If curriculum alignment is that important, as it surely is, the next logical step in that progression is the creation and use of a common assessment system. Teachers have taught students the same skills; now let's develop common assessments, scored on a common scale to measure how well students learned the skills that were taught: Did they learn those skills?

Formative assessments. *Common* is the first part of the required common formative assessments; that is, the assessments are used and scored by everyone, using common scoring and rating systems. The second part, *formative*, is equally important and, perhaps, far more misunderstood. This new system of standards-based instruction is changing years if not centuries of curriculum, instruction, and assessment practice. As discussed earlier, the old "teach, test, move on" cycle has dominated public education forever. Such a model was important, especially if the teacher was expected to finish the entire book—whether everyone could learn the whole book or not was not important. Such practices, supported by and supportive of the bell curve, created the results we all expected—some learned and some didn't. No problem, the factories need help.

In this old system, tests have for years employed a kind of secretive finality as part of their use. The contents of the assessments (expectations) were completely secret; it wouldn't be fair to let the students know what was "on the test." Then, there was also finality to the test—whatever the grade, it was final—it signaled the end of the learning experience. The student passed or failed, and the class moved on to the next learning experience.

When judging the success of such formative assessments, it is important to see how these assessments and the information they provide are received and used by teachers. The feedback below from teachers who are using the system shows the value and power of formative assessments.

I feel the strengths of this effort are . . .

- Once it all comes together, it will be really good to use
- Standard curriculum
- Digital copies/footprint
- Interesting information the assessments provide
- I was involved in making assessments for Language Arts
- Training is provided
- Training is comprehensible

These unedited replies from teachers who have been using the common formative assessments for one semester show that teachers are really getting it. They are getting information in real time to guide their instruction and increase student learning.

That is not what formative assessments are about; formative assessments inform instruction and give teachers and students important information about what was learned and what wasn't learned, so that the instruction can be revised to improve learning. By agreeing on the expected learnings for a grade level or course and limiting the amount of expected learnings to the essential learnings discussed in the first chapter and lots of research, we provide time to ensure that those critical skills are learned by all.

Formative assessments provide us information on which students did and did not learn a skill and which instructional strategies worked and didn't work.

Addressing Formative Assessments Within the Assessment Development Cycle

It is here, in the development and use of the common, formative assessments that the instructional leader will need to provide patient, supportive leadership as new skills are learned and current skills are honed. In my years of doing this work, I find the concept of common formative assessments to be one of the most difficult pieces of this work. It is worth spending some more time on here and to provide a special notice to the reader to make sure this issue of formative versus summative assessments is addressed completely and readdressed several times as you move through this process.

The use of common formative assessments represents a change in thinking for many but not all teachers. As the transition to a standards-based curriculum and the introduction of standards to be mastered replaces content to be covered, the change in thinking required here can be particularly challenging. For years, public education has used the "teach, test, move on" cycle as the "correct" way to assess students. Grades are then averaged, and a final, averaged grade becomes the grade for the course. There was no evil intention, but, rather, an acceptance as to the way to grade students fairly and impartially.

This new standards-based curriculum model has standards that all students are expected to master. The purpose of the formative assessments (assessments given during the academic term to measure student mastery of the intended curriculum) has changed significantly: Are students mastering the intended curriculum? What changes in instruction need to be made? This is a fundamental change in assessment practice in the district and must be addressed early and often during this process. Staff development and discussions to help teachers and everyone else understand this fundamental shift is mandatory. In the box below, the reader can see where instructional leadership, myself included, failed to help people understand this fundamental change in assessment.

Formative assessments? I didn't know that! While I was working with an early-implementation district, for lots of reasons on both sides of the partnership, the scoring software and process was giving everyone fits. The software is designed to give not only information on who passed and who failed the assessments, but also on which instructional objectives were mastered and which were not—to enable the reteaching, tutorial loop. While talking to several teachers, I found they were scoring the assessments themselves, before they even turned the assessments in to be scanned by the software. When I asked how they could do that scoring and reporting for each instructional objective, they looked at me very puzzled and asked. "Why would we want to do that?" They were only interested in who passed and failed each assessment so they could enter the grade in the grade book and move on to the next unit. Leadership, myself included, had done a terrible job of helping them understand the role of common *formative* assessments; they got the common part, but had no clue on the formative part. Old ways die hard!

Here is where the instructional leader must really be persistent and forward leaning. There are in every organization people who really get it, and this is also true in the correct use of common formative assessments. Many teachers are currently using such practices very effectively, and these are the people who can help move this forward far faster and far more efficiently than any outside consultant. Lots of teachers have been doing this kind of formative assessment to monitor and measure student learning to then address concerns for a long time. Make sure to know who those people are and use them to help move the process forward.

Formative assessments? I already do those! While working with a district, I addressed the entire staff on the need for and use of common formative assessments. Following my remarks, one of the English teachers came to me and invited me to her classroom to see her current assessment system. There it was, in full, living color, a complete set of assessments used in the writing process to assess student abilities in all the areas of writing used for the state assessment and writing in general. There were assessments, rubrics, scoring guidelines, and reassessments based on the same skills to give students a chance to try again and demonstrate mastery or at least improve performance on the second try. This is an incredibly valuable resource within the school community that can be invaluable in moving this initiative forward. Instructional leaders should use their own people whenever possible.

There is certainly a place for final evaluations, called summative evaluations, that measure what was learned and what wasn't learned, and those assessments absolutely have a place in the educational cycle. The state assessments, the ACT, the SAT, and all the other summative assessments measure student mastery of the intended curriculum. Students have one, final chance to demonstrate mastery of that intended curriculum, and significant decisions are made based on their performance on those assessments.

Those summative assessments will always have a place in education, just like final exams and board exams have a place in medicine, law, flying, and so on. Can the person do the things they are expected to do as a result of their schooling and in preparation for their career? This summative assessment is a necessary and appropriate part of education.

The use of formative assessments, those assessments intended to measure progress toward the intended learning, are one of education's most powerful tools in overcoming the bell curve. By first identifying the critical learnings and then assessing along the way to identify strengths and weaknesses in student mastery of sequenced, requisite parts of those intended learnings, this proposed system enables both the students and the teachers to readdress those weaknesses through different learning and instructional approaches.

Students now have an opportunity to own their learning and to use feedback from formative assessments to improve their own performance and mastery of the intended curriculum, what Rick Stiggins calls assessment for learning. Students now have the tools and the opportunity to get engaged in their own learning. They tried it, got feedback, and tried again to improve their performance. There is not a penalty for failing; there is only the requirement to do it over again until they get it right.

Using only the state test to measure student performance is like going on a diet and only getting weighed once a year—the learner and the teacher need data along the way to see if what they are doing is working. Our students need and deserve formative data along the way to help them and the teacher redesign and alter instruction to maximize learning. When formative assessments are used, the ability and opportunity for the student to really engage in learning grow exponentially, and the chance to help students see ways to improve their performance enriches the professional lives of educators.

In this new system, assessments are aligned to the instructional objectives, and one assessment may contain multiple instructional objectives—that is, reducing fractions, finding the lowest common factor, converting decimals to fractions, and so on. While students may have earned passing scores on the overall assessment, they may have failed to demonstrate mastery of one of the instructional objectives. Now there is a chance, a reason, a process, and the data to go back and reteach and reassess this skill. Good teachers have been doing this for years; this system merely provides the data and the process to facilitate this work. We became teachers to help students learn, and this formative assessment loop presents the perfect opportunity to do so.

The learning gains through the proper use of formative assessments were discussed in the first chapter, but it is equally critical to realize the professional and personal gains that this cycle of instruction and assessment offer. All of us who have taught remember the heartbreak we have seen when handing back tests. The huge disappointment we saw in some faces as students saw the results of all their work resulted in an *F* on the test. For whatever reason, that *F* has a finality and a judgment that hurts kids, and we did not get into this profession to hurt kids. Additionally, we all know that after some kids get enough *Fs*, they begin to understand they don't fit in this system and withdraw from it.

But in this old system, there really isn't much a teacher can do but offer extra credit, when possible, or bend the grading scale to help the student at least pass the course. In a system of formative assessments, specific strengths and weaknesses can be identified and addressed, retaught, and reassessed. The penalty for not learning it the first time is doing it again until the student learns it. In a standards-based environment, the issue is learning the standard, not how quickly the standard is learned.

This incredibly fundamental new use of assessments to inform instruction and to help students master the intended curriculum is foundational to standards-based education; however, leadership must be absolutely certain to help teachers understand this new role of assessment and to internalize that new role as the project moves forward.

Frequently, the first step in this new curriculum, instruction, and assessment system is the development of quarterly or semester assessments. These first rounds of assessments generally are of the more summative nature—end-of-quarter or semester assessments, designed to close the learning activities and assess student mastery of the intended curriculum. The leader is reminded to be patient and allow the teachers to "grow into" this new formative assessment work and to work with people to help them understand the overall system before they move into the real formative use of those assessments. It takes time to create such sweeping change in thought and practice.

Address Issues in Creating Common Formative Assessments

Teacher trepidation. The creation of local common formative assessments might create issues at the local level. Teacher resistance/reluctance to do this work is not at all uncommon. While teachers always have and continue to develop their own classroom assessments for their own classes, the thought of developing these common assessments for use by other teachers as a common measure of student performance intimidates some educators.

There are several reasons for the issues created by asking teachers to develop common formative assessments at the local level, and we'll discuss those issues and some proposed solutions and realities. Most teachers I speak with fear the creation of local assessments more than any other piece of this work. Whether it is their memories of the statistics courses they were required to take in college and graduate school, or their fear of psychometrics, or the fear of proving validity and reliability, or the natural fear of developing assessments for use by others beyond their own students, the reality remains that many teachers really see the development of the local assessments as the deal breaker in creating a new system.

Using premade national assessments. There is no question that the use of nationally normed standardized assessments is less disruptive of the entire district and less work for the classroom teacher. Local people spend no time (or fear) developing these purchased tests; there is no question of the validity or reliability of these standardized assessments; there is no questioning the results of these national standardized assessments. The district simply buys them, administers them, scores them, and reports out the scores. As I have alluded to before, that is exactly what is wrong with those assessments; they are not an integral part of the instruction/assessment/reteaching loop so important to standards-based learning.

These really work! I have experienced this resistance in the past, and one district really comes to mind as a great example of opportunities exploited. This district was particularly reticent to develop its own assessments but moved forward with the project. After creating local CCSS and instructional objectives and using them for a year, the teachers began to develop assessments based on the instructional objectives they had developed, tried, and revised during this first year. As they felt more comfortable with the learning targets they had designed, they began to challenge the textbook unit tests with comments like these: "That is not the skill we were trying to emphasize." "That item is not related to our instructional objectives." "I don't like that item." They were, of course, given permission to develop their own assessments and use items from the textbook assessments or not as they deemed appropriate. They really got it and moved forward with developing their own assessments, enjoying the professional empowerment, and getting excited about their great work. Instructional leaders need to make sure to take the time and give the support to foster change.

For example, let's look at using these premade national assessments. In the typical fourth grade, teachers across the district are very busy teaching this particular set of skills (although we know those skills may or may not be the same skills across all fourth-grade classes in a district) when it is time to administer a set of standardized national assessments. While the district teachers have been busy teaching this particular set of skills (and as we've discussed, there is variance between classrooms as to the skills taught), the national assessment may or may not test these same skills that the fourth-grade teachers have been teaching but, rather, tests a completely different set of skills or tests those skills at a different cognitive level than those skills are being taught.

Designing Local Assessments

Using the instructional objectives. The instructional objectives address and solve this problem of assessment alignment within the district/building and alignment to the CCSS. Since the instructional objectives very clearly identify the skill to be learned, the level at which it is to be learned, and the time frame in which it is to be learned, the design of a common assessment based on those instructional objectives is greatly enhanced.

In the new CCSS model of curriculum, instruction, and assessment alignment, these instructional objectives are deliberately aligned to the domains, clusters, and standards in the CCSS, so these assessment items, when designed appropriately, will directly align and reflect the skills in the CCSS. This allows a real national conversation about skills students are learning and a way to report those skills in terms directly aligned to the CCSS.

The design of the instructional objectives themselves may answer the lack-of-direction issue mentioned earlier, but the lack of time remains as an issue. Released-time days, extra-duty contracts, and other uses of non-school time need to be explored and used.

This design of the instructional objectives themselves also addresses a concern of classroom teachers in creating common assessments, the issue of aligning the questions to the level of Bloom's Taxonomy that is expected in the CCSS. Most teachers have received little, if any, instruction in designing assessment items, and the fear of creating assessment items at the appropriate level of Bloom's Taxonomy to reflect the performance demanded in the CCSS tends to intimidate classroom teachers.

That is why some districts I work with choose to implement the local assessments over the period of a year or two. As they try the local CCSS and instructional objectives to make sure they have designed them appropriately and realistically, they build teacher confidence and experiences with standards-based instruction. Once the district has tried the local CCSS and instructional objectives, gathered feedback on them, and is confident those local CCSS and instructional objectives are appropriate and teachers are familiar with them, the assessment development begins. Often, some teachers just cannot wait to get started and begin to design assessments on their own, getting pretty good at it and sharing that expertise with other teachers. Administrators need to keep a close eye on that whole process and help these early starters get some help and share what they learn.

What about validity and reliability? Careful work was done in the selection of the verb used in the quarterly instructional objectives to align that learning expectation to the performance expected in the standard. The noun, in this case "causes of the Civil War," is the content students will be dealing with, and the verb identifies at what level of Bloom's Taxonomy they are to do that work. Are they to list the causes of the Civil War? Analyze them? Evaluate them? Remember, too, that the verbs used in the quarterly instructional objectives may frequently show a progression from one quarter to the next as the verbs used in the instructional objectives intentionally create an increasingly complex task for learners as they move through the academic year. The skill may begin with listing, move to describing, and finish with analyzing as the year progresses, so the assessments will measure that skill at the appropriate level as the academic year progresses.

Also, the feedback gathered as the assessments are developed and administered will help the task force continuously improve its work as it administers the assessments, gathers feedback, and applies that feedback to improve its work. This entire curriculum, instruction, and assessment process is about using the Plan, Do, Check, Act cycle, and the assessments phase must also have that cycle built in. Forms that are helpful in this process are in Resource B.

Since these local common, formative assessments are not part of a national norm-referenced assessment system, the issue of validity and reliability is somewhat different than in national norm-referenced assessments. The local assessments are not intended to be administered nationally, nor are they intended to produce a standard distribution (bell curve). Rather, their validity and reliability are tied to the issue of assessing the specific skill designated in the instructional objective.

For example, if the instructional objective expects students to "add, subtract, and multiply polynomials" (from the instructional objectives in Chapter 1), the issue being considered is, do the items used in the assessment assess that particular skill at the appropriate cognitive level? As the items are used over time, and adjustments are made to those items where student performance and assessment results demonstrate a need to do so, validity and reliability will be established. Again, let's not forget that teachers are designing and using their own classroom assessments constantly. Just as validity and reliability are not the identified issues under these circumstances, they shouldn't distract us from whether the items assess the correct skills, either.

Hand scored versus machine scored. As any district develops common formative assessments, the issue of hand scoring versus machine scoring quickly comes to the surface. Hand scoring, especially of essays and complex math problems, enables teachers to feel better about testing higher-order skills and true performance assessments. However, the realities involved in hand scoring—that is, interrater reliability and a common reporting process—quickly become overwhelming.

The use of common scoring rubrics is very helpful here, but again interrater reliability must be addressed as must the common reporting piece. If all 10 English teachers grade a writing assessment, how are those scores recorded, posted, and reported? Whenever hand-scored assessments with rubrics are used, it is imperative that the district build interrater reliability into the scoring process. That process requires scoring of student work and spending the time to work with staff to ensure that the performance definitions and assigned scores are constant across scorers.

Some districts struggle with doing this reporting work manually, but I have yet to see a manual reporting process that is timely and that works. By the time all the teachers score their assessments, regardless of whether they do it by hand or machine, the task of reporting those scores in a timely, readable manner has always been overwhelming. Additionally, the issue of separating the individual scores into reports based on instructional objectives or rubric-based criteria is far too complicated and needs some kind of electronic reporting help. The website www.partners4results.org/demo can show more of these reports. Sign in, click on sample reports, and see how this software reports student performance results.

Bubble sheets? Another area that raises concerns among local educators is the tendency of electronically scored assessments to use traditional bubble sheets. Many teachers feel constantly barraging students with bubble sheet exams somehow diminishes the quality and academic appropriateness of the assessments. If we are to move forward with performance-based assessments, how can we constantly use bubble sheets? Additionally, for teachers in Pre-K and primary grades, students that young simply do not have the fine motor skills to deal with such tiny bubble sheets and such a huge array of questions and answers on assessments. Both of these concerns are valid and need to be addressed.

While it is true that bubble sheets questions can be low level, asking students to list, identify, and so on, the reality is they do not have to be. Almost all national assessment use bubble sheets yet are assessing students at high intellectual levels. The design of the items themselves is key here, and again, teachers using this curriculum, instruction, and alignment system must be sure to address the verb used in the instructional objective and to align the assessment item to the verb in the instructional objective. If the verbs used in the instructional objectives are appropriate, the assessment items that directly assess those skills will be appropriate as well. If the verbs used are not appropriate, that will come out in the Plan, Do, Check, Act cycle as it is applied to the assessment work (see Resource B6).

Custom bubble sheets. When addressing the bubble sheet issues in Pre-K through the primary grades, again alternatives to traditional bubble sheets need to be explored. Frequently, assessments designed for use with this age group are done verbally, and the results are recorded by the teacher or an aide. This is not always possible based on money and available help for the teacher, but it can be considered when possible. Such scoring practices create opportunities for custom bubble sheet usage, and some examples of these will be shown later.

Custom bubble sheets, designed specifically for both the age and developmental level of the students and the task to be performed, have to be part of the answer here. Bubble sheets can and must be designed that address the individual, age-appropriate needs of the students. Some of the ways we can address this bubble sheet issue are listed below:

- Larger bubbles in general
- Larger bubbles that appear directly on the assessments themselves, avoiding the transfer issues of going from the question to a separate answer sheet
- Rubrics with bubbles to allow teachers to score rubrics and feed the resulting answer sheets through for electronic reading, scoring, and reporting
- Teacher-scored items within the assessments that allow teacher scoring on a predetermined scale of certain items in the assessment
- Direct entry of teacher judgment of student performance on assessment items
- Other designs as developed and deemed appropriate

Samples of some of these custom bubble sheets are shown in the coming pages. The first one (Figure 3.1) is a rubric for speech. The teacher scores the writing sample based on the rubric, and the machine scores the rubric, thus giving the printouts on the categories defined in the rubric.

Figure 3.2 allows quick machine scoring of these early primary answer sheets. Figure 3.3 is an arithmetic exercise; the student simply bubbles in the chosen answer. This allows for individual input and electronic scoring.

Such electronic scoring gives the teacher real-time data on the categories reflected in a rubric and allows for the comparison of student achievement results based on instructional objectives. This, in turn, helps identify the instructional strategies that work, as well as individual student performance strengths and weaknesses. The electronic process used allows for instant reporting and the creation of reports that show student performance based on instructional objectives and compares student performance across building, grade levels/courses, and the district.

Figure 3.1

Student: 110338 — 1/4/2011

Teacher: Teacher — v1.0

Class: Gr: 12 Trm: T1 Crs: Speech Period: 1(A)

Student name:

Speech Common Assessment

	TIME	EYE CONTACT	VOCAL VARIETY, GESTURE, POSTURE	CONTENT	ORGANIZATION	DELIVERY/FLOW/P PREPARATION
5 Exemplary	Student meets time requirements without being overly rushed or slow in delivery	Student makes and sustains eye contact with others around the room. Almost no reliance on notes or sources	Student's message is significantly enhanced by changes in vocal tones and gestures. Posture communicates message well.	Student chooses audience-appropriate examples that illicit a noticeable recognition from the audience.	Student begins speech in an original manner. Opening of speech is relevant to the audience. Content of speech is logical. Conclusion of speech is parallel with opening.	Strong evidence of preparation. Student transitions between ideas in a comfortable and conversational manner. Visual aids and props, if used, enhance message and don't distract attention.
4 Commendable	Student meets time requirements.	Student makes eye contact with audience. Little reliance on notes or sources.	Student changes vocal tones and gestures to communicate points. Changes are placed appropriately in the speech. Posture communicates message well.	Student includes a variety of well-planned examples in speech that are appropriate for the audience. Speech is a topic that matches the student's personality and interests.	Student opens and closes speech with a parallel opening and closing. Content of the speech is logical.	Evidence of preparation. Student demonstrates a comfortable presence and relates to audience well. Visual aids and props, if used, enhance message minimally.

	TIME	EYE CONTACT	VOCAL VARIETY, GESTURE, POSTURE	CONTENT	ORGANIZATION	DELIVERY/FLOW/P PREPARATION
3 Effective	Student falls short or goes over time requirements within a reasonable time window.	Student makes eye contact with audience members, glancing at notes or sources occasionally.	Student uses vocal variety and gestures occasionally, but returns to a default delivery manner.	Student includes examples in speech that support the main idea. The main idea of the speech is clear.	Student opens and closes speech with a clear idea. Content of the speech has an overall logical structure, but could use some revision.	Evidence of preparation. Student demonstrates a comfortable presence.
2 Approaches Effective	Student significantly falls short or goes over time requirements.	Student's focus is split relatively equally between audience and notes.	Student attempts to change vocal tones and gestures but still appears restricted and confined.	Student uses vague examples that do very little to support the main premise or idea. Main idea is present, but needs focus.	Speech is organized with a logical structure, but some elements are out of place. Attempt is made to open and close with a parallel idea.	Little evidence of preparation.
1 Not effective	Student significantly falls short or goes over time requirements due to lack of preparation.	Student relies fully on notes for speech delivery.	Student does not include changes in vocal variety or gesture in speech. Posture is weak.	Student examples have little or no meaning. Main idea is absent.	Structure of speech is scattered. Opening and closing of speech is cumbersome or absent.	No evidence of preparation. Student stammers and is clearly unfamiliar with the material.
	① ② ③ ④ ⑤	① ② ③ ④ ⑤	① ② ③ ④ ⑤	① ② ③ ④ ⑤	① ② ③ ④ ⑤	① ② ③ ④ ⑤

Figure 3.2

Author's Purpose Q2

Student: Student A	1/4/2011
Teacher: Teacher	1
Class: Gr: 03 Trm: YR Crs: READING Period:0	

Read the passages. Then choose the best answer for each question.

Protect Your Head

Many people enjoy riding bikes. They ride for fun and for exercise. However, a fall from a bike is not fun. You can be hurt badly. That's why you should wear a helmet each time you ride a bike. When you wear a bike helmet, you lower your risk of brain injury. If you fall off your bike while wearing a helmet, you are almost 85 percent less likely to have a brain injury than if you were without a helmet. Be a smart bike rider, and wear a helmet each time you ride a bike.

1. What is the author's purpose?

Ⓐ to entertain readers with a story of a bike ride
Ⓑ to explain to readers how to ride a bike
Ⓒ to persuade readers to wear a bike helmet
Ⓓ to tell readers how to choose a bike helmet

2. Which sentence from the story gives you a clue about the author's purpose?

Ⓐ Many people enjoy riding bikes.
Ⓑ They ride for fun and for exercise.
Ⓒ However, a fall from a bike is not fun.
Ⓓ When you wear a bike helmet, you lower your rish of brain injury.

Figure 3.3

Count Sets Nickel/Dime

Student: Student A 1/4/2011

Teacher: Teacher 1

Class: Gr: 01 Trm: YR Crs: MATH Period: 1

Money

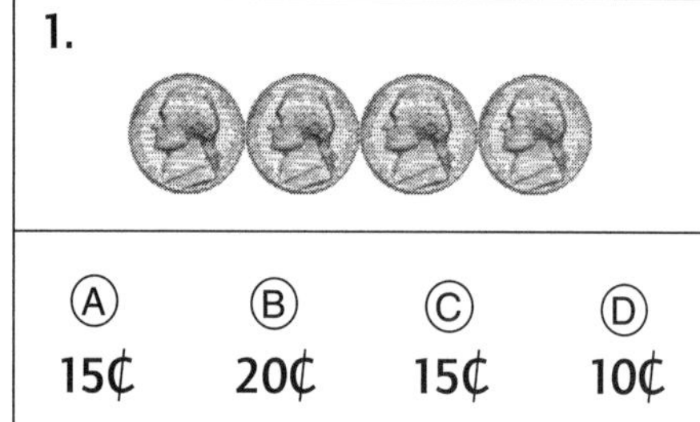
1.

Ⓐ 15¢ Ⓑ 20¢ Ⓒ 15¢ Ⓓ 10¢

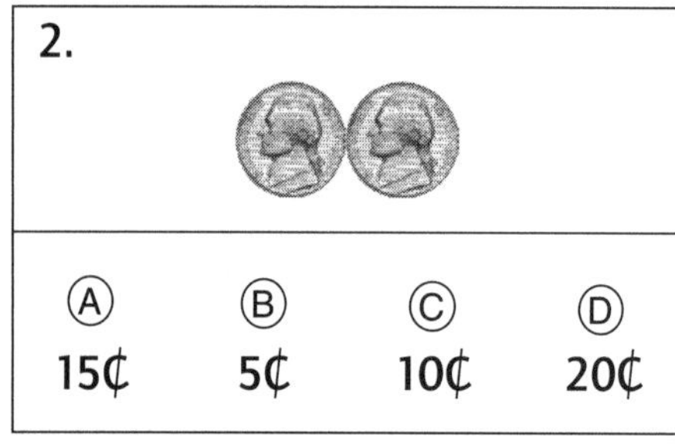
2.

Ⓐ 15¢ Ⓑ 5¢ Ⓒ 10¢ Ⓓ 20¢

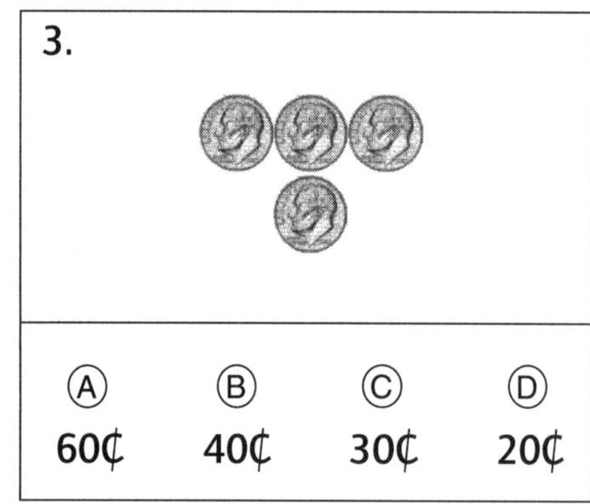
3.

Ⓐ 60¢ Ⓑ 40¢ Ⓒ 30¢ Ⓓ 20¢

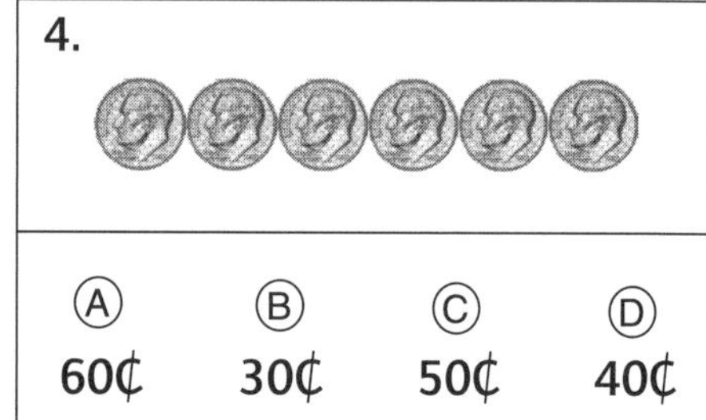
4.

Ⓐ 60¢ Ⓑ 30¢ Ⓒ 50¢ Ⓓ 40¢

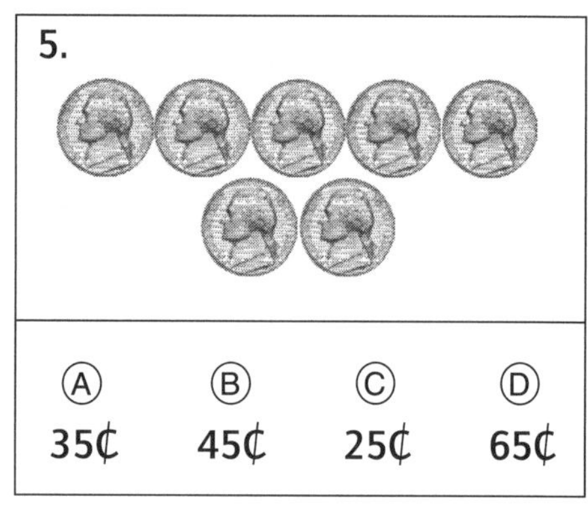
5.

Ⓐ 35¢ Ⓑ 45¢ Ⓒ 25¢ Ⓓ 65¢

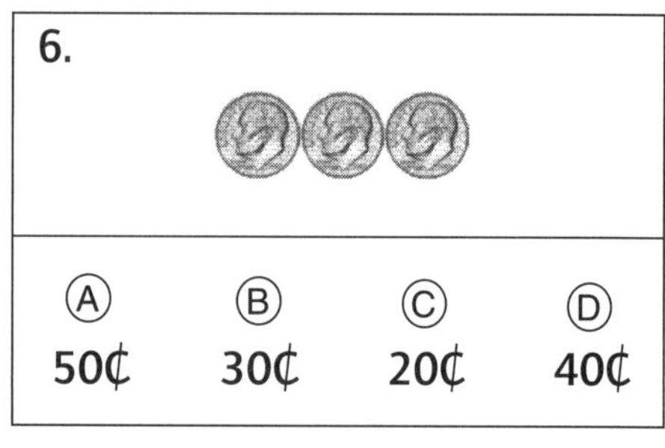
6.

Ⓐ 50¢ Ⓑ 30¢ Ⓒ 20¢ Ⓓ 40¢

The development and use of such custom bubble sheets are definitely part of the answer to this assessment question, and the samples shown here are just the beginning of the possibilities. If an answer sheet can be produced in Word, PDF, RTF, or another format, a custom bubble sheet can and should be developed for such important progressive uses of technology. The samples used here are from some of the districts I have worked with and are actually used by those districts in this process. They are published here as examples of possibilities for doing this work electronically.

As discussed often in this book, www.partners4results.org/demo offers an electronic way to do all of this creation of custom bubble sheets and posting and reporting of scores, and that may be viewed by going to the site, clicking on ASSESSMENT MAINTENANCE and SAMPLE BUBBLE SHEETS.

PROCESS SUMMARY

The work of designing the local CCSS, instructional objectives, and common formative assessments, as well as the issues involved in the work have been reviewed, and the issues associated with that work have been discussed. The design work and the need for staff development and support during that process were discussed in depth, and the need to and potential for tying all of this work directly to the CCSS through the assessment and reporting system were also discussed.

America has a chance to build its own assessment and reporting system around the skills outlined in the CCSS, so it is imperative that the assessments and reporting system use the same language as the domains, clusters, and standards in the CCSS. This enables student reports to move with the student from district to district and even state to state and allows the receiving building to better understand that student's current functioning level.

The use of custom bubble sheets or some kind of electronic scoring capability is a given in this part of the work. The scoring and reporting of this work in such a large setting as a building or district demand some kind of electronic support to be able to provide real-time data in a common, usable, and understandable format. The ability to report out by teacher and by instructional objective (aligned to the CCSS) gives educators huge new possibilities for improving student performance, identifying instructional strategies that work (and don't work) and have real, meaningful professional learning community conversations.

PROCESS CHECKLIST

Make sure you have addressed or at least considered each of these tasks and used this in the design of your work:

- ❒ Built among the group doing the work a common understanding of the design, structure, and expectations of the CCSS
- ❒ Paid particular attention to the domains, clusters, and standards in the CCSS
- ❒ Attached every element in your local CCSS to a domain in the CCSS
- ❒ Ensured that the skills in your local CCSS elements represent the most critical, most important learnings that all students must know and be able to do
- ❒ Ensured that the curriculum expectations represent a learnable not teachable amount of learning
- ❒ Articulated the grade-level and course-specific learning expectations among grade levels
- ❒ Allowed the time and the permission to change and finalize the elements to best reflect the CCSS
- ❒ Developed your local instructional objectives based on the local CCSS elements
- ❒ Ensured that the instructional objectives appropriately scaffold the learning to ensure mastery of the end-of-the year learning expectations
- ❒ Ensured that assessment items can be developed based on your instructional objectives
- ❒ Provided the time and the resources to facilitate common formative assessment development
- ❒ Decided on the process and/or software for publishing, scoring, reporting, and analyzing of the common formative assessments
- ❒ Looked at and developed a process for using custom bubble sheets or some such age-appropriate method for assessing primary and all other age levels of students in all subject areas

4 A Sample K–12 Curriculum

CHAPTER EXPECTATIONS

This chapter will share a sample K–12 curriculum in English Language Arts /and Math that is based on the Common Core State Standards. These documents were developed by local school districts partnering with us and using the processes advocated in this book. This sample K–12 curriculum represents the work of local educators responding to the challenges of CCSS. This will give teachers and educators everywhere a chance to see and understand how the CCSS can be used to create curriculum for specific grade levels/courses.

ACTION STEPS

Steps to consider and address in doing this phase of the work:

- Read and Understand the New Model
  - Spend the time on this sample and make sure you fully understand its structure, design, and intent.
  - Make this model available to your district as a place to begin this conversation.
  - Make hard copies available or use an electronic posting to ensure ready access for all to the model.
  - Make sure everyone understands the model.
  - Ensure the task force identified to do this work understands and accepts this model or an alternative model.
  - Spend the time with the task force to discuss this model fully to ensure they understand the model and their role in developing the new curriculum documents.

- Allow for full exchange of ideas and concerns.
    - Provide time for grade-level/course-specific conversations of the corresponding grade level/course sample as appropriate and where possible.
    - Set aside some time early in the process for grade-level/course-specific conversations about the content and format of the sample.
    - Encourage discussion to promote understanding of the model.
    - Revise the sample as local needs dictate.
    - The sample is exactly that, a sample. Allow/encourage your people to amend change as local conditions, state assessment systems, and so on dictate.
    - Remember, the students will continue to take the state assessment for several more years; if a skill is on the state assessment, we want to make sure we continue to teach that skill, even if it is not a CCSS
- Accept the Realities of a Sample From Several Districts
    - While looking at the model, this is the work of several districts, so the articulation work does not apply, and the writing style will be different.

READ AND UNDERSTAND THE NEW MODEL

The sample curricula that follow are developed and based on the new model of a national curriculum suggested and defined in Chapter 1. Any curriculum, whether it is local or national, should fit the following criteria:

- Based on and aligned to the CCSS
- Standards based, not content based
- Be a learnable, not a teachable, curriculum
- Nonprescriptive
- Address the *what* and the *when* of student learning
- Encourage creativity and use of alternative learning sources
- Result in common, formative assessments

These are the criteria used in developing this curriculum model, and these criteria are reflected in the work that follows. It must also be said that this is work done by local educators in response to a brand-new set of national standards; that is, to say the least, a formidable challenge, but they were willing to do this difficult work *and* put it out there for everyone to see and react to. That work and that willingness to share their work, in and of itself, is to be admired and appreciated. My special thanks to them for both the willingness and fortitude to do the work and the willingness and courage to share that work with a national audience.

Most readers are probably amazed that a K–12 curriculum in one area can be presented without consuming an entire book, much less two major curricular areas being presented in a single chapter of a book. That is one of the beauties of this new model; it is clean and lean, describing the skills to be learned and when those skills are to be learned. That allows for easy reading and clear expectations.

Please remember that in this model of curriculum design, the complications of lesson designs, instructional approaches, assessment strategies, and the other elements needed to guide and assist in the design of instruction and assessments are contained elsewhere. A clear and concise explanation of the learning expectations is presented for everyone in the professional learning community, parents, teachers, administrators—everyone—to read, understand, and work to improve. The technicalities and the details of implementation will be worked out by the local teachers and professional learning communities and shared as technology and local commitment allow and encourage. It will be shared, but not necessarily as part of the curriculum documents themselves.

These local educators have applied the criteria suggested above and throughout this book and present their work for the readers' information and input. Please enjoy it and recognize it for what it is—a place to begin the national conversation on implementing the CCSS. It is not presented as perfect or as the only solution but, rather, as a place to begin a civil conversation about ways to implement the CCSS and ultimately improve learning for all.

To facilitate this conversation at the national level, this model may be found at www.partners4results.org/demo. Feel free to visit that site, sign in, click on the New Curriculum Model icon and use the software to post your comments and exchange ideas with fellow educators.

ACCEPT THE REALITIES OF A SAMPLE FROM SEVERAL DISTRICTS

I have selected grade levels and subjects from several of the school districts we have worked with in this developmental process. As a result of the sampling from various sources, the reader should be aware of several issues:

- Grade-level articulation activities described in this book were not necessarily applied to these samples. You may be looking at the second-grade local CCSS from Geneseo, Illinois, and the third-grade local CCSS from Sauk Village, Illinois, so the vertical articulation we are working on may or may not be represented in the samples being viewed.

- I deliberately selected local CCSS and instructional objectives that represent various writing styles and preferences. Some people prefer to have much more detail in their student performance descriptors, while others prefer broader strokes to describe their expectations, so I present here samples of both. I hope the reader will not find those stylistic differences too distracting.
- There are many different configurations used in scheduling classes and grade levels. Some districts have separate reading and literature and writing classes scheduled within the day. As a result of these varied grade-level and course configurations, the reader may see a reading local CCSS that addresses reading skills exclusively while another set of descriptors addresses reading and literature. The concept is the same; the application is different under different applications.
- There are several variances on the high school math system as well. Some districts have several levels of Algebra 2, for example, and multiple math courses beyond Algebra 1. The courses shown here are for example and understanding of the process and its results only and represent no intended preference or recommendation for curricular organization.

How to Read These Samples

In this proposed model, there is a lead-in line, "By the end of whatever course, the student will . . ." followed by several elements. In the sample curriculum documents that follow, in the local CCSS sections, the first column contains the number of the element, then the exact language of the local CCSS element, and the last column references the domain of the CCSS used to develop that local CCSS element.

In the instructional objectives section, the first column contains the academic term (in this case, the quarter), followed by the instructional objective number (O1.1 means first term, first instructional objective, O1.2 means first term, second instructional objective, and so on). The next column contains the language defining the learner expectation in that specific instructional objective (the numbers in parentheses indicate the CCSS used in developing this instructional objective), and the final column shows the local CCSS element this instructional objective is tied to. Please remember each local CCSS element is tied to a domain in the CCSS.

SAMPLE K–12 ELA CURRICULUM

Table 4.1 Kindergarten

By the end of Kindergarten English Language Arts, the student will . . .		
Power Standard Element	**Local Common Core State Standard**	**Common Core Domain**
1	Print many uppercase and lowercase letters	Language
2	Use capital letters at the beginning of names	Language
3	Write letters for sounds heard in isolation and in words	Language
4	Sort objects into categories and name the categories	Language
5	Demonstrate the use of basic print concepts	Foundational skills
6	Recognize all uppercase and lowercase letters	Foundational skills
7	Recognize and produce rhyming words	Foundational skills
8	Read common, high-frequency words by sight	Foundational skills
9	Produce correct sounds for letters	Foundational skills
10	Identify parts of a book and know the roles of the author and illustrator	Informational text
11	Describe the relationship between illustrations and the text in a story and in the student's own writing	Informational text
12	Be able to identify the main topic and make a self-connection	Informational text
13	With prompting, identify characters and details of a story	Literature
14	Follow the rules for classroom discussion (raise a hand to speak and listen to others)	Speaking and listening
15	Use combinations of drawing, dictating, and writing to express ideas on a topic	Writing

Kindergarten English Language Arts Instructional Objectives (End-of-Term Expectations)[a]

Term	IO Number	Instructional Objective (CCSS)	LCCSS Element
1	O1.1	Participate in the rules of classroom discussion (SL.K.1a)	14
1	O1.2	Sort objects into categories and names the category (L.K.5a, L.K.5c)	4
1	O1.3	Recognize six letters (uppercase and lowercase) presented during the quarter (RF.K.1d)	6
1	O1.4	Produce sounds for six letters presented during the quarter (RF.K.3a)	9
1	O1.5	Able to print six uppercase letters presented during the quarter (L.K.1a)	1
1	O1.6	Able to write at least six letters presented during the quarter for sounds in isolation (L.K.2c, L.K.2d)	3
2	O2.1	Recognize 12 letters (uppercase and lowercase) (RF.K.1d)	6
2	O2.2	Produce sounds for 12 letters (RF.K.3a)	9
2	O2.3	Able to print 12 uppercase and some lowercase letters (L.K.1a)	1
2	O2.4	Able to write at least 12 letters for sounds in isolation (L.K.2c, L.K.2d)	3
3	O3.1	Recognize 19 letters (uppercase and lowercase) (RF.K.1d)	6
3	O3.2	Produce sounds for 19 letters (RF.K.3a)	9
3	O3.3	Able to print 19 uppercase and some lowercase letters (L.K.1a)	1
3	O3.4	Able to write at least 19 letters for sounds in isolation (L.K.2c, L.K.2d)	3
3	O3.5	Identify whether 2 words rhyme (RF.K.2a)	7

Term	IO Number	Instructional Objective (CCSS)	LCCSS Element
3	O3.6	Can read at least 10 kindergarten sight words (RF.K.3c)	8
3	O3.7	Choose the main topic of a story (RI.K.2, RI.K.3)	12
3	O3.8	Identify main characters of a story (RL.K.3)	13
4	O4.1	Recognize all 26 uppercase and lowercase letters (RF.K.1d)	6
4	O4.2	Produce sounds for 26 letters (RF.K.3a)	9
4	O4.3	Able to print 26 uppercase and most lowercase letters (L.K.1a)	1
4	O4.4	Able to write all 26 letters for sounds in isolation (L.K.2c, L.K.2d)	3
4	O4.5	Produce rhyming pairs (RF.K.2a)	7
4	O4.6	Can read at least 20 kindergarten sight words (RF.K.3c)	8
4	O4.7	Track print, read from left to right and top to bottom, and return sweep (RF.K.1, RF.K.1a, RF.K.1b, RF.K.1c)	5
4	O4.8	Identify front cover, back cover, role of author, and role of illustrator (RI.K.5, RI.K.6)	10
4	O4.9	Use capitalization at the beginning of names when writing (L.K.2, L.K.2a)	2
4	O4.10	State a self-connection to a story we have read (RI.K.2, RI.K.3)	12
4	O4.11	Dictate and/or write text to describe their illustrations (RI.K.7)	11
4	O4.12	Identify main characters and three details of a story (RL.K.3)	13
4	O4.13	Produce a combination of drawing, dictation and writing to support a topic (W.K.1, W.K.2, W.K.3)	15

a. IO = instructional objective; LCCSS = local Common Core State Standards; SL.K.1a = Item 1, Point a, in the Speaking & Listening subset of the English Language Arts section for kindergartners in the CCSS; L.K.2c = Item 2, Point c, in the Language subset of the English Language Arts section; RF.K.2a = Item 2, Point a, in the Reading Foundation Skills subset of the English Language Arts section.

Table 4.2 First Grade

By the end of Grade 1 English Language Arts, the student will . . .		
Power Standard Element	**Local Common Core State Standard**	**Common Core Domain**
1	Know and apply the basic elements of phonemic awareness and phonological awareness in reading texts	Foundational skills
2	Decode and read grade level material using word analysis skills	Foundational skills
3	Read grade-level texts with accuracy, expression, and appropriate rate to support comprehension	Foundational skills
4	Read grade-level texts with accuracy, expression, and appropriate rate to support comprehension	Foundational skills
5	Write for a variety of purposes (narrative, expository, opinion, etc.) using appropriate sequence of events or details as well as providing some sense of closure	Writing
6	Demonstrate writing with guidance and support from adults, focus on a topic, gather information, respond to questions and suggestions from peers, and add details to strengthen writing as needed	Writing
7	Participate in and lead collaborative conversations with peers and adults in a small or large group setting	Speaking and listening
8	Create a simple story using beginning, middle, and end with complete sentence structure, grade-appropriate grammar, spelling, punctuation, and capitalization in written language	Language
9	Determine the meaning of unknown words or phrases using word relationships and context while reading and listening	Language

Power Standard Element	Local Common Core State Standard	Common Core Domain
10	Read grade-level material using a variety of reading strategies (phonics/decoding, monitor/clarify, predict/infer, questioning, summarizing, making connections, visualizing)	Literature
11	Retell texts using story elements (setting, characters, plot, conflict/resolution) and compare/contrast selections, characters, and experiences	Literature
12	Read informational texts and utilize various text features to locate key facts or information in a text and identify connections between key ideas	Informational text

1ELA Instructional Objectives (End-of-Term Expectations)[a]

Term	IO Number	Instructional Objective (CCSS)	LCCSS Element
1	O1.1	Read Fountas-Pinnell high-frequency Word List 1 (20 words total) (RF.1.3b, RF.1.3g)	4
1	O1.2	Identify the beginning and ending sounds in words (RF.1.2, RF.1.2a, RF.1.2b, RF.1.2c, RF.1.2d)	1
1	O1.3	Read 3-4 letter CVC and CVCC short vowel words (RF.1.2, RF.1.2a, RF.1.2b, RF.1.2c, RF.1.2d)	1
1	O1.4	Use initial consonant as a clue to decode unknown words (RF.1.3, RF.1.3a, RF.1.3b, RF.1.3c, RF.1.3d, RF.1.3e, RF.1.3f, RF.1.3g)	2
1	O1.5	Reread to identify unknown words (RF.1.3, RF.1.3a, RF.1.3b, RF.1.3c, RF.1.3d, RF.1.3e, RF.1.3f, RF.1.3g)	2
1	O1.6	Use picture cues to build meaning when reading (L.1.4, L.1.4a, L.1.5, L.1.5a, L.1.5b, L.1.5c, L.1.5d, L.1.6)	9

Term	IO Number	Instructional Objective (CCSS)	LCCSS Element
1	O1.7	Answer simple recall questions after hearing read-alouds (SL.1.1, SL.1.1a, SL.1.1b, SL.1.1c, SL.1.2, SL.1.3, SL.1.4, SL.1.5, SL.1.6)	7
1	O1.8	Demonstrate reading fluency during small-group guided reading (RF.1.4, RF.1.4a, RF.1.4b, RF.1.4c)	3
1	O1.9	Distinguish between fiction and nonfiction during a read-aloud (RI.1.1, RI.1.10, RI.1.2, RI.1.3, RI.1.4, RI.1.5, RI.1.6, RI.1.7, RI.1.8)	12
1	O1.10	Distinguish between sentences and fragments (L.1.1, L.1.1a, L.1.1b, L.1.1c, L.1.1d, L.1.1e, L.1.1f, L.1.1g, L.1.1h, L.1.1j, L.1.2, L.1.2a, L.1.2b, L.1.2c, L.1.2d, L.1.2e)	8
1	O1.11	Demonstrate correct spacing between letters and words in a sentence (L.1.1, L.1.1a, L.1.1b, L.1.1c, L.1.1d, L.1.1e, L.1.1f, L.1.1g, L.1.1h, L.1.1j, L.1.2, L.1.2a, L.1.2b, L.1.2c, L.1.2d, L.1.2e)	8
1	O1.12	Utilize journals for daily writing using invented spelling (W.1.1, W.1.2, W.1.3)	5
1	O1.13	Create a shared story with a beginning, middle, and end (W.1.5, W.1.7, W.1.8)	6
1	O1.14	Participate in collaborative conversations about Grade 1 topics and texts with peers and adults in both small- and large-group settings (SL.1.1, SL.1.1a, SL.1.1b, SL.1.1c, SL.1.2, SL.1.3, SL.1.4, SL.1.5, SL.1.6)	7
2	O2.1	Read Fountas-Pinnell high-frequency Word List 2 (40 words total) (RF.1.3b, RF.1.3g)	4
2	O2.2	Identify the "sentence stopper" (ending punctuation) as a question mark, exclamation point, or period (L.1.1, L.1.1a, L.1.1b, L.1.1c, L.1.1d, L.1.1e, L.1.1f, L.1.1g, L.1.1h, L.1.1j, L.1.2, L.1.2a, L.1.2b, L.1.2c, L.1.2d, L.1.2e)	8
2	O2.3	Capitalize the first word in sentences (L.1.1, L.1.1a, L.1.1b, L.1.1c, L.1.1d, L.1.1e, L.1.1f, L.1.1g, L.1.1h, L.1.1j, L.1.2, L.1.2a, L.1.2b, L.1.2c, L.1.2d, L.1.2e)	8

Term	IO Number	Instructional Objective (CCSS)	LCCSS Element
2	O2.4	Identify main characters, setting, and sequence of events of a story (RL.1.3, RL.1.5, RL.1.6, RL.1.7, RL.1.9)	11
2	O2.5	Begin to recognize and self-correct miscues that interfere with fluency and comprehension while reading (RL.1.1, RL.1.2, RL.1.4)	10
2	O2.6	Demonstrate reading fluency in small-group guided reading (RF.1.4, RF.1.4a, RF.1.4b, RF.1.4c)	3
2	O2.7	Utilize journal writing for applying capitals and punctuation while responding to texts (W.1.1, W.1.2, W.1.3)	5
2	O2.8	Create a shared written story with a beginning, middle, and end using a story starter or a graphic organizer (W.1.5, W.1.7, W.1.8)	6
2	O2.9	Utilize journals for daily writing using invented spelling while incorporating conventional spelling of words studied in spelling units (L.1.1, L.1.1a, L.1.1b, L.1.1c, L.1.1d, L.1.1e, L.1.1f, L.1.1g, L.1.1h, L.1.1j, L.1.2, L.1.2a, L.1.2b, L.1.2c, L.1.2d, L.1.2e)	8
3	O3.1	Read Fountas-Pinnell high-frequency Word List 3 (60 words total) (RF.1.3b, RF.1.3g)	4
3	O3.2	Read beginning blends and digraphs in short vowel words (RF.1.2, RF.1.2a, RF.1.2b, RF.1.2c, RF.1.2d)	1
3	O3.3	Reread to clarify meaning (L.1.4, L.1.4a, L.1.5, L.1.5a, L.1.5b, L.1.5c, L.1.5d, L.1.6)	9
3	O3.4	Identify elements of a story such as problem/solution, characters, setting, and main events/details (RL.1.3, RL.1.5, RL.1.6, RL.1.7, RL.1.9)	11
3	O3.5	Use nonfiction text features (tables of contents, glossary, index, picture captions, tables, graphs, etc.) to derive meaning (RI.1.1, RI.1.10, RI.1.2, RI.1.3, RI.1.4, RI.1.5, RI.1.6, RI.1.7, RI.1.8)	12

Term	IO Number	Instructional Objective (CCSS)	LCCSS Element
3	O3.6	Demonstrate reading fluency during small-group guided reading (RF.1.4, RF.1.4a, RF.1.4b, RF.1.4c)	3
3	O3.7	Develop a short story with a beginning, middle, and end using a story starter or a graphic organizer (W.1.1, W.1.2, W.1.3)	5
3	O3.8	Utilize journals for writing three or more sentences using invented spelling and correct punctuation, capitalization, and conventional spelling of words learned in spelling units. Demonstrate proper letter/word spacing (W.1.1, W.1.2, W.1.3)	5
3	O3.9	Apply the reading strategies taught to effectively self-monitor while reading grade-level texts (RF.1.4, RF.1.4a, RF.1.4b, RF.1.4c)	3
3	O3.10	Demonstrate reading fluency during small-group guided reading (RF.1.4, RF.1.4a, RF.1.4b, RF.1.4c)	3
4	O4.1	Read Fountas-Pinnell high-frequency Word Lists 4 and 5 (100 words total) (RF.1.3b, RF.1.3g)	4
4	O4.2	Apply knowledge of decoding skills (chunking, blending, onset, rhymes) to read unknown words while self-correcting miscues that interfere with comprehension and fluency while reading (RL.1.1, RL.1.2, RL.1.4)	10
4	O4.3	Utilize journals for writing four or more connected sentences while using background knowledge, grammar skills, conventional spelling of words learned in spelling units, and conventions (capitalization, punctuation, spacing) (L.1.1, L.1.1a, L.1.1b, L.1.1c, L.1.1d, L.1.1e, L.1.1f, L.1.1g, L.1.1h, L.1.1j, L.1.2, L.1.2a, L.1.2b, L.1.2c, L.1.2d, L.1.2e)	8
4	O4.4	Determine the meaning of unknown words or phrases using word relationships and context clues while reading and listening (L.1.4, L.1.4a, L.1.5, L.1.5a, L.1.5b, L.1.5c, L.1.5d, L.1.6)	9

Term	IO Number	Instructional Objective (CCSS)	LCCSS Element
4	O4.5	Read grade-level material using a variety of reading strategies (phonics/decoding, monitor/ clarify, predict/infer, questioning, summarizing, making connections, visualizing) (RL.1.1, RL.1.2, RL.1.4)	10
4	O4.6	Participate and lead collaborative conversations with peers and adults in a small- or large-group setting (SL.1.1, SL.1.1a, SL.1.1b, SL.1.1c, SL.1.2, SL.1.3, SL.1.4, SL.1.5, SL.1.6)	7
4	O4.7	Retell texts using story elements (setting, characters, plot, conflict/resolution,) and compare/ contrast selections, characters, and experiences (RL.1.3, RL.1.5, RL.1.6, RL.1.7, RL.1.9)	11
4	O4.8	Write for a variety of purposes (narrative, expository, opinion, etc.) using appropriate sequence of events or details as well as providing some sense of closure (W.1.1, W.1.2, W.1.3)	5
4	O4.9	Demonstrate writing with guidance and support from adults, focus on a topic, gather information, respond to questions and suggestions from peers, and add details to strengthen writing as needed (W.1.5, W.1.7, W.1.8)	6
4	O4.10	Read informational texts and utilize various text features to locate key facts or information in a text and identify connections between key ideas (RI.1.1, RI.1.10, RI.1.2, RI.1.3, RI.1.4, RI.1.5, RI.1.6, RI.1.7, RI.1.8)	12

a. IO = instructional objective; LCCSS = local Common Core State Standards; RF.1.3b = Item 1, Point 3b, in the Reading Foundational Skills subset of the English Language Arts section for Grade 1 in the CCSS; L.1.4 = Item 1, Point 4, in the Language subset of the English Language Arts section; RI.1.1 = Item 1 in the Reading Informational Text subset of the English Language Arts section; W.1.1 = Item 1 in the Writing subset of the English Language Arts section.

Table 4.3 Second Grade

By the end of Grade 2 English Language Arts, the student will . . .		
Power Standard Element	**Local Common Core State Standard**	**Common Core Domain**
1	Demonstrate correct conventions by using irregular plural nouns, irregular past tense verbs, proper capitalization at the beginning of the sentence and with holidays and names, use periods at the end of a sentence, and use commas in greetings and closings of letters	Language
2	Use context clues within a sentence to determine the meaning of a word or phrase	Language
3	Apply phonics to read one-syllable words with long and short vowels and vowel pairs, recognize and read high-frequency words, identify words with inconsistent but common spelling-sound correspondences, decode words with common prefixes and suffixes, and apply spelling patterns in writing	Foundational skills
4	Read second-grade text orally with accuracy, rate, expression, and understanding	Foundational skills
5	Identify the topic and main idea of a one-paragraph text and answer questions such as who, what, when, where, why, and how	Informational text
6	Use text features such as captions, bold print, headings, glossaries, charts, diagrams, and images to locate information and clarify text	Informational text
7	Summarize fiction, including fables and folktales, by describing the story structure and identify the theme	Literature
8	Implement agreed-upon rules for discussion, such as speaking one at a time, listening to others with care, and gaining the floor in respectful ways to participate in large- and small-group discussions	Speaking and listening

Power Standard Element	Local Common Core State Standard	Common Core Domain
9	Write, revise, and edit an expository four-square paper and participate in a research project	Writing
10	Use illustrations and text to describe or infer the elements of fiction such as characters, setting, and plot	Literature

2ELA Instructional Objectives (End-of-Term Expectations)[a]

Term	IO Number	Instructional Objective (CCSS)	LCCSS Element
1	O1.1	Follow agreed-upon rules for discussion, such as speaking one at a time, listening to others with care, and gaining the floor in respectuful ways to participate in large- and small-group discussions (SL.2.1, SL.2.1a)	8
1	O1.2	Capitalize the beginning of a sentence (L.2.1b, L.2.1d, L.2.2, L.2.2a, L.2.2b, L.2.2d)	1
1	O1.3	Use a period at the end of a statement (L.2.1b, L.2.1d, L.2.2, L.2.2a, L.2.2b, L.2.2d)	1
1	O1.4	Use context clues within a sentence to figure out an unknown word (L.2.4a)	2
1	O1.5	Use first-quarter spelling patterns in writing (RF.2.3a, RF.2.3b, RF.2.3d, RF.2.3e, RF.2.3f)	3
1	O1.6	Read 60 WCPM (RF.2.4a, RF.2.4b)	4
1	O1.7	Read 27 high-frequency words (RF.2.3a, RF.2.3b, RF.2.3d, RF.2.3e, RF.2.3f)	3
1	O1.8	Make predictions to read second-grade text with understanding (RF.2.4a, RF.2.4b)	4
1	O1.9	Summarize fiction, including fables, folktales, by describing the story structure and identify the theme (RL.2.2, RL.2.5)	7

Term	IO Number	Instructional Objective (CCSS)	LCCSS Element
1	O1.10	Write a five-sentence four-square paper (W.2.2, W.2.5, W.2.7)	9
2	O2.1	Use commas in greeting and closing of letters (L.2.1b, L.2.1d, L.2.2, L.2.2a, L.2.2b, L.2.2d)	1
2	O2.2	Use proper capitalization with holidays and names (L.2.1b, L.2.1d, L.2.2, L.2.2a, L.2.2b, L.2.2d)	1
2	O2.3	Use second-quarter spelling patterns in writing (RF.2.3a, RF.2.3b, RF.2.3d, RF.2.3e, RF.2.3f)	3
2	O2.4	Read 70 WCPM (RF.2.4a, RF.2.4b)	4
2	O2.5	Read 53 high-frequency words (RF.2.3a, RF.2.3b, RF.2.3d, RF.2.3e, RF.2.3f)	3
2	O2.6	Summarize nonfiction by identifying the topic and main idea of a one-paragraph text (RI.2.2, RI.2.1)	5
2	O2.7	Summarize nonfiction using text features such as captions, bold print, headings, glossaries, charts, diagrams, and images (RI.2.5, RI.2.7)	6
2	O2.8	Use connecting to read second-grade text with understanding (RF.2.4a, RF.2.4b)	4
3	O3.1	Demonstrate correct conventions by using irregular past-tense verbs (L.2.1b, L.2.1d, L.2.2, L.2.2a, L.2.2b, L.2.2d)	1
3	O3.2	Use third-quarter spelling patterns in writing (RF.2.3a, RF.2.3b, RF.2.3d, RF.2.3e, RF.2.3f)	3
3	O3.3	Read 80 WCPM (RF.2.4a, RF.2.4b)	4
3	O3.4	Read 86 high-frequency words (RF.2.3a, RF.2.3b, RF.2.3d, RF.2.3e, RF.2.3f)	3
3	O3.5	Ask and answer questions such as who, what, when, where, why, and how (RI.2.2, RI.2.1)	5
3	O3.6	Use context clues within a sentence to determine the meaning of a word or phrase (L.2.4a)	2

Term	IO Number	Instructional Objective (CCSS)	LCCSS Element
3	O3.7	Make inferences when reading (RL.2.7)	10
3	O3.8	Write an eight-sentence four-square paper (W.2.2, W.2.5, W.2.7)	9
4	O4.1	Demonstrate correct conventions by using irregular plural nouns (L.2.1b, L.2.1d, L.2.2, L.2.2a, L.2.2b, L.2.2d)	1
4	O4.2	Use fourth-quarter spelling patterns in writing (RF.2.3a, RF.2.3b, RF.2.3d, RF.2.3e, RF.2.3f)	3
4	O4.3	Read 90 WCPM (RF.2.4a, RF.2.4b)	4
4	O4.4	Read 120 high-frequency words (RF.2.3a, RF.2.3b, RF.2.3d, RF.2.3e, RF.2.3f)	3
4	O4.5	Use imaging to read second-grade text with understanding (RF.2.4a, RF.2.4b)	4

a. IO = instructional objective; LCCSS = local Common Core State Standards; SL.2.1 = Item 1 in the Speaking and Listening subset of the English Language Arts section for Grade 2 in the CCSS; L.21b = Item 1, Point b, in the Language subset of the English Language Arts section; RF.2.3a = Item 3, Point a in the Reading Foundational Skills subset of the English Language Arts section; RL.2.2 = Item 2 in the Readings Standards for Literature section; W.2.2= Item 2 in the Writing subset of the English Language Arts section; RI.2.2 = Item 2 in the Reading Informational Text subset of the English Language Arts section.

Used with permission.

Table 4.4 Third Grade

By the end of Grade 3 English Language Arts, the student will . . .		
Power Standard Element	**Local Common Core State Standard**	**Common Core Domain**
1	Apply language conventions when writing and speaking	Language
3	Read and comprehend grade-level informational text by asking and answering questions based on the text	Informational text

(Continued)

Table 4.4 (Continued)

Power Standard Element	Local Common Core State Standard	Common Core Domain
4	Ask and answer questions to demonstrate understanding of a text, referring explicitly to the text as the basis for the answers	Literature
5	Effectively engage in a range of collaborative discussions on third-grade topics and texts by building on others' ideas and expressing their own ideas using complete sentences and following agreed rules for discussion time	Speaking and listening
6	Write routinely over short and extended time frames for a range of tasks and purposes	Writing
7	Know and apply grade-level phonics and word analysis skills in decoding words	Foundational skills

3ELA Instructional Objectives (End-of-Term Expectations)[a]

Term	IO Number	Instructional Objective (CCSS)	LCCSS Element
1	O1.1	Identify three types of sentences: statement, commands, questions (L.3.1, L.3.2, L.3.3)	1
1	O1.2	Model correct capitalization and punctuation in writing using periods, exclamations, and question marks (L.3.1, L.3.2, L.3.3)	1
1	O1.3	Collaborate in small-group discussions or with partners to express ideas and follow the rules for discussions (SL.3.1, SL.3.1a, SL.3.1b, SL.3.6)	5
1	O1.4	Identify characters and setting in a given story (RL.3.1)	4
1	O1.5	Write one paragraph using correct capitalization and punctuation (W.3.10)	6
1	O1.6	Identify the problem and solution in a story (RL.3.1)	4
1	O1.7	Identify the main idea of the story (RL.3.1)	4

Term	IO Number	Instructional Objective (CCSS)	LCCSS Element
2	O2.1	Define the meaning of prefixes *dis-*, *re-*, and *un-* (RF.3.3)	7
2	O2.2	Label the base word and identify the prefixes *dis-*, *re-*, *un-* (RF.3.3)	7
2	O2.3	Define the meanings of the suffixes *able, less, ful, ly,* and identify the base/root word (RF.3.3)	7
2	O2.4	Read leveled mystery book and answer questions based on each chapter, going back to check answers in the text (RL.3.1)	4
2	O2.5	Write a two-paragraph story with a topic sentence using correct punctuation and capitalization (W.3.10)	6
2	O2.6	Distinguish between fact and opinion (RL.3.1)	4
2	O2.7	Identify the author's purpose for writing a story (RL.3.1)	4
2	O2.8	Identify and explain nouns and verbs in grammar and usage (L.3.1, L.3.2, L.3.3)	1
3	O3.1	Make predictions and draw conclusions on the story and review predictions and conclusions (RL.3.1)	4
3	O3.2	Write a three- to four-paragraph paper with an introduction, supporting details, and conclusion (W.3.10)	6
3	O3.3	Identify common singular and plural pronouns (L.3.1, L.3.2, L.3.3)	1
3	O3.4	Identify synonyms, antonyms, and homophones (RF.3.3)	7
4	O4.1	Write an opinion piece on a topic with supporting points and reasons; introduce the topic and create an organized paragraph with two or more details and an ending sentence (W.3.10)	6

a. IO = instructional objective; LCCSS = local Common Core State Standards; L.3.1 = Item 1 in the Language subset of the English Language Arts section for Grade 3 in the CCSS; SL.3.1 = Item 1 in the Speaking and Listening subset of the English Language Arts section for Grade 3 in the CCSS; RL.3.1 = Item 1 in the Readings Standards for Literature section; RF.3.3 = Item 3 in the Reading Foundational Skills subset of the English Language Arts section; W.3.10 = Item 10 in the Writing subset of the English Language Arts section.

Used with permission.

Table 4.5 Fourth Grade

By the end of Grade 4 English Language Arts, the student will . . .		
Power Standard Element	**Local Common Core State Standard**	**Common Core Domain**
1	Provide details and examples from fictional and informational text when describing and analyzing in depth a character, setting, or event in the story or drama (e.g., a character's thoughts, words, or actions) and when applying strategies (e.g., inferring, summarizing, comparing/contrasting) to various grade-level texts	Literature
2	Demonstrate command of the conventions of standard English grammar and usage including progressive verb tenses (e.g., *was walking, am walking, will be walking*), recognition of sentences, fragments, and run-ons and frequently confused words (e.g., *to, too, two; their, there*) when writing or speaking	Language
3	Determine the main idea of a text by sight details and examples from the text	Informational text
4	Interpret information presented visually, orally, or quantitatively (i.e., in chats, graphs, diagrams, timelines)	Informational text
5	Produce clear and coherent writing in which the development and organization are appropriate to task, purpose, and audience for fourth grade	Writing
6	Effectively discuss topics and texts that build on ideas and also effectively express their feelings (one-on-one, in groups, and teacher-led)	Speaking and listening

4ELA Instructional Objectives (End-of-Term Expectations)[a]

Term	IO Number	Instructional Objective (CCSS)	LCCSS Element
1	O1.1	Identify and classify sentences as statements, questions, commands, and exclamations (RL.4.1, RL.4.10)	2
1	O1.2	Identify simple subjects and simple predicates (RL.4.1, RL.4.10)	2
1	O1.3	Construct sentences identifying simple subjects and simple predicates (RL.4.1, RL.4.10)	2
1	O1.4	Construct a well-organized paragraph with a clear main idea sentence and supporting details (W.4.1, W.4.2, W.4.4)	5
1	O1.5	Describe in depth a character, setting, or event in a story, drawing on specific details within various literary selections (RL.4.3)	1
1	O1.6	Summarize the text using a variety of literary selections (RL.4.3)	1
1	O1.7	Explain information presented in charts, graphs, diagrams, time-lines, maps, and data (RI.4.7)	4
1	O1.8	Explain connections (e.g., text to text, text to self, text to world) using a variety of grade-level reading materials (SL.4.1)	6
1	O1.9	Describe and give examples of written responses (W.4.1, W.4.2, W.4.4)	5
2	O2.1	Identify and give examples of run-on and compound sentences (RL.4.1, RL.4.10)	2
2	O2.2	Write sentences using commas in a series (RL.4.1, RL.4.10)	2
2	O2.3	Identify common and proper nouns (RL.4.3)	1
2	O2.4	Construct a well-organized expository which introduces a topic and develops the topic with related paragraphs (e.g., clear topic, supporting paragraphs, conclusion) (W.4.1, W.4.2, W.4.4)	5

Term	IO Number	Instructional Objective (CCSS)	LCCSS Element
2	O2.5	Determine the main idea of an informational text and explain how it is supported by key details (RL.4.3)	1
2	O2.6	Explain events, procedures, ideas, or concepts in historical or scientific text including what happened and why (e.g., cause and effect) (RL.4.3)	1
2	O2.7	Interpret information presented visually, orally, or quantitatively (e.g., in charts, graphs diagrams, time-lines) and explain how the information contributes to an understanding of the text (RI.4.7)	4
2	O2.8	Describe the overall text structure (e.g., chronology, compare/contrast, cause/effect, problem/solution) (RL.4.3)	1
2	O2.9	Construct written responses related to a variety of topics (W.4.1, W.4.2, W.4.4)	5
3	O3.1	Identify and construct sentences using progressive verb tenses (e.g., *I was walking, I am walking, I will be walking*) (W.4.1, W.4.2, W.4.4)	5
3	O3.2	Research and construct a well-organized expository that introduces a topic clearly and groups related information in paragraphs using fact, definitions, quotations, or other related examples to the topic and links ideas using words and phrases (e.g., *another, also, because*) (W.4.1, W.4.2, W.4.4)	5
3	O3.3	Produce and publish a piece of writing (W.4.1, W.4.2, W.4.4)	5
3	O3.4	Make connections (text to text, text to self, text to world) using a variety of grade-level reading materials (RL.4.3)	1
3	O3.5	Discuss and analyze responses written to a variety of topics (W.4.1, W.4.2, W.4.4)	5

Term	IO Number	Instructional Objective (CCSS)	LCCSS Element
3	O3.6	Construct connections (e.g., text to text, text to self, text to world) using a variety of grade-level materials (RL.4.3)	1
3	O3.7	Determine the overall text structure of a variety of grade-level reading materials (e.g., chronology, compare/contrast, cause/effect, problem/solution) (RL.4.3)	1
3	O3.8	Compare and contrast two or more characters, settings, or events in grade-level text (RL.4.3)	1
4	O4.1	Order adjectives within sentences according to conventional patterns (e.g., *a small red wagon* rather than *a red small wagon*) (RL.4.1, RL.4.10)	2
4	O4.2	Identify and write examples of sentences including adverbs (RL.4.1, RL.4.10)	2
4	O4.3	Debate a topic and then produce a well-organized persuasive that provides reasons supported by facts and details and that links opinion and reasons using words and phrases (e.g., *for instances, in order to, in addition*) (W.4.1, W.4.2, W.4.4)	5
4	O4.4	Compare and contrast a variety of literary elements (W.4.1, W.4.2, W.4.4)	5
4	O4.5	Engage in collaborative group discussions (e.g., literature circles, book clubs, guided reading groups) (SL.4.1)	6
4	O4.6	Discuss and analyze responses written to a variety of topics (W.4.1, W.4.2, W.4.4)	5

a. IO = instructional objective; LCCSS = local Common Core State Standards; RL.4.1 = Item 1 in the Readings Standards for Literature section for Grade 4 in the CCSS; W.4.1 = Item 1 in the Writing subset of the English Language Arts section; RI.4.7 = Item 7 in the Reading Informational Text subset of the English Language Arts section; SL.4.1 = Item 1 in the Speaking and Listening subset of the English Language Arts section.

Table 4.6 Fifth Grade

By the end of Grade 5 English Language Arts, the student will . . .		
Power Standard Element	**Local Common Core State Standard**	**Common Core Domain**
1	Read and interpret literary elements including theme, characters, setting, climax, plot, and conflict/resolution, as well as techniques (e.g., connections and compare/contrast) used to convey meaning in a variety of grade-level literary works	Literature
2	Incorporate a broad range of grade-level reading materials and apply reading strategies (e.g., using context clues, cause/effect, inferencing, and compare and contrast) to improve comprehension	Informational text
3	Produce clear and coherent writing in which the development and organization are appropriate to task, purpose, and audience for fifth-grade level	Writing
4	Engage effectively in a range of collaborative discussions with diverse partners on Grade 5 topics and texts, building on others' ideas and expressing their own clearly	Speaking and listening
5	Demonstrate command of the conventions of standard English grammar and usage, including conjunctions, prepositions, interjections, and verb tense when writing or speaking.	Language

5ELA Instructional Objectives (End-of-Term Expectations)[a]

Term	IO Number	Instructional Objective (CCSS)	LCCSS Element
1	O1.1	Identify literary elements of plot, theme, characters (main and minor), and setting within various literary selections (RL.5.1, RL.5.10, RL.5.2, RL.5.3)	1
1	O1.2	Describe text-to-text, text-to-self, and text-to-world connections and find connections within grade-level text (RL.5.1, RL.5.10, RL.5.2, RL.5.3)	1

Term	IO Number	Instructional Objective (CCSS)	LCCSS Element
1	O1.3	Using context clues, determine the meaning of words and phrases as they are used in a text (RI.5.4, RI.5.5, RI.5.6)	2
1	O1.4	Identify writing organization appropriate to task, purpose, and audience (W.5.1, W.5.10, W.5.2)	3
1	O1.5	Orally list information relevant to effective grade-level discussions. (SL.5.1a, SL.5.1b, SL.5.1c, SL.5.1d)	4
1	O1.6	Identify and effectively apply conjunctions in sentences when writing or speaking (L.5.1a, L.5.1e, L.5.2, L.5.2a, L.5.2e)	5
2	O2.1	Explain literary elements of plot, theme, characters (main and minor), and setting within various literary selections (RL.5.1, RL.5.10, RL.5.2, RL.5.3)	1
2	O2.2	Compare and contrast two or more characters, settings, or events in a grade-level text (RL.5.1, RL.5.10, RL.5.2, RL.5.3)	1
2	O2.3	Recognize the cause/effect relationship between a variety of events in a grade-level text (RI.5.4, RI.5.5, RI.5.6)	2
2	O2.4	Explain writing organization appropriate to task, purpose, and audience (W.5.1, W.5.10, W.5.2)	3
2	O2.5	Discuss grade-level information in various groupings pertaining to teacher-generated topics while expressing the student's own thoughts clearly (SL.5.1a, SL.5.1b, SL.5.1c, SL.5.1d)	4
2	O2.6	Identify and effectively apply prepositions in sentences when writing or speaking (L.5.1a, L.5.1e, L.5.2, L.5.2a, L.5.2e)	5
3	O3.1	Given a piece of grade-level information/literature, determine literary elements of plot, theme, characters (main and minor), and setting within various literary selections (RL.5.1, RL.5.10, RL.5.2, RL.5.3)	1
3	O3.2	Compare and contrast stories in the same genre on their approaches to similar themes and topics (RL.5.1, RL.5.10, RL.5.2, RL.5.3)	1

Term	IO Number	Instructional Objective (CCSS)	LCCSS Element
3	O3.3	Model the cause/effect relationship between a variety of events in a grade-level text (RI.5.4, RI.5.5, RI.5.6)	2
3	O3.4	Produce writing samples appropriate to teacher-selected variables of task, purpose, and audience (W.5.1, W.5.10, W.5.2)	3
3	O3.5	Recognize diversity among discussion participants and utilize this newfound information to produce ideas to converse effectively (SL.5.1a, SL.5.1b, SL.5.1c, SL.5.1d)	4
3	O3.6	Identify and effectively apply interjections in sentences when writing or speaking (L.5.1a, L.5.1e, L.5.2, L.5.2a, L.5.2e)	5
4	O4.1	Interpret literary elements of plot, theme, characters (main and minor), and setting within various literary selections (RL.5.1, RL.5.10, RL.5.2, RL.5.3)	1
4	O4.2	Infer information based upon prior knowledge as well as grade-level text (RI.5.4, RI.5.5, RI.5.6)	2
4	O4.3	Analyze different writing samples of peers to determine and classify clear and coherent writing with appropriate writing organization (W.5.1, W.5.10, W.5.2)	3
4	O4.4	Participate in group discussions and reflect upon personal performance pertaining to clear expression of ideas while taking into account others' diversities (SL.5.1a, SL.5.1b, SL.5.1c, SL.5.1d)	4
4	O4.5	Identify and effectively apply verb tenses in sentences when writing or speaking (L.5.1a, L.5.1e, L.5.2, L.5.2a, L.5.2e)	5

a. IO = instructional objective; LCCSS = local Common Core State Standards; RL.5.1 = Item 1 in the Reading Literature subset of the English Language Arts section for Grade 5 in the CCSS; W.5.1 = Item 1 in the Writing subset of the English Language Arts section; SL.5.1a = Item 1, Point a, in the Speaking and Listening subset of the English Language Arts section; L.5.1a = Item 1, Point a, in the Language subset of the English Language Arts section; RI.5.4 = Item 4 in the Reading Informational Text subset of the English Language Arts section.

Used with permission.

Table 4.7 Sixth Grade

By the end of Grade 6 English Language Arts, the student will . . .		
Power Standard Element	**Local Common Core State Standard**	**Common Core Domain**
1	Use a variety of word-identification strategies (context, affixes and roots, reference materials) to determine the figurative, connotative, and multiple meaning of words and phrases as used in grade-level text and explain its impact on text meaning and tone	Literature
2	Cite textual evidence to support analysis of what the text says explicitly as well as inferences drawn from the text	Literature
3	Compare, contrast and evaluate the arguments, claims, and events in different media and formats	Informational text
4	Use the main idea and details within a piece of text to create an objective summary	Informational text
5	Through the development of skills (prediction, summarization, and connections) compare and contrast theme/topic, point of view, setting, characters, and plot present in various genres including stories, poems, historical novels, informational text, and fantasy as read and comprehended in the Grade 6 text complexity band proficiently	Literature
6	Demonstrate command of standard English grammar through the proper use of pronouns (intensive, vague, and shifts in person) and punctuation (comma, parentheses, dash)	Language
7	Conduct short research projects to answer a stated question, locating, evaluating, using, and citing information to produce and publish writing	Writing

(Continued)

Table 4.7 (Continued)

Power Standard Element	Local Common Core State Standard	Common Core Domain
8	Through 6+ and the writing process, produce a variety of text in which idea development, organization, word choice, and style are appropriate to task, purpose, and audience at a sixth-grade level while writing to support a claim and with clear reasons and relevant evidence, writing to inform/explain a topic (comparison/ contrast, cause/effect), and writing narratives to develop real or imagined experiences	Writing
9	Pose and respond to Grade 6–specific questions with elaboration and detail, and engage in collaborative discussions (one on one, groups, and teacher led) to build on the ideas of others through reflection and paraphrasing.	Speaking and listening

6ELA Instructional Objectives (End-of-Term Expectations)[a]

Term	IO Number	Instructional Objective (CCSS)	LCCSS Element
1	O1.1	Use reference materials and contextual clues to determine the connotative and multiple meaning of words and phrases as used in grade-level text (RL.6.4)	1
1	O1.2	Determine key points to answer an explicitly stated question within fiction and nonfiction text, providing support through textual evidence (RL.6.1)	2
1	O1.3	Identify subcategories of genre (including short stories, poems, historical novels, fantasy); identify informational text as narrative, expository, or persuasive; and recognize character, setting, plot, point of view, and theme/topic present in various Grade 6 genres (RL.6.9)	5

Term	IO Number	Instructional Objective (CCSS)	LCCSS Element
1	O1.4	View information presented in different media (visually, words) and compare/contrast the information to fully understand the topic/issue (RI.6.7, RI.6.8)	3
1	O1.5	Utilize fiction and nonfiction summarizing strategies (including informational text features . . . charts, maps, diagrams, tables, and headings) to distinguish key points/main idea and supporting details in fiction/nonfiction text (RI.6.2, RI.6.3)	4
1	O1.6	Demonstrate command of standard English plural and possessive nouns, possessive pronouns, and punctuation (commas) to set off appositives (L.6.1, L.6.1a, L.6.1b, L.6.1c, L.6.1d, L.6.2a)	6
1	O1.7	By using prewriting strategies, writing, revising, editing, and publishing, the learner will compose a well-focused and elaborated narrative essay with the development of ideas and using specific, descriptive words, characters/narrator utilizing dialogue and point of view, and well-structured event sequences to develop real or imagined experiences/events (W.6.1, W.6.2, W.6.3, W.6.4, W.6.5, W.6.6)	10
1	O1.8	Conduct a short research project to answer a question, drawing on several print and digital sources (W.6.7, W.6.8)	9
1	O1.9	The learner will pose and respond to specific questions with clear expression, elaboration, and detail, making comments that contribute to the topic/text/issue in a teacher-led collaborative discussion (SL.6.1, SL.6.1c, SL.6.1d)	13
2	O2.1	Additionally, use root-word meanings to determine the connotative and multiple meaning of words and phrases as used in grade-level text and explain its impact on text meaning (RL.6.4)	1

Term	IO Number	Instructional Objective (CCSS)	LCCSS Element
2	O2.2	Combine multiple key points to answer an explicitly stated question within fiction and nonfiction text, providing support through textual evidence (RL.6.1)	2
2	O2.3	Explain the meaning of argument, claim, and evidence to support and recognize these elements in text (RI.6.7, RI.6.8)	3
2	O2.4	Make and verify predictions and connections to compare/contrast one author's presentation of events with another's within informational text (e.g., memoir to biography), and identify the author's purpose in various types of informational text (RL.6.9)	5
2	O2.5	By using prewriting strategies, writing, revising, editing, and publishing, the learner will compose an informative/explanatory essay to examine a topic, convey ideas and information, utilizing an organizational pattern (classification, sequence, compare/contrast, cause/effect), a clear main idea, support and transitions, and using specific, descriptive words (W.6.1, W.6.2, W.6.3, W.6.4, W.6.5, W.6.6)	10
2	O2.8	Demonstrate command of standard English verb tense, subjective and objective pronouns, and punctuation (commas, parentheses, dashes) to set off parenthetical elements (L.6.1, L.6.1a, L.6.1b, L.6.1c, L.6.1d, L.6.2a)	6
2	O2.9	Create an objective summary of text using fiction and nonfiction summarizing strategies to identify key points in text (RI.6.2, RI.6.3)	4
2	O2.10	Conduct a short research project to answer a question, using several print and digital sources and quoting or paraphrasing the data and conclusions of others while avoiding plagiarism (W.6.7, W.6.8)	9
2	O2.11	Pose and respond to specific questions with expression, elaboration, and detail, utilizing defined individual roles through a collaborative discussion in small, diverse groups (SL.6.1, SL.6.1c, SL.6.1d)	13

Term	IO Number	Instructional Objective (CCSS)	LCCSS Element
3	O3.1	Additionally use affixes to determine the connotative and multiple meaning of words and phrases as used in grade-level text, explain the impact on text meaning, and identify and interpret figurative language (RL.6.4)	1
3	O3.2	Infer to draw conclusions based on textual evidence and connected knowledge and determine the answer to inferential questions (RL.6.1)	2
3	O3.3	Use inferencing skills while reading various Grade 6 fiction/nonfiction genres to recognize changes in character, events important to the development of the plot and leading to a resolution, and the development of point of view in text (RL.6.9)	5
3	O3.4	View opposing arguments and claims, with evidence, and compare/contrast the evidence for each side (RI.6.7, RI.6.8)	3
3	O3.5	Demonstrate command of standard English pronouns by using intensive pronouns, recognizing and correcting inappropriate shifts in pronoun number and person, and recognizing and correcting vague pronouns (i.e., ones with unclear or ambiguous antecedents) (L.6.1, L.6.1a, L.6.1b, L.6.1c, L.6.1d, L.6.2a)	6
3	O3.6	Produce clear and coherent writing with an effective style in which a consistent voice is maintained throughout, pronouns demonstrate coherence and cohesion, and sentence structure is varied (W.6.1, W.6.2, W.6.3, W.6.4, W.6.5, W.6.6)	10
3	O3.7	Conduct a short research project to answer a question, using several print and digital sources, refocusing the inquiry when appropriate, quoting or paraphrasing the data, and citing basic bibliographic information for sources (W.6.7, W.6.8)	9

Term	IO Number	Instructional Objective (CCSS)	LCCSS Element
3	O3.8	Pose and respond to specific questions with elaboration and detail, through a collaborative discussion in small, diverse groups, paraphrasing others' ideas and expressing the student's own ideas clearly (SL.6.1, SL.6.1c, SL.6.1d)	13
4	O4.1	Use a variety of word-identification strategies to determine the meaning of words and phrases as used in grade-level text and analyze its impact on text meaning and tone (RL.6.4)	1
4	O4.2	Compose inferential questions based on drawn conclusions from text evidence and connected knowledge (RL.6.1)	2
4	O4.3	Compare/contrast fictional elements (character, setting, plot, point of view, theme) in various Grade 6 fiction genres (stories, poems, historical novels, fantasy) (RL.6.9)	5
4	O4.4	Compare/contrast and evaluate opposing claims for support and soundness (RI.6.7, RI.6.8)	3
4	O4.5	By using prewriting strategies, writing, revising, editing, and publishing, the learner will compose an argument to support a claim with clear, organized reasons and clear, relevant evidence using credible sources (W.6.1, W.6.2, W.6.3, W.6.4, W.6.5, W.6.6)	10
4	O4.6	Conduct a short research project to answer a question, using several print and digital sources, assessing the credibility of each source, quoting or paraphrasing the data, and citing basic bibliographic information for sources (W.6.7, W.6.8)	9
4	O4.7	Demonstrate understanding of multiple perspectives by posing and responding to specific questions with elaboration and detail, through a one-on-one collaborative discussion, reflecting and building on others' ideas (SL.6.1, SL.6.1c, SL.6.1d)	13

a. IO = instructional objective; LCCSS = local Common Core State Standards; RL.6.4 = Item 4 in the Reading Literature subset of the English Language Arts section for Grade 6 in the CCSS; RI.6.7 = Item 7 in the Reading Informational Text subset of the English Language Arts section; L.6.1 = Item 1 in the Language subset of the English Language Arts section; W.6.1 = Item 1 in the Writing subset of the English Language Arts section; SL.6.1 = Item 1 in the Speaking and Listening subset of the English Language Arts section.

Used with permission.

Table 4.8 Seventh Grade

By the end of English Language Arts 7, the student will . . .		
Power Standard Element	**Local Common Core State Standard**	**Common Core Domain**
1	Analyze fiction and nonfiction text to determine a theme or central idea and its development over the course of the text. Provide an objective summary of the text. Cite textual evidence that most strongly supports an analysis of what the text says explicitly as well as inferences drawn from the text	Literature
2	Analyze a poem's form and structure and how it contributes to the overall meaning of the poem. Determine the meaning of words and phrases as they are used in a text, including figurative and connotative meanings; analyze the impact of rhymes and other repetitions of sounds on a specific verse or stanza of a poem	Literature
3	Read and comprehend a variety of literature and informational text at the high end of the sixth-to-eighth-grade complexity band proficiently	Literature
4	Use a variety of strategies to determine the meaning of grade-appropriate unknown and multiple-meaning words and figures of speech (e.g., context clues, reference materials, nuances, word relationships, allusions)	Language
5	Draw evidence from literary or informational texts to support analysis and reflection; produce clear and coherent writing in which the development, organization, and style are appropriate to the task, purpose, and audience	Writing

7ELA Instructional Objectives (End-of-Term Expectations)[a]

Term	IO Number	Instructional Objective (CCSS)	LCCSS Element
1	O1.1	Define and identify story elements in works of literature (plot, characterization, theme, symbolism) (RL.7.1, RL.7.2, RL.7.3)	1
1	O1.2	Preview, make, and adjust predictions regarding text (RL.7.1, RL.7.2, RL.7.3)	1
1	O1.3	Write a summary from literature and nonfiction text, including key information from text (RL.7.1, RL.7.2, RL.7.3)	1
1	O1.4	Identify a variety of figurative language (e.g., simile, metaphor, personification, hyperbole) (RL.7.4, RL.7.5)	2
1	O1.5	Draw evidence and clearly communicate reasoning in sentence format (W.7.4, W.7.9)	5
1	O1.6	Read and comprehend literature and informational text in the sixth-to-eighth-grade complexity band (RL.7.10)	3
1	O1.7	Use the dictionary and context clues to determine the meaning of unfamiliar words (L.7.4, L.7.4a, L.7.4c, L.7.4d, L.7.5, L.7.5a)	4
2	O2.1	Relate text to background knowledge (RL.7.1, RL.7.2, RL.7.3)	1
2	O2.2	Using background knowledge, develop, ask, and answer questions to improve comprehension; use Bloom's Taxonomy verbs (RL.7.1, RL.7.2, RL.7.3)	1
2	O2.3	Identify and select matching synonyms and antonyms that correspond to meanings of words found in text (L.7.4, L.7.4a, L.7.4c, L.7.4d, L.7.5, L.7.5a)	4
2	O2.4	Draw evidence from the text to support analysis and reflection in a written format (at least two-to-three supports) (W.7.4, W.7.9)	5

Term	IO Number	Instructional Objective (CCSS)	LCCSS Element
2	O2.5	Identify, define, and use poetry terms (e.g., simile, metaphor, personification, hyperbole, assonance, alliteration, rhyme, rhyme scheme, repetition, stanza, free verse, prose, clerihew, diamante, acrostic, double acrostic, limerick, part-of-speech poem, bio poem, metaphor poem, cinquain, haiku, tanka, color poem, and pantoum poem) (RL.7.4, RL.7.5)	2
2	O2.6	Read and comprehend literature and informational text in the sixth-to-eighth-grade complexity band proficiently (RL.7.10)	3
3	O3.1	Use questions and connections to anticipate authors intent (RL.7.1, RL.7.2, RL.7.3)	1
3	O3.2	Predict and verify meaning of unfamiliar words in text using context clues and reference materials (L.7.4, L.7.4a, L.7.4c, L.7.4d, L.7.5, L.7.5a)	4
3	O3.3	Using textual evidence, express and defend theme choice and relate it to the real world (RL.7.1, RL.7.2, RL.7.3)	1
3	O3.4	Read and comprehend literature and informational text in the sixth-to-eighth-grade complexity band proficiently (RL.7.10)	3
3	O3.5	Draw evidence from the text to support analysis and reflection in a written format (at least three-to-five supports) (W.7.4, W.7.9)	5
4	O4.1	Use sensory and conceptual imagery to comprehend the text (RL.7.1, RL.7.2, RL.7.3)	1
4	O4.2	Use a variety of strategies to determine the meaning of grade-appropriate unknown and multiple-meaning words and figures of speech (L.7.4, L.7.4a, L.7.4c, L.7.4d, L.7.5, L.7.5a)	4

Term	IO Number	Instructional Objective (CCSS)	LCCSS Element
4	O4.3	Evaluate the effectiveness of the story elements used by the author to develop the theme; support reasoning (RL.7.1, RL.7.2, RL.7.3)	1
4	O4.4	Read and comprehend a variety of literature and informational text at the high end of sixth-to-eighth-grade complexity band proficiently (RL.7.10)	3
4	O4.5	Draw evidence from the text to support analysis and reflection in a written format (at least three-to-five supports); produce clear and coherent writing appropriate to task (W.7.4, W.7.9)	5

a. IO = instructional objective; LCCSS = local Common Core State Standards; RL.7.1 = Item 1 in the Reading Literature subset of the English Language Arts section for Grade 7 in the CCSS; W.7.4 = Item 4 in the Writing subset of the English Language Arts section; L.7.4 = Item 4 in the Language subset of the English Language Arts section.

Used with permission.

Table 4.9 Eighth Grade

By the end of Grade 8 English Langauge Arts, the student will . . .		
Power Standard Element	**Local Common Core State Standard**	**Common Core Domain**
1	Cite the textual evidence that most strongly supports an analysis of what the text says explicitly as well as inferences drawn from the text	Literature
2	Delineate and evaluate the argument and specific claims in a text, assessing whether the reasoning is sound and the evidence is relevant and sufficient; recognize when irrelevant evidence is introduced	Informational text

Power Standard Element	Local Common Core State Standard	Common Core Domain
3	With some guidance and support from peers and adults, use 6 Traits +1 and the writing process to develop and strengthen writing at an eight-grade level, as needed by planning, revising, editing, rewriting, or trying a new approach, focusing on how well purpose and audience have been addressed	Writing
4	At an eighth-grade level, gather relevant information from multiple print and digital sources, using search terms effectively; assess the credibility and accuracy of each source; and quote or paraphrase the data and conclusions of others while avoiding plagiarism and following a standard format for citation	Writing
5	Engage effectively in a range of collaborative discussions (one-on-one, in groups, and teacher-led) with diverse partners on Grade 8 topics, texts, and issues, building on others' ideas and expressing the learner's own clearly	Speaking and listening
6	Demonstrate understanding of figurative language, word relationships, and nuances in word meanings, using a variety of strategies, including analyzing the impact of specific word choices on meaning as used in grade-level text	Language

8ELA Instructional Objectives (End-of-Term Expectations)[a]

Term	IO Number	Instructional Objective (CCSS)	LCCSS Element
1	O1.1	Preview the text to create and monitor predictions (RL.8.1, RL.8.2, RL.8.3, RL.8.6)	1
1	O1.2	Make simple inferences using textual clues and background knowledge (RL.8.1, RL.8.2, RL.8.3, RL.8.6)	1

Term	IO Number	Instructional Objective (CCSS)	LCCSS Element
1	O1.3	Create multiple inferences explaining contextual clues and background knowledge (RL.8.1, RL.8.2, RL.8.3, RL.8.6)	1
1	O1.4	Summarize multiple key points/concepts in a nonfiction text (RI.8.1, RI.8.2, RI.8.6, RI.8.8, RI.8.9)	2
1	O1.5	Connect to text using background knowledge or personal experiences (RL.8.1, RL.8.2, RL.8.3, RL.8.6)	1
1	O1.6	Identify character traits (RL.8.1, RL.8.2, RL.8.3, RL.8.6)	1
1	O1.7	Identify and summarize plot, character, and setting (RL.8.1, RL.8.2, RL.8.3, RL.8.6)	1
1	O1.8	Plan, revise, edit, and rewrite a piece of writing focusing on openings, ideas, organization, and conventions (W.8.1, W.8.1e, W.8.2, W.8.2f, W.8.3, W.8.3e, W.8.5)	3
1	O1.9	Identify figurative language in grade-level text (L.8.3, L.8.5, L.8.6)	6
1	O1.10	Examine striking, powerful word choice that catches the reader's eye and lingers in mind (L.8.3, L.8.5, L.8.6)	6
1	O1.11	With some guidance from peers and adults, the learner will ask questions that refer to literal aspects of the text or discussion, including clarifying, predicting, and pondering (SL.8.1, SL.8.4)	5
1	O1.12	Draw evidence from literary or informational texts to support analysis, reflection, and research (W.8.1, W.8.7, W.8.8, W.8.9)	4
2	O2.1	Identify the elements of fiction: exposition, rising action, climax, falling action, and resolution (RL.8.1, RL.8.2, RL.8.3, RL.8.6)	1

Term	IO Number	Instructional Objective (CCSS)	LCCSS Element
2	O2.2	Create inferences that are consistent with text and background knowledge (RL.8.1, RL.8.2, RL.8.3, RL.8.6)	1
2	O2.3	Summarize the effects of a character's personality on the plot or conflict of a story (RL.8.1, RL.8.2, RL.8.3, RL.8.6)	1
2	O2.4	Explain connections made from text to other texts, the learner, the learner's community, or the world (RL.8.1, RL.8.2, RL.8.3, RL.8.6)	1
2	O2.5	Explain the summary of multiple key points/ concepts in a text (RI.8.1, RI.8.2, RI.8.6, RI.8.8, RI.8.9)	2
2	O2.6	Summarize types of conflict contained in a text (RL.8.1, RL.8.2, RL.8.3, RL.8.6)	1
2	O2.7	Plan, revise, edit, and rewrite a piece of writing, focusing on ideas, support, organization, and conventions (W.8.1, W.8.1e, W.8.2, W.8.2f, W.8.3, W.8.3e, W.8.5)	3
2	O2.8	Given an example, imitate figurative language used in grade-level text (L.8.3, L.8.5, L.8.6)	6
2	O2.9	Examine striking, powerful word choice that catches the reader's eye and lingers in the mind, focusing on specific nouns and modifiers and vivid verbs to add depth and clarity (L.8.3, L.8.5, L.8.6)	6
2	O2.10	During reading or discussion, with some guidance from peers and adults, the learner will ask and answer questions that clarify understanding, predict and monitor outcomes, and ponder possibilities (SL.8.1, SL.8.4)	5
2	O2.11	Draw evidence from literary or informational texts to support analysis, reflection, and research; identify false statements and fallacious reasoning (W.8.1, W.8.7, W.8.8, W.8.9)	4

Term	IO Number	Instructional Objective (CCSS)	LCCSS Element
3	O3.1	Explain inferences using text and background knowledge (RL.8.1, RL.8.2, RL.8.3, RL.8.6)	1
3	O3.2	Construct an argument using notes from multiple sources (RI.8.1, RI.8.2, RI.8.6, RI.8.8, RI.8.9)	2
3	O3.3	Summarize different points of view relating to a text or event (RI.8.1, RI.8.2, RI.8.6, RI.8.8, RI.8.9)	2
3	O3.4	Prioritize multiple key points/concepts in a nonfiction text (RI.8.1, RI.8.2, RI.8.6, RI.8.8, RI.8.9)	2
3	O3.5	Evaluate the effects of conflict on plot (RL.8.1, RL.8.2, RL.8.3, RL.8.6)	1
3	O3.6	Compare/contrast the effects of a character's personality on the plot or conflict of a story (RL.8.1, RL.8.2, RL.8.3, RL.8.6)	1
3	O3.7	Explain multiple connections made from text to other texts, the learner, the learner's community, or the world (RL.8.1, RL.8.2, RL.8.3, RL.8.6)	1
3	O3.8	Identify theme with textual support (RL.8.1, RL.8.2, RL.8.3, RL.8.6)	1
3	O3.9	Plan, revise, edit, and rewrite a piece of writing focusing on support, word choice, closings, and conventions (W.8.1, W.8.1e, W.8.2, W.8.2f, W.8.3, W.8.3e, W.8.5)	3
3	O3.10	Create multiple writings using figurative language (L.8.3, L.8.5, L.8.6)	6
3	O3.11	Identify grade-level affixes and root words (L.8.3, L.8.5, L.8.6)	6
3	O3.12	Examine striking, powerful word choice that catches the reader's eye and lingers in mind, focusing on specific nouns and modifiers to add depth and clarity (L.8.3, L.8.5, L.8.6)	6

Term	IO Number	Instructional Objective (CCSS)	LCCSS Element
3	O3.13	With some guidance from peers and adults, the learner will ask and answer a variety of questions that explore important ideas/issues in text or discussion, including clarifying, predicting, inferring, and pondering (SL.8.1, SL.8.4)	5
3	O3.14	Gather relevant information from multiple print and digital sources using search terms effectively, assess the credibility and accuracy of each source, and quote or paraphrase the data and conclusions of others while avoiding plagiarism and following a standard format for citation (W.8.1, W.8.7, W.8.8, W.8.9)	4
4	O4.1	Analyze multiple key points/concepts in a text (RL.8.1, RL.8.2, RL.8.3, RL.8.6)	1
4	O4.2	Defend an argument using notes from multiple sources (RI.8.1, RI.8.2, RI.8.6, RI.8.8, RI.8.9)	2
4	O4.3	Explain why multiple connections made from text to other texts, the learner, the learner's community, or the world matter to other people (RL.8.1, RL.8.2, RL.8.3, RL.8.6)	1
4	O4.4	Analyze theme with textual support (RL.8.1, RL.8.2, RL.8.3, RL.8.6)	1
4	O4.5	Plan, revise, edit, and rewrite a piece of writing focusing on 6 + 1 Traits: ideas, support, openings, organization, word choice, closings, and conventions (W.8.1, W.8.1e, W.8.2, W.8.2f, W.8.3, W.8.3e, W.8.5)	3
4	O4.6	Critique an author's use of figurative language, including peers or established writers (L.8.3, L.8.5, L.8.6)	6
4	O4.7	Utilize grade-level affixes and root words to comprehend unfamiliar words (L.8.3, L.8.5, L.8.6)	6

Term	IO Number	Instructional Objective (CCSS)	LCCSS Element
4	O4.8	Create multiple writings using striking, powerful word choice that catches the reader's eye and lingers in mind, focusing on specific nouns and modifiers, sensory details, and vivid verbs to add depth and clarity (L.8.3, L.8.5, L.8.6)	6
4	O4.9	Independently ask and answer a variety of questions that explore important ideas/issues in text or discussion, including clarifying, predicting, inferring, and pondering (SL.8.1, SL.8.4)	5
4	O4.10	Conduct short research projects to answer a question (including a self-generated question) or to solve a problem, drawing on several sources and generating additional related, focused questions that allow for multiple avenues of exploration (W.8.1, W.8.7, W.8.8, W.8.9)	4

a. IO = instructional objective; LCCSS = local Common Core State Standards; RL.8.1 = Item 1 in the Reading Literature subset of the English Language Arts section for Grade 8 in the CCSS; RI.8.1 = Item 1 in the Reading Informational Text subset of the English Language Arts section; W.8.1 = Item 1 in the Writing subset of the English Language Arts section; L.8.3 = Item 3 in the Language subset of the English Language Arts section; SL.8.1 = Item 1 in the Speaking and Listening subset of the English Language Arts section.

Used with permission.

Table 4.10 Ninth Grade

By the end of Grade 9 English Language Arts, the student will . . .		
Power Standard Element	**Local Common Core State Standard**	**Common Core Domain**
1	Apply specific reading strategies (i.e., connect, infer, predict, etc.) to a variety of literary and informational texts	Literature
2	Use context clues, a dictionary, and a thesaurus to determine appropriate word use, meaning, and function; students will demonstrate mastery of new vocabulary by incorporating new terms into the learner's writing and speaking	Language

Power Standard Element	Local Common Core State Standard	Common Core Domain
2	Recognize figurative language in literary texts and analyze the function of these devices in the written text	Literature
3	Integrate textual evidence into analytical writings through the use of the quotation sandwich organizational method (i.e., claim, signal phrase, quote, commentary)	Writing
4	Practice the skill of annotation as a means of transcribing an inner monologue while reading literary and informational texts	Literature
6	Recognize universal themes in literature from pre-21st-century texts (i.e., Shakespeare, Edgar Allan Poe,etc.)	Literature
7	Write a literary analysis that focuses on a particular element of fiction and incorporates specific literary devices taught in the course of the semester (i.e., metaphor, simile, allusion, etc.)	Writing
8	Use the MLA style guidelines to understand the purpose and structure of parenthetical citation in a literary analysis	Language
9	Identify the writer, audience, subject, and purpose (WASP) of nonfiction essays in order to understand and summarize the main idea of literary nonfiction texts	Informational text
10	Recognize a common theme that develops over multiple pieces of literary nonfiction	Informational text
11	The learner will, in multi-draft essays, demonstrate command of the conventions of standard English capitalization, punctuation, and spelling by clarifying errors that impede understanding by the reader	Language

9ELA Instructional Objectives (End-of-Term Expectations)[a]

Term	IO Number	Instructional Objective (CCSS)	LCCSS Element
1	O1.1	Demonstrate understanding of the reading strategies of *question, connect, visualize, predict, infer, evaluate, analyze* in relation to short stories using a variety of teacher-created graphic organizers (RL.9-10.4, RL.9-10.5, RL.9-10.6, RL.9-10.7, RL.9-10.9)	1
1	O1.2	Write purposeful, qualitative annotations using the reading strategies to demonstrate comprehension of literary and informational texts, which grow increasingly more sophisticated over time (RL.9-10.1, RL.9-10.2, RL.9-10.3, RL.9-10.4, RL.9-10.5)	4
1	O1.3	Define and use 20 teacher-provided, thematic vocabulary terms per quarter in all assigned writing. In addition, students will gather, record, and write using "organic" vocabulary words from their independent reading (L.9-10.3, L.9-10.4, L.9-10.4a, L.9-10.4b, L.9-10.4c, L.9-10.4d, L.9-10.5)	2
1	O1.4	Describe how the elements of fiction are illustrated in short stories by using an increasingly specific Freytag model (RL.9-10.4, RL.9-10.5, RL.9-10.9)	2
1	O1.5	Begin to craft specific claims, short signal phrases, relevant quotes, and simple commentary to analyze elements of short stories (W.9-10.1, W.9-10.10, W.9-10.1a, W.9-10.1b, W.9-10.1c, W.9-10.1d, W.9-10.2b, W.9-10.2c, W.9-10.2d, W.9-10.4, W.9-10.5, W.9-10.9)	3
1	O1.6	Learn of the existence and purpose of MLA style; use correct parenthetical citations with increasing accuracy across all writing modes addressed at this level (L.9-10.3a)	8

Term	IO Number	Instructional Objective (CCSS)	LCCSS Element
2	O2.1	Choose an element of fiction (i.e., characterization, plot, etc.) to write a literary analysis paper, using two quotation sandwiches joined with a constructive transition logically linking the two and at least two literary devices (W.9-10.1, W.9-10.1a, W.9-10.1b, W.9-10.1c, W.9-10.1d, W.9-10.1e, W.9-10.9, W.9-10.9a)	7
2	O2.2	Demonstrate understanding of the reading strategies of *question, connect, visualize, predict, infer, evaluate, analyze* in relation to the whole-class novel using a variety of assessments, such as graphic organizers and small-group discussions (RL.9-10.4, RL.9-10.5, RL.9-10.6, RL.9-10.7, RL.9-10.9)	1
2	O2.3	Write specific and insightful claims, short signal phrases, relevant quotes, and more advanced commentary to analyze elements of a novel (W.9-10.1, W.9-10.10, W.9-10.1a, W.9-10.1b, W.9-10.1c, W.9-10.1d, W.9-10.2b, W.9-10.2c, W.9-10.2d, W.9-10.4, W.9-10.5, W.9-10.9)	3
3	O3.1	Read a pre-21st century drama (e.g., *Romeo and Juliet*) to acquire an understanding of varied time periods as a means of better understanding enduring themes (RL.9-10.2, RL.9-10.3, RL.9-10.6, RL.9-10.7)	6
3	O3.2	Write specific and insightful claims, short signal phrases, relevant quotes, and more analytical commentary to analyze elements of a play (L.9-10.1, L.9-10.2, L.9-10.2a, L.9-10.3a, L.9-10.4c)	11
3	O3.3	Choose an element of drama (e.g., characterization, plot, etc.) to write a literary analysis paper, using two quotation sandwiches joined with a constructive transition logically linking the two and at least two literary devices (W.9-10.1, W.9-10.10, W.9-10.1a, W.9-10.1b, W.9-10.1c, W.9-10.1d, W.9-10.2b, W.9-10.2c, W.9-10.2d, W.9-10.4, W.9-10.5, W.9-10.9)	3

Term	IO Number	Instructional Objective (CCSS)	LCCSS Element
4	O4.1	Interpret how all of the texts provided center on particular themes, with the overarching theme being self-discovery (RI.9-10.2, RI.9-10.3, RI.9-10.7)	10
4	O4.2	Write a multi-draft essay that demonstrates an understanding of conventions of standard English (L.9-10.1, L.9-10.2, L.9-10.2a, L.9-10.3a, L.9-10.4c)	11
4	O4.3	Read a variety of teacher-vetted essays focused on determining the main idea through the exploration of the writer, audience, subject, and purpose of each nonfiction essay (RI.9-10.6, RI.9-10.8)	9
4	O4.4	Write a reflective essay that synthesizes an understanding of a particular theme and how the texts and materials studied helped to define a sense of self (RI.9-10.2, RI.9-10.3, RI.9-10.7)	10

a. IO = instructional objective; LCCSS = local Common Core State Standards; RL9-10.4 = Item 4 in the Reading Literature subset of the English Language Arts section for Grades 9–10 in the CCSS; L.9-10.3 = Item 3 in the Language subset of the English Language Arts section; W.9-10.1 = Item 1 in the Writing subset of the English Language Arts section; RI. 9-10.2 = Item 2 in the Reading Informational Text subset of the English Language Arts section.

Used with permission.

Table 4.11 Tenth Grade

By the end of Grade 10 English Language Arts, the student will . . .		
Power Standard Element	**Local Common Core State Standard**	**Common Core Domain**
1	Identify a common theme in both literary and nonfiction texts and analyze in detail its development over the course of the texts	Informational text
2	Produce a concise paraphrase of the ideas in a nonfiction text that can be incorporated as evidence into a quotation sandwich	Writing

Power Standard Element	Local Common Core State Standard	Common Core Domain
3	Sophisticate the integration of paraphrased and quoted evidence into persuasive writing	Writing
4	Conduct short as well as more sustained research projects using a credible database as a main source of gathering information	Writing
5	Use the MLA style guidelines to cite articles from a database	Language
6	Generate essential questions for research	Writing
7	Develop improved comfort in speaking in front of a variety of audiences (i.e., informational, persuasive, and interviewing)	Speaking and listening
8	Recognize the importance of audience and purpose in determining the process, product, and presentation of communication	Speaking and listening
9	Produce clear and coherent outlines that structure the listener's reception of the spoken presentation	Writing
10	Analyze the impact of word choice on a particular audience (i.e., connotations, figurative language, technical jargon, etc.)	Informational text

10ELA Instructional Objectives (End-of-Term Expectations)[a]

Term	IO Number	Instructional Objective (CCSS)	LCCSS Element
1	O1.1	Learn several models of basic communication theory that interpret the roles of the sender and receiver in the process of communication (SL.9-10.4, SL.9-10.5, SL.9-10.6)	8
1	O1.2	Discuss how the connotations of a speaker's language influences an audience (RI.9-10.4, RI.9-10.5, RI.9-10.6, RI.9-10.9)	10

Term	IO Number	Instructional Objective (CCSS)	LCCSS Element
1	O1.3	Give a first speech of the semester, focusing on gauging the learner's initial comfort level in speaking in front of peers (SL.9-10.4)	7
1	O1.4	Practice various methods of confidence-boosting techniques, including relaxation and breathing exercises (SL.9-10.4)	7
1	O1.5	Write a specific informational-speech objective, keeping in mind the prior knowledge of the audience on this topic (SL.9-10.4, SL.9-10.5, SL.9-10.6)	8
1	O1.6	Demonstrate basic outlining structure, including the three main parts of a speech (introduction, body, conclusion), as well as the conventions of formal outlining labels and indentation (W.9-10.10, W.9-10.1c, W.9-10.1d, W.9-10.1e, W.9-10.2, W.9-10.2a, W.9-10.2b, W.9-10.2c, W.9-10.2d, W.9-10.2f, W.9-10.4, W.9-10.5, W.9-10.6, W.9-10.7)	9
1	O1.7	Produce an outline and speech presentation that effectively incorporates presentation software technology, such as PowerPoint or Keynote (SL.9-10.4, SL.9-10.5, SL.9-10.6)	8
1	O1.8	Sophisticate their use of attention-getter and conclusion techniques (W.9-10.10, W.9-10.1c, W.9-10.1d, W.9-10.1e, W.9-10.2, W.9-10.2a, W.9-10.2b, W.9-10.2c, W.9-10.2d, W.9-10.2f, W.9-10.4, W.9-10.5, W.9-10.6, W.9-10.7)	9
2	O2.9	Incorporate transition sentences to smoothly link the three main parts of a speech (W.9-10.10, W.9-10.1c, W.9-10.1d, W.9-10.1e, W.9-10.2, W.9-10.2a, W.9-10.2b, W.9-10.2c, W.9-10.2d, W.9-10.2f, W.9-10.4, W.9-10.5, W.9-10.6, W.9-10.7)	9
2	O2.1	Model the completion of the documents necessary to gaining employment, including the job application and resume (SL.9-10.4, SL.9-10.5, SL.9-10.6)	8

Term	IO Number	Instructional Objective (CCSS)	LCCSS Element
2	O2.2	Discuss the dress code, speech, and behavior conventions associated with participating in a job interview (SL.9-10.4, SL.9-10.5, SL.9-10.6)	8
2	O2.3	Perform a simulated job interview (SL.9-10.4)	7
2	O2.4	Recognize the four main categories of persuasive audiences and how their needs influence the strategies of the persuasive speaker (SL.9-10.4, SL.9-10.5, SL.9-10.6)	8
2	O2.5	Analyze how an effective persuasive speaker uses connotations to create an emotional connection to the audience (RI.9-10.4, RI.9-10.5, RI.9-10.6, RI.9-10.9)	10
2	O2.6	Create a speech outline that utilizes an organizational pattern appropriate to persuasive speaking (W.9-10.10, W.9-10.1c, W.9-10.1d, W.9-10.1e, W.9-10.2, W.9-10.2a, W.9-10.2b, W.9-10.2c, W.9-10.2d, W.9-10.2f, W.9-10.4, W.9-10.5, W.9-10.6, W.9-10.7)	9
2	O2.7	Present a persuasive speech (SL.9-10.4)	7
3	O3.1	Read and analyze multiple short selections of nonfiction and literature to establish one of the following theme possibilities: family relationships, faith, forgiveness, the meaning of life, exploration of genocide (RI.9-10.1, RI.9-10.2, RI.9-10.3, RI.9-10.4, RI.9-10.5, RI.9-10.6)	1
3	O3.2	Review knowledge of basic quotation sandwich structure (W.9-10.1, W.9-10.1a, W.9-10.1c, W.9-10.1d, W.9-10.1e, W.9-10.2a, W.9-10.2b, W.9-10.2c, W.9-10.2d, W.9-10.2e, W.9-10.2f, W.9-10.5, W.9-10.8, W.9-10.9)	3
3	O3.3	Demonstrate the ability to choose an effective signal phrase based on the contextual details needed to clarify the source of the quote (W.9-10.1, W.9-10.1a, W.9-10.1c, W.9-10.1d, W.9-10.1e, W.9-10.2a, W.9-10.2b, W.9-10.2c, W.9-10.2d, W.9-10.2e, W.9-10.2f, W.9-10.5, W.9-10.8, W.9-10.9)	3

Term	IO Number	Instructional Objective (CCSS)	LCCSS Element
3	O3.4	Refine the commentary portion of the quotation sandwich by connecting more smoothly between the quote and the explanation and avoiding irrelevant tangents (W.9-10.1, W.9-10.1a, W.9-10.1c, W.9-10.1d, W.9-10.1e, W.9-10.2a, W.9-10.2b, W.9-10.2c, W.9-10.2d, W.9-10.2e, W.9-10.2f, W.9-10.5, W.9-10.8, W.9-10.9)	3
3	O3.5	Practice paraphrasing the main idea of a short nonfiction text (W.9-10.10, W.9-10.2, W.9-10.2d, W.9-10.4, W.9-10.5, W.9-10.9)	2
3	O3.6	Write a 12-part essay that explores one of the selected themes and utilizes the incorporation of textual support through the use of quotation sandwiches (W.9-10.1, W.9-10.1a, W.9-10.1c, W.9-10.1d, W.9-10.1e, W.9-10.2a, W.9-10.2b, W.9-10.2c, W.9-10.2d, W.9-10.2e, W.9-10.2f, W.9-10.5, W.9-10.8, W.9-10.9)	3
3	O3.7	Conduct a short research project on modern genocides to introduce the mechanics of using a computerized database (i.e., SIRS) (W.9-10.10, W.9-10.6, W.9-10.7, W.9-10.8, W.9-10.9)	4
4	O4.1	Read and annotate the book *Night* by Elie Wiesel and make connections to themes presented in the first term of the course (RI.9-10.1, RI.9-10.2, RI.9-10.3, RI.9-10.4, RI.9-10.5, RI.9-10.6)	1
4	O4.2	Master the skill of paraphrasing a text using selections from either *Night* or various nonfiction texts (W.9-10.10, W.9-10.2, W.9-10.2d, W.9-10.4, W.9-10.5, W.9-10.9)	2
4	O4.3	Practice incorporating paraphrased evidence in place of direct quotations in the quotation sandwich model (W.9-10.10, W.9-10.2, W.9-10.2d, W.9-10.4, W.9-10.5, W.9-10.9)	2
4	O4.4	As a whole-class exercise, generate essential questions to be used as the basis for an extended research project (W.9-10.7)	6

Term	IO Number	Instructional Objective (CCSS)	LCCSS Element
4	O4.5	Conduct independent research through a computerized database to explore class-generated essential questions (W.9-10.10, W.9-10.6, W.9-10.7, W.9-10.8, W.9-10.9)	4
4	O4.6	Practice writing correct MLA works-cited entries for articles accessed through a computerized database (L.9-10.3, L.9-10.3a)	5
4	O4.7	Write an extended multi-draft essay that responds to their essential questions by incorporating textual evidence gathered from class readings and personal research (This also supports PS element 3.W for ELA 10.) (W.9-10.10, W.9-10.6, W.9-10.7, W.9-10.8, W.9-10.9)	4
4	O4.8	Incorporate correct parenthetical citations that correspond to an accurate works-cited list that follows MLA style guidelines (L.9-10.3, L.9-10.3a)	5

a. IO = instructional objective; LCCSS = local Common Core State Standards; SL.9-10.4 = Item 4 in the Speaking and Listening subset of the English Language Arts section for Grades 9–10 in the CCSS; RI.9-10.4 = Item 4 in the Reading Informational Text subset of the English Language Arts section; W.9-10.10 = Item 10 in the Writing subset of the English Language Arts section; L.9-10.3 = Item 3 in the Language subset of the English Language Arts section.

Used with permission.

Table 4.12 Eleventh Grade

By the end of Grade 11 English Language Arts, the student will . . .		
Power Standard Element	**Local Common Core State Standard**	**Common Core Domain**
1	Analyze 17th-, 18th-, and 19th-century foundational U.S. documents of historical and literary significance for themes, purposes, and rhetorical features	Informational text
2	Demonstrate knowledge of 18th-, 19th-, 20th-, and 21st-century works of American literature; focus on how two or more texts from the same period treat similar themes or topics	Literature

(Continued)

Table 4.12 (Continued)

Power Standard Element	Local Common Core State Standard	Common Core Domain
3	Identify writer, audience, subject, and purpose of texts, analyzing how style and content contribute to the power, persuasiveness, or beauty of the literary nonfiction	Informational text
4	Write a narrative to develop real experiences or events using effective techniques, well-chosen details, and well-structured event sequences	Writing
5	Analyze the relationship between culture and fiction through examining various pieces related to one theme	Literature
6	Generate a thesis for both research and literary writing	Writing
7	Write arguments to support claims in literary analysis	Writing
8	Synthesize information from books, databases, and credible websites to create a multi-draft research essay	Writing
9	Use the MLA style guidelines to cite articles from books, databases, and credible websites and incorporate correct parenthetical citations to research essays for the purpose of avoiding plagiarism	Language
10	Sophisticate the integration of textual evidence in both literary analysis and synthesis writing by building arguments through multiple quotation sandwiches that support a central thesis	Writing

ELA11 Instructional Objectives (End-of-Term Expectations)[a]

Term	IO Number	Instructional Objective (CCSS)	LCCSS Element
1	O1.1	Read and annotate documents from Puritan era America: for example, William Bradford, Edward Taylor, Anne Bradstreet, and Jonathan Edwards (RI.11-12.3, RI.11-12.4, RI.11-12.5, RI.11-12.9)	1
1	O1.2	Read and annotate documents from the Revolutionary War era (RI.11-12.3, RI.11-12.4, RI.11-12.5, RI.11-12.9)	1
1	O1.3	Read and annotate documents from early American philosophers: for example, Emerson and Thoreau (RI.11-12.3, RI.11-12.4, RI.11-12.5, RI.11-12.9)	1
1	O1.4	Review and identify writer, audience, subject, and purpose of nonfiction texts through annotation (RI.11-12.5, RI.11-12.6)	3
1	O1.5	Illustrate author's purpose by making claims (RI.11-12.5, RI.11-12.6)	3
1	O1.6	Analyze the impact of writer, audience, subject, and purpose by writing quote sandwiches (RI.11-12.5, RI.11-12.6)	3
1	O1.7	Compare and contrast nonfiction texts through class discussion (RI.11-12.5, RI.11-12.6)	3
2	O2.1	Read and annotate Native American texts: for example, myths, speeches, and essays (RL.11-12.2, RL.11-12.3, RL.11-12.5, RL.11-12.7, RL.11-12.9)	2
2	O2.2	Read and annotate a book-length text written by a minority voice (RL.11-12.2, RL.11-12.3, RL.11-12.5, RL.11-12.7, RL.11-12.9)	2
2	O2.3	Read and annotate African American texts: for example, Olaudah Equiano, Frederick Douglass, Sojourner Truth, Langston Hughes, Alex Haley, and Toni Cade Bambara (RL.11-12.2, RL.11-12.3, RL.11-12.5, RL.11-12.7, RL.11-12.9)	2

Term	IO Number	Instructional Objective (CCSS)	LCCSS Element
2	O2.4	Read and annotate American texts by female writers: for example, Sandra Cisneros, Amy Tan, Louise Erdrich, and Jhampa Lahiri (RL.11-12.2, RL.11-12.3, RL.11-12.5, RL.11-12.7, RL.11-12.9)	2
2	O2.5	Compare and contrast themes of "minority texts" through class discussion (RL.11-12.2, RL.11-12.3, RL.11-12.5, RL.11-12.7, RL.11-12.9)	2
2	O2.6	Write a narrative to develop real-life experiences or events using effective techniques, well-chosen details, and well-structured event sequences (W.11-12.2d, W.11-12.3, W.11-12.3b, W.11-12.3c, W.11-12.3d)	4
2	O2.7	Analyze relationships between culture and fiction by writing 12-part essays that incorporate quote sandwiches and parenthetical citations (RL.11-12.3, RL.11-12.4, RL.11-12.5, RL.11-12.6, RL.11-12.9)	5
3	O3.1	Read and annotate a classic, American novel (RL.11-12.2, RL.11-12.3, RL.11-12.5, RL.11-12.7, RL.11-12.9)	2
3	O3.2	Analyze how fiction of a particular time and place in America reflects cultural values, both past and present (RL.11-12.2, RL.11-12.3, RL.11-12.5, RL.11-12.7, RL.11-12.9)	2
3	O3.3	Identify authors' purpose for writing and focus on impact of purpose on audience through class discussion (RL.11-12.3, RL.11-12.4, RL.11-12.5, RL.11-12.6, RL.11-12.9)	5
3	O3.4	Generate thesis for literary analysis writing (W.11-12.1a, W.11-12.1b)	6
3	O3.5	Write arguments to support claims in literary analysis (W.11-12.1, W.11-12.9, W.11-12.9a)	7

Term	IO Number	Instructional Objective (CCSS)	LCCSS Element
3	O3.6	Sophisticate integration of textual evidence in literary analysis by building arguments through multiple quotation sandwiches that support a central thesis (W.11-12.1, W.11-12.1c, W.11-12.1d, W.11-12.1e, W.11-12.2, W.11-12.2c, W.11-12.8)	10
4	O4.1	Generate an essential question that can be studied from multiple angles (W.11-12.1a, W.11-12.1b)	6
4	O4.2	Evaluate nonfiction resources, both print and nonprint materials (L.11-12.1, L.11-12.2, L.11-12.3, L.11-12.6)	9
4	O4.3	Formulate a thesis based off the research (W.11-12.1a, W.11-12.1b)	6
4	O4.4	Incorporate documented sources through the quotation-sandwich organizational tool (W.11-12.1, W.11-12.1c, W.11-12.1d, W.11-12.1e, W.11-12.2, W.11-12.2c, W.11-12.8)	10
4	O4.5	Produce a five-to-seven page, multi-draft, position paper based off the sources available to the students (W.11-12.10, W.11-12.2, W.11-12.2a, W.11-12.2b, W.11-12.5, W.11-12.7, W.11-12.8, W.11-12.9)	8
4	O4.6	Navigate and apply MLA standards as method of academic citation philosophy through header, parenthetical citation, and works-cited page (L.11-12.1, L.11-12.2, L.11-12.3, L.11-12.6)	9

a. IO = instructional objective; LCCSS = local Common Core State Standards; RI.11-12.3 = Item 3 in the Reading Informational Text subset of the English Language Arts section for Grades 11–12 in the CCSS; RL.11-12.3 = Item 3 in the Reading Literature subset of the English Language Arts section; W.11-12.2b = Item 2, Point b, in the Writing subset of the English Language Arts section; L.11-12.1 = Item 1 in the Language subset of the English Language Arts section.

Table 4.13 Twelfth Grade

By the end of Grade 12 English Language Arts, the student will . . .		
Power Standard Element	**Local Common Core State Standard**	**Common Core Domain**
1	Cite strong and thorough textual evidence in both written and verbal discussions, demonstrating mastery of the quotation-sandwich organizational tool in both single-draft and multi-draft writings (i.e., clear claims, strong evidence, use of signal phrases, coherent commentary sentences)	Writing
2	Determine two central ideas of a literary text and analyze their development over the course of the piece	Literature
3	Analyze multiple interpretations of a story, drama, or poem, evaluating how each version interprets the source text (i.e., a film version or short story adaptation of a play or novel compared with its original source)	Literature
4	Analyze an author's use of sarcasm or irony for various rhetorical purposes (i.e., humor, instruction, emphasis, and satire)	Literature
5	Write a multi-draft literary analysis of a major text	Writing
6	In multi-draft essays, demonstrate command of the conventions of standard English capitalization, punctuation, and spelling by clarifying errors that impede understanding by the reader	Language
7	Recognize the differences in audience, purpose, and publishing sequence between the following types of informational texts: newspapers, magazines, blogs, academic journals, books, and reference texts	Writing
8	Determine an author's point of view or purpose in a nonfiction text and demonstrate how the presence of bias influences both the composition of the text and its effect on the reader	Informational text

Power Standard Element	Local Common Core State Standard	Common Core Domain
9	On a more independent level, perform the tasks necessary to complete a research-based synthesis essay	Writing
10	Demonstrate mastery of MLA style-guide rules for in-text documentation of works cited in a research or literary analysis	Language

ELA12 Instructional Objectives (End-of-Term Expectations)[a]

Term	IO Number	Instructional Objective (CCSS)	LCCSS Element
1	O1.1	Review and brainstorm the purposes of the written word: communication of information, ideas, experiences, historical documentation of events, entertainment, and so on (RL.11-12.1, RL.11-12.2, RL.11-12.3, RL.11-12.4)	2
1	O1.2	Review short pieces (beginning with children's stories) looking for a central idea of the piece; 100% of the class will be able to write a short, clear statement explaining one central idea (RL.11-12.1, RL.11-12.2, RL.11-12.3, RL.11-12.4)	2
1	O1.3	Read longer, grade-level text as a class, tracing one main idea throughout; working in small groups, students will identify one central idea of a short, complex piece (RL.11-12.1, RL.11-12.2, RL.11-12.3, RL.11-12.4)	2
1	O1.4	Provide two or three main ideas at the beginning of a long piece of fiction (play); read as a class, tracing main ideas throughout the piece, completing outline of detailed examples (RL.11-12.1, RL.11-12.2, RL.11-12.3, RL.11-12.4)	2

Term	IO Number	Instructional Objective (CCSS)	LCCSS Element
1	O1.5	Read a college-level novel and trace at least two main ideas throughout the work. (RL.11-12.1, RL.11-12.2, RL.11-12.3, RL.11-12.4)	2
1	O1.6	Review and clarify expectations and information of claim, quote, and commentary; use quotation sandwich (W.11-12.1, W.11-12.1a, W.11-12.1b, W.11-12.1c, W.11-12.1e, W.11-12.2, W.11-12.2a, W.11-12.9)	1
1	O1.7	Write rough draft of central-ideas piece using textual support gathered individually, in small groups, and as a class (W.11-12.1, W.11-12.1a, W.11-12.1b, W.11-12.1c, W.11-12.1e, W.11-12.2, W.11-12.2a, W.11-12.9)	1
1	O1.8	Peer edit, revise, and type final draft of central-ideas piece using minimum of three quotations sandwiches to support claims (W.11-12.1, W.11-12.1a, W.11-12.1b, W.11-12.1c, W.11-12.1e, W.11-12.2, W.11-12.2a, W.11-12.9)	1
1	O1.9	Review the components of a compare and contrast paper (RL.11-12.1, RL.11-12.7)	3
1	O1.10	Read or view one or more secondary texts or films adapted from an original source text (RL.11-12.1, RL.11-12.7)	3
1	O1.11	Venn-diagram original text compared to secondary source[s] (RL.11-12.1, RL.11-12.7)	3
1	O1.12	Peer edit, revise, and type final draft of comparison piece (RL.11-12.1, RL.11-12.7)	3
2	O2.1	Introduce students to various forms of satire: poems, *Onion* pieces, and so on (RL.11-12.1, RL.11-12.4, RL.11-12.6)	4
2	O2.2	Determine the purpose of various satirical pieces (RL.11-12.1, RL.11-12.4, RL.11-12.6)	4

Term	IO Number	Instructional Objective (CCSS)	LCCSS Element
2	O2.3	Using a complex piece, such as *A Modest Proposal*, understand complex historical satires (RL.11-12.1, RL.11-12.4, RL.11-12.6)	4
2	O2.4	Complete a satirical piece (RL.11-12.1, RL.11-12.4, RL.11-12.6)	4
2	O2.5	Identify the most important stylistic techniques from a self-chosen work of literature (W.11-12.1, W.11-12.10, W.11-12.1b, W.11-12.1c, W.11-12.2b, W.11-12.4, W.11-12.5, W.11-12.9a)	5
2	O2.6	Identify the most important literary devices from the self-chosen work of literature (W.11-12.1, W.11-12.10, W.11-12.1b, W.11-12.1c, W.11-12.2b, W.11-12.4, W.11-12.5, W.11-12.9a)	5
2	O2.7	Identify two or more important symbols from the work of literature (W.11-12.1, W.11-12.10, W.11-12.1b, W.11-12.1c, W.11-12.2b, W.11-12.4, W.11-12.5, W.11-12.9a)	5
2	O2.8	Synthesize book-talk information into a multi-draft analysis (W.11-12.1, W.11-12.10, W.11-12.1b, W.11-12.1c, W.11-12.2b, W.11-12.4, W.11-12.5, W.11-12.9a)	5
2	O2.9	Use Grammar Bytes to determine baseline of grammatical understanding and then review capitalization, punctuation, spelling, S-V agreement, pronoun usage, commas, parallel structure, irregular verbs, fragments, comma splices, fused sentences, and sentence style; students will work at 80% mastery at each level before moving forward to next topic (L.11-12.1, L.11-12.1b, L.11-12.2, L.11-12.2a, L.11-12.2b)	6
2	O2.9	Transition from Grammar Bytes into identifying similar errors in the papers of their classmates and their own writings (L.11-12.1, L.11-12.1b, L.11-12.2, L.11-12.2a, L.11-12.2b)	6

Term	IO Number	Instructional Objective (CCSS)	LCCSS Element
3	O3.1	Identify the target audience of a particular commercial, media advertisement, blog, newspaper article, academic journal, book, or reference text (W.11-12.8)	7
3	O3.2	Identify the intended purpose of a particular commercial, media advertisement, blog, newspaper article, academic journal, book, or reference text (W.11-12.8)	7
3	O3.3	Evaluate how time alters the information cycle of a particular event (W.11-12.8)	7
3	O3.4	Pinpoint examples of author bias in the following types of informational texts: newspapers, magazines, blogs, academic journals, books, and reference texts (RI.11-12.1, RI.11-12.2, RI.11-12.6)	8
3	O3.5	Use research of author to determine what factors might make the author both an expert on the subject and/or biased about the topic (RI.11-12.1, RI.11-12.2, RI.11-12.6)	8
3	O3.6	Support claims by using quotation sandwich or some other support format to analyze the point of view or purpose of a piece (RI.11-12.1, RI.11-12.2, RI.11-12.6)	8
4	O4.1	Use previous experience and teacher facilitation to research an assigned topic and incorporate accurate MLA sources into an annotated bibliography (W.11-12.5, W.11-12.6, W.11-12.7, W.11-12.8, W.11-12.9)	9
4	O4.2	Use annotated bibliography to complete a research paper (W.11-12.5, W.11-12.6, W.11-12.7, W.11-12.8, W.11-12.9)	9

Term	IO Number	Instructional Objective (CCSS)	LCCSS Element
4	O4.3	Be assigned a teacher-selected moment in recent history that can be followed over the course of time through multiple sources up to the present; after independently searching for specific types of sources, students will participate in a whole-class discussion of the impact of the event (W.11-12.5, W.11-12.6, W.11-12.7, W.11-12.8, W.11-12.9)	9
4	O4.4	Review MLA style (L.11-12.1a, L.11-12.1b, L.11-12.3a)	10
4	O4.5	Create accurate works-cited list that connects to correct parenthetical in-text citations (L.11-12.1a, L.11-12.1b, L.11-12.3a)	10
4	O4.6	Use technology and peer editing to complete final project (L.11-12.1, L.11-12.1b, L.11-12.2, L.11-12.2a, L.11-12.2b)	6

a. IO = instructional objective; LCCSS = local Common Core State Standards; RL.11-12.1 = Item 1 in the Reading Literature subset of the English Language Arts section for Grades 11–12 in the CCSS; W.11-12.1 = Item 1 in the Writing subset of the English Language Arts section; L.11-12.1 = Item 1 in the Language subset of the English Language Arts section; RI.11-12.1 = Item 1 in the Reading Informational Text subset of the English Language Arts section.

SAMPLE K–12 MATH CURRICULUM

Table 4.14 Kindergarten

By the end of Kindergarten Math, the student will . . .

PS Element	Local Common Core State Standard	Common Core Domain
1	Count to 100 by *1s* and by *10s* and from any given number	Counting and cardinality
2	Recognize and write numbers 0–20	Counting and cardinality

(Continued)

PS Element	Local Common Core State Standard	Common Core Domain
3	Count to tell the number of objects up to 20	Counting and cardinality
4	Compare quantities and numbers to know if they are more than, less than, or equal to each other	Counting and cardinality
5	Demonstrate the sequence order in patterns	Counting and cardinality
6	Identify shapes: square, rectangle, circle, triangle, oval, heart, diamond, star, and hexagon	Geometry
7	Describe two- and three-dimensional shapes	Geometry
8	Describe objects by using measurement vocabulary, such as longer, shorter, heavier, and lighter	Measurement and data
9	Demonstrate that addition is putting together and adding to and subtraction is taking apart and taking from	Operations and algebraic thinking

KM Instructional Objectives (End-of-Term Expectations)[a]

Term	IO Number	Instructional Objective (CCSS)	LCCSS Element
1	O1.1	Count from 1 to 25 (K.CC.1, K.CC.2)	1
1	O1.2	Count the number of objects in a group up to 10 (K.CC.3, K.CC.4, K.CC.4a, K.CC.4b, K.CC.4c, K. CC.5)	3
1	O1.3	Recognize and complete AB patterns (K.CC.2)	5
1	O1.4	Identify shapes: square, rectangle, circle, triangle, oval, heart, diamond, and star (K.G.1, K.G.2, K.G.3)	6

Term	IO Number	Instructional Objective (CCSS)	LCCSS Element
2	O2.1	Count from 1 to 50 (K.CC.1, K.CC.2)	1
2	O2.2	Count to 50 by *10s* (K.CC.1, K.CC.2)	1
2	O2.3	Able to recognize and complete more complex patterns (ABB, AAB, ABC) (K.CC.2)	5
2	O2.4	Recognizes and writes numbers 0–10 (K.CC.3)	2
3	O3.1	Count to 100 by *10s* (K.CC.1, K.CC.2)	1
3	O3.2	Recognizes and writes numbers 10–20 (K.CC.3)	2
3	O3.3	Count from 1 to 75 (K.CC.1, K.CC.2)	1
3	O3.4	Count the number of objects in a group up to 20 (K.CC.3, K.CC.4, K.CC.4a, K.CC.4b, K.CC.4c, K. CC.5)	3
3	O3.5	Describe two- and three-dimensional shapes: rolls, slides, stacks, sides, and corners (K.G.4, K.G.5)	7
4	O4.1	Identify that addition is putting together and subtraction is taking apart (K.OA.1)	9
4	O4.2	Compare groups of objects to tell more than, less than, or equal to (K.CC.6, K.CC.7)	4
4	O4.3	Compare objects by using measurement vocabulary (K.MD.1, K.MD.2)	8
4	O4.4	Count from 1 to 100 (K.CC.1, K.CC.2)	1

a. IO = instructional objective; LCCSS = local Common Core State Standards; K.CC.1 = Item 1 in the Counting and Cardinality subset of the Mathematics section for kindergartners in the CCSS; K.G.4 = Item 1 in the Geometry subset; K.OA.1 = Item 1 in the Operations and Algebraic Thinking subset; K. MD.1 = Item 1 in the Measurement and Data subset.

Table 4.15 First Grade

By the end of Grade 1 Mathematics, the student will . . .		
Power Standard Element	**Local Common Core State Standard**	**Common Core Domain**
1	Measure objects using formal and informal units and order objects in a set by length from shortest to longest	Measurement and data
2	Tell and write time to the hour and half hour using analog and digital clocks	Measurement and data
3	Collect data using tally marks, construct simple graphs, and interpret information using picture and bar graphs and tables	Number and operations in base 10
4	Describe and extend patterns, including writing and skip counting by *1s, 2s, 5s,* and *10s* up to 120.	Number and operations in base 10
5	Identify and describe that the two digits of a two-digit number represent amounts of *10s* and *1s*, such as 10 single cubes is equivalent to one unit of 10, and compare two numbers based upon the amount of *10s* and *1s* each has, recording the results of the comparison with the symbols >, <, and =	Number and operations in base 10
6	Add and subtract while using place value	Number and operations in base 10
7	Use the worth of U.S. money coins (pennies, nickels, dimes, and quarters) to skip count a given collection's worth	Number and operations in base 10
8	Add and subtract within 20 with automaticity	Operations and algebraic thinking
9	Apply strategies of problem solving and estimation to solve story problems using addition and subtraction up to 20	Operations and algebraic thinking
10	Identify attributes of geometric shapes	Geometry
11	Divide shapes into two and four equal parts and describe/illustrate them as part of the whole	Geometry

1M Instructional Objectives (End-of-Term Expectations)[a]

Term	IO Number	Instructional Objective (CCSS)	LCCSS Element
1	O1.1	Demonstrate basic addition and subtraction math facts to 10 (1.OA.5, 1.OA.6)	8
1	O1.2	Create a number sentence given pictures, operations, or a story problem with sums to 10 (1.OA.1, 1.OA.2)	9
1	O1.3	Identify and write numbers by *1s* to 50 (1.NBT.1)	4
2	O2.1	Demonstrate basic addition and subtraction math facts to 12 (1.OA.5, 1.OA.6)	8
2	O2.2	Identify and complete simple geometric and numeric patterns (1.NBT.1)	4
2	O2.3	Identify the attributes of a variety of graphs and charts (1.NBT.4)	3
2	O2.4	Organize, label, and display data using pictographs, bar graphs, and tally charts (1.NBT.4)	3
2	O2.5	Identify and write by *1s* to 100 (1.NBT.1)	4
2	O2.6	Identify plane (circle, square, rectangle, triangle, oval) and space shapes (rectangular prism, cube, sphere, cone, pyramid, cylinder) and their attributes (sides, faces, and vertices) (1.G.1, 1.G.2)	10
2	O2.7	Create a number sentence given pictures, operations, or a story problem with sums to 12 (1.OA.1, 1.OA.2)	9
3	O3.1	Identify days of the week and months of the year and locate specific information on the calendar (1.NBT.4)	3
3	O3.2	Determine the correct operation to use when given a story problem (1.OA.1, 1.OA.2)	9
3	O3.3	Identify place value of *1s* and *10s* in two-digit numbers (1.NBT.2, 1.NBT.2a, 1.NBT.2b, 1.NBT.2c, 1.NBT.3)	5

Term	IO Number	Instructional Objective (CCSS)	LCCSS Element
3	O3.4	Compare pairs of two-digit numbers using place value and record the results of the comparison with the symbols >, <, and = (1.NBT.2, 1.NBT.2a, 1.NBT.2b, 1.NBT.2c, 1.NBT.3)	5
3	O3.5	Make up and generate basic addition and subtraction number sentences to 15 (1.OA.5, 1. OA.6)	8
3	O3.6	Identify penny, nickel, dime, and quarter and the value of each coin (1.NBT.1)	7
3	O3.7	Interpret and write time to the half hour and hour using analog/digital clocks (1.MD.3)	2
4	O4.1	Add 3 one-digit numbers with an answer of 15 or less (1.OA.5, 1.OA.6)	8
4	O4.2	Count collections of coins containing pennies, nickels, dimes, and quarters up to $1 (1.NBT.1)	7
4	O4.3	Prove skip-counting abilities by *2s, 5s,* and *10s* to 120 (1.NBT.1)	4
4	O4.4	Demonstrate basic addition and subtraction math facts to 20 (1.OA.5, 1.OA.6)	8
4	O4.5	Measure length informally and order objects in a set from shortest to longest (1.MD.1, 1.MD.2)	1
4	O4.6	Measure length using rulers (1.MD.1, 1.MD.2)	1
4	O4.7	Add and subtract two-digit numbers without regrouping with an answer of 20 or less (1.NBT.4)	6
4	O4.8	Solve simple addition and subtraction word problems involving money (1.NBT.1)	7
4	O4.8	Divide shapes into equal parts, shade one part, and express the amount shaded as part of the whole by writing a fraction (1.G.3)	11

a. IO = instructional objective; LCCSS = local Common Core State Standards; 1.OA.5 = Item 5 in the Operations and Algebraic Thinking subset for Grade 1 in the CCSS; 1.NBT.1 = Item 1 in the Number and Operations in Base 10 subset of the Mathematics section; 1.G.1 = Item 1 in the Geometry subset; 1.MD.3 = Item 3 in the Measurement and Data subset.

Table 4.16 Second Grade

By the end of Grade 2 Mathematics, the student will . . .

Power Standard Element	Local Common Core State Standard	Common Core Domain
1	Illustrate partitioning circles and rectangles into two, three, or four equal shares using descriptive words such as halves, thirds, two halves, three thirds, and so on	Geometry
2	Choose the appropriate length estimation using the units of inches, feet, centimeters, and meters	Measurement and data
3	Tell and write time from analog and digital clocks to the nearest five minutes, using a.m. and p.m.	Measurement and data
4	Solve word problems involving dollar bills, quarters, dimes, nickels, and pennies, using dollar and cent symbols appropriately. Example, if you have 2 dimes and 3 pennies, how many cents do you have?	Measurement and data
5	Interpret data from picture and bar graphs with a single-unit scale	Measurement and data
6	Identify that the three digits of a three-digit number represent amounts of hundreds, tens, and ones; 706 equals 7 hundreds, 0 tens, and 6 ones	Number and operations in base 10
7	Solve addition and subtraction problems within 100 using strategies based on place value, properties of operations, and/or the relationship between addition and subtraction	Number and operations in base 10
8	Compare 2 three-digit numbers based on meanings of the hundreds, tens, and ones digits using >, =, and < symbols to record the results of comparisons	Number and operations in base 10
9	Solve one-step addition and subtraction word problems within 100	Operations and algebraic thinking
10	Fluently add and subtract within 20 using mental strategies	Operations and algebraic thinking

2M Instructional Objectives (End-of-Term Expectations)[a]

Term	IO Number	Instructional Objective (CCSS)	LCCSS Element
1	2M-O1.1	Use a number line to demonstrate addition and subtraction facts up to 20 (2.OA.2)	10
1	2M-O1.2	Use mental strategies to demonstrate addition and subtraction facts up to 20 (2.OA.2)	10
1	2M-O1.3	Demonstrate the value of a three-digit number by using manipulatives (100 blocks, 10 rods, one unit) (2.NBT.1)	6
1	2M-O1.4	Identify the value of any given underlined digit in a three-digit number (2.NBT.1)	6
1	2M-O1.5	Review <, >, = signs by comparing one- and two-digit numbers (2.NBT.4)	8
1	2M-O1.6	Demonstrate place-value knowledge to compare three-digit numbers by using <, >, = (2.NBT.4)	8
2	2M-O1.1	Compute two-digit addition problems without regrouping (2.NBT.5)	7
2	2M-O1.2	Compute two-digit addition problems with regrouping (2.NBT.5)	7
2	2M-O1.3	Compute two-digit subtraction problems without regrouping (2.NBT.5)	7
2	2M-O1.4	Compute two-digit subtraction problems with regrouping (2.NBT.5)	7
2	2M-O1.5	Identify what the problems is asking and the key words to determine whether to add or subtract (2.OA.1)	9
2	2M-O1.6	Implement the correct computation to correctly label solve and the problem (2.OA.1)	9
2	2M-O1.7	Identify the different parts of a graph (2.MD.10)	5
2	2M-01.8	Interpret, make sense of, and discuss the data from picture and bar graphs with a single-unit scale (2.MD.10)	5

Term	IO Number	Instructional Objective (CCSS)	LCCSS Element
3	2M-O3.1	Identify all coins and their value (2.MD.8)	4
3	2M-O3.2	Demonstrate counting and grouping to show value of a collection of coins (2.MD.8)	4
3	2M-O3.3	Identify what the problem is asking and the key words to determine whether to add or subtract (2.MD.8)	4
3	2M-O3.4	Implement the correct computation to correctly label solve the problem (2.MD.8)	4
3	2M-O3.5	Review minute hand, hour hand, a.m., p.m., and skip counting as well as telling time to the hour and half hour (2.MD.7)	3
3	2M-O3.6	Tell and record the time to the quarter hour using a.m. and p.m (2.MD.7)	3
3	2M-O3.7	Tell and record the time to the nearest 5 minutes using a.m. and p.m. (2.MD.7)	3
4	2M-O4.1	Identify basic shapes (2.G.3)	1
4	2M-O4.2	Partition circles and rectangles into equal shares using descriptive words such as halves, thirds, fourths, and so on (2.G.3)	1
4	2M-O4.3	Demonstrate fractions by the partitioning and shading of circles and rectangles (2.G.3)	1
4	2M-O4.4	View examples of 1 inch, 1 foot, 1 centimeter, 1 meter, and so on (2.MD.3)	2
4	2M-O4.5	Give examples of objects that are of an approximate length; that is, a paper clip is about 1 inch, a water bottle is about 1 foot (2.MD.3)	2

a. IO = instructional objective; LCCSS = local Common Core State Standards; 2.OA.2 = Item 2 in the Operations and Algebraic Thinking subset for Grade 2 in the CCSS; 2.NBT.1 = Item 1 in the Number and Operations in Base 10 subset of the Mathematics section; 2.MD.10 = Item 10 in the Measurement and Data subset; 2.G.3 = Item 2 in the Geometry subset.

Used with permission.

Table 4.17 Third Grade

By the end of Grade 3 Mathematics, the student will . . .		
Power Standard Element	**Local Common Core State Standard**	**Common Core Domain**
1	Recognize rhombuses, rectangles, and squares as examples of quadrilaterals and draw examples of quadrilaterals	Geometry
2	Demonstrate and recognize the area of plane figures	Measurement and data
3	Use place-value understanding to round, add, and subtract whole numbers to the nearest 10 or 100	Number and operations in base 10
5	Apply properties of multiplication and the relationship between multiplication and division	Operations and algebraic thinking
6	Tell and write time to the nearest minute and measure time intervals in minutes	Measurement and data
7	Solve problems involving perimeters of polygons	Measurement and data

3M Instructional Objectives (End-of-Term Expectations)[a]

Term	IO Number	Instructional Objective (CCSS)	LCCSS Element
1	O1.1	Identify the thousands place and know its value (3.NBT.1, 3.NBT.2)	3
1	O1.2	Identify the ten-thousands place and know its value (3.NBT.1, 3.NBT.2)	3
1	O1.3	Identify the hundred-thousands place and know its value (3.NBT.1, 3.NBT.2)	3

Term	IO Number	Instructional Objective (CCSS)	LCCSS Element
1	O1.4	Recite and write numbers to hundred-thousands place in standard, expanded, and word form (3.NBT.1, 3.NBT.2)	3
1	O1.5	Using place value to round numbers to the nearest 100 and 1000 (3.NBT.1, 3.NBT.2)	3
1	O1.6	Compare numbers using greater, less than, and equal to with whole numbers and money (3.NBT.1, 3.NBT.2)	3
1	O1.7	Add two- and three-digit numbers with and without regrouping (3.NBT.1, 3.NBT.2)	3
1	O1.8	Subtract two- and three-digit numbers with and without regrouping (3.NBT.1, 3.NBT.2)	3
1	O1.9	Compare numbers using even and odd (3.NBT.1, 3.NBT.2)	3
1	O1.10	Estimate addition problems by rounding to the nearest ten-thousandth place and check for accuracy (3.NBT.1, 3.NBT.2)	3
1	O1.11	Estimate subtraction problems by rounding to the nearest ten-thousandth place and check for accuracy (3.NBT.1, 3.NBT.2)	3
1	O1.12	Subtract across zeros (3.NBT.1, 3.NBT.2)	3
2	O2.1	Add four-digit numbers with and without regrouping (3.NBT.1, 3.NBT.2)	3
2	O2.2	Subtract four-digit dollar amounts (3.NBT.1, 3.NBT.2)	3
2	O2.3	Subtract four-digit numbers with and without regrouping (3.NBT.1, 3.NBT.2)	3
2	O2.4	Add four-digit dollar amounts (3.NBT.1, 3.NBT.2)	3

Term	IO Number	Instructional Objective (CCSS)	LCCSS Element
2	O2.5	Tell and write time to the nearest minute (3.MD.1)	6
2	O2.6	Convert minutes to hours (3.MD.1)	6
2	O2.7	Locate weeks and days between events using a calendar (3.MD.1)	6
2	O2.8	Identify and write elapsed time (3.MD.1)	6
2	O2.9	Compare analog and digital times (3.MD.1)	6
3	O3.10	Identify and describe geometric figures (3.G.1)	1
3	O3.11	Identify two- and three-dimensional shapes (3.G.1)	1
3	O3.12	Compare and contrast quadrilaterals with plane figures (3.G.1)	1
3	O3.13	Identify and draw lines of symmetry (3.G.1)	1
3	O3.14	Identify and reproduce parallel lines (3.G.1)	1
3	O3.15	Compare and contrast congruent and similar figures (3.G.1)	1
3	O3.16	Identify flips, slides, and turns (3.G.1)	1
3	O3.17	Determine and write the area of plane figures (3.MD.5, 3.MD.5a, 3.MD.6, 3.MD.7b)	2
4	O4.1	Calculate and write the perimeter for polygons (3.MD.8)	7
4	O4.2	Model multiplication facts using an array (3.OA.1, 3.OA.2, 3.OA.4)	5
4	O4.3	Solve simple multiplication problems (3.OA.1, 3.OA.2, 3.OA.4)	5
4	O4.4	Solve simple division problems and relate to multiplication: for example, 72/9 = 8; 8 × 9 = 72 (3.OA.1, 3.OA.2, 3.OA.4)	5

a. IO = instructional objective; LCCSS = local Common Core State Standards; 3.NBT.1 = Item 1 in the Number and Operations in Base 10 subset of the Mathematics section for Grade 3 in the CCSS; 3.MD.1 = Item 1 in the Measurement and Data subset; 3.G.1 = Item 1 in the Geometry subset; 3.OA = Item 1 in the Operations and Algebraic Thinking subset.

Used with permission.

Table 4.18 Fourth Grade

By the end of Grade 4 Mathematics, the student will . . .		
Power Standard Element	**Local Common Core State Standard**	**Common Core Domain**
1	Solve problems using all four operations (addition, subtraction, multiplication, division) with whole numbers and apply across all content areas	Operations and algebraic thinking
2	Read, write, compute, and compare multi-digit whole numbers using the four operations up to four-digit numbers	Number and operations in base 10
3	Add and subtract fractions and mixed numbers with like denominators using visual fraction models and equations; compose (e.g., 3/8 = 1/8 + 1/8 + 1/8) fractions with like denominators in a variety of ways	Number and operations-fractions
4	Identify and demonstrate lines of symmetry for a two-dimensional figure; differentiate points, lines, line segments, rays, and angles	Geometry
5	Calculate and explain perimeter and area; identify angles and demonstrate concepts of angle measurement	Measurement and data

4M Instructional Objectives (End-of-Term Expectations)[a]

Term	IO Number	Instructional Objective (CCSS)	LCCSS Element
1	O1.1	Compare whole numbers using <, >, = (4.NBT.2, 4.NBT.4, 4.NBT.5, 4.NBT.6)	2
1	O1.2	Determine place value through millions (4.NBT.2, 4.NBT.4, 4.NBT.5, 4.NBT.6)	2
1	O1.3	Add and subtract four-digit numbers (4.NBT.2, 4.NBT.4, 4.NBT.5, 4.NBT.6)	2

Term	IO Number	Instructional Objective (CCSS)	LCCSS Element
1	O1.4	Subtract with zero and regrouping (4.NBT.2, 4.NBT.4, 4.NBT.5, 4.NBT.6)	2
1	O1.5	Break down numbers into their various forms (e.g., standard, word, expanded) (4.NBT.2, 4.NBT.4, 4.NBT.5, 4.NBT.6)	2
1	O1.6	Identify key words, terms, and phrases for each operation (e.g., in all, how much left, difference, sum) (4.OA.1, 4.OA.3)	1
2	O2.1	Draw and differentiate lines of symmetry (4.G.1, 4.G.3)	4
2	O2.2	Compare and contrast similarity and congruency (4.G.1, 4.G.3)	4
2	O2.3	Draw and describe points, lines, line segments, rays, and angles (4.G.1, 4.G.3)	4
2	O2.4	Solve multi-digit multiplication problems (e.g., 3645 × 23) (4.NBT.2, 4.NBT.4, 4.NBT.5, 4. NBT.6)	2
2	O2.5	Solve division problems with two-digit divisors (4.NBT.2, 4.NBT.4, 4.NBT.5, 4.NBT.6)	2
2	O2.6	Interpret word problems and determine steps in the process of solving (4.OA.1, 4.OA.3)	1
3	O3.1	Compare mixed numbers using <, >, and = (4.NF.3a, 4.NF.3b, 4.NF.3c, 4.NF.3d)	3
3	O3.2	Add and subtract mixed numbers with like denominators (4.NF.3a, 4.NF.3b, 4.NF.3c, 4.NF.3d)	3
3	O3.3	Break down fractions with like denominators (4.NF.3a, 4.NF.3b, 4.NF.3c, 4.NF.3d)	3

Term	IO Number	Instructional Objective (CCSS)	LCCSS Element
3	O3.4	Write probability as a fraction and identify possible outcomes (likely, unlikely, equally likely, certain) (4.NF.3a, 4.NF.3b, 4.NF.3c, 4.NF.3d)	3
3	O3.5	Apply strategies in solving real-to-life extended word problems (4.OA.1, 4.OA.3)	1
3	O3.6	Use the four operations to solve a variety of extended response word problems (4.OA.1, 4.OA.3)	1
4	O4.1	Explain and calculate perimeter and area (4.MD.1, 4.MD.3, 4.MD.5, 4.MD.6)	5
4	O4.2	Measure angles using a protractor (4.MD.1, 4.MD.3, 4.MD.5, 4.MD.6)	5
4	O4.3	Name types of angles and their properties (e.g., acute = less than 90 degrees, obtuse = more than 90 degrees, and right = 90 degrees) (4.MD.1, 4.MD.3, 4.MD.5, 4.MD.6)	5
4	O4.4	Interpret data from a variety of sources (4.MD.1, 4.MD.3, 4.MD.5, 4.MD.6)	5
4	O4.5	Solve problems involving measurement and conversion within one system of units (e.g., km, m, cm; hr, min, sec) (4.MD.1, 4.MD.3, 4.MD.5, 4.MD.6)	5
4	O4.6	Illustrate, apply, and solve extended response word problems using previously taught strategies in all four basic operations of math (4.OA.1, 4.OA.3)	1

a. IO = instructional objective; LCCSS = local Common Core State Standards; 4.NBT.2 = Item 2 in the Number and Operations in Base 10 subset of the Mathematics section for Grade 4 in the CCSS; 4.OA.1 = Item 1 in the Operations and Algebraic Thinking subset; 4.G.1 = Item 1 in the Geometry subset; 4.NF.3a = Item 3, Point a, in the Number and Operations-Fractions subset; 4.MD.1 = Item 1 in the Measurement and Data subset.

Table 4.19 Fifth Grade

By the end of Grade 5 Mathematics, the student will . . .		
Power Standard Element	**Local Common Core State Standard**	**Common Core Domain**
1	Demonstrate knowledge of number sense involving whole numbers and decimals (Goal 6)	Number and operations in base 10
2	Apply computational skills to whole numbers and decimals	Number and operations in base 10
3	Select and apply appropriate tools and standard units of measure to solve perimeter, area, volume (including unit conversions) (Goal 7)	Measurement and data
4	Write and solve algebraic expressions using one variable (Goal 8)	Operations and algebraic thinking
5	Identify missing terms and errors in a given sequence description and demonstrate how a change in one quantity results in a change in another quantity (Goal 8)	Operations and algebraic thinking
6	Identify and describe two- and three-dimensional shapes and analyze their properties (Goal 9)	Geometry
7	Graph, locate, identify, and determine the distance between two points on a horizontal and vertical graph using ordered pairs (Goal 9)	Geometry
8	Read, interpret, create, and display different types of graphs to make predictions representing given data. Apply the probabilities of events (Goal 10)	Geometry
9	Demonstrate knowledge of number sense involving fractions and percents (Goal 6)	Number and operations-fractions
10	Apply computational skills to fractions and percents (Goal 6)	Number and operations-fractions

5M Instructional Objectives (End-of-Term Expectations)[a]

Term	IO Number	Instructional Objective (CCSS)	LCCSS Element
1	O1.1	Interpret numerical expressions from a given description or situation for whole numbers (up to 100,000,000) and decimals (up to the hundredths place) (5.NBT.1, 5.NBT.2, 5.NBT.3, 5.NBT.3b)	1
1	O1.2	Write and evaluate algebraic expressions using variables to represent known (e.g., n + 5 + n when n = 4) and unknown quantities (e.g., 3 + n = 9) (5.OA.1, 5.OA.2)	4
1	O1.3	Read, write, recognize, and draw a relationship between decimals and fractions (5.NBT.1, 5. NBT.2, 5.NBT.3, 5.NBT.3b)	1
1	O1.4	Demonstrate how a change in one quantity results in a change in another quantity (input-output tables) (5.OA.3)	5
1	O1.5	Solve problems and identify commutative, distributive, identity, and associative properties and order of operations (5.NBT.5, 5.NBT.6, 5. NBT.7)	2
1	O1.6	Solve an equation or word problem and explain how and why (5.NBT.5, 5.NBT.6, 5.NBT.7)	2
1	O1.7	Compare and order fractions having like and unlike denominators (5.NBT.5, 5.NBT.6, 5. NBT.7)	2
1	O1.8	Apply addition and subtraction skills to add and subtract fractions with like and unlike denominators (5.NBT.5, 5.NBT.6, 5.NBT.7)	2
2	O2.1	Describe relationships in a simple scale drawing-map interpretation (e.g. 1 in. = 5 mi., so 2 in. = 10 mi.) (5.G.1, 5.G.2)	7
2	O2.2	Read, interpret, and create a stem and leaf plot, frequency table, and line graph for a given set of data (5.G.2)	8

Term	IO Number	Instructional Objective (CCSS)	LCCSS Element
2	O2.3	Select and apply appropriate tools and standard units of measure (including weight/mass, volume, and capacity) (5.MD.3a, 5.MD.3b, 5.MD.4, 5.MD.5, 5.MD.5b)	3
2	O2.4	Calculate and construct figures for perimeter and area (5.MD.3a, 5.MD.3b, 5.MD.4, 5.MD.5, 5.MD.5b)	3
2	O2.5	Determine mean, median, mode, and range of a given data set (5.G.2)	8
2	O2.6	Estimate and convert standard and metric measurements (5.OA.1, 5.OA.2)	4
2	O2.7	Solve an equation or word problem and explain how and why the learner chose to solve as you did (5.NBT.1, 5.NBT.2, 5.NBT.3, 5.NBT.3b)	1
2	O2.8	Identify radius and diameter (5.G.3, 5.G.4)	6
2	O2.9	Graph, locate, identify points, and describe paths using ordered pairs (5.G.1, 5.G.2)	7
3	O3.1	Classify and identify two- and three-dimensional polygons according to faces, edges, verticies (angles), and sides (5.G.3, 5.G.4)	6
3	O3.2	Determine three-dimensional polygon using a net (flat shape) and then construct (5.G.3, 5.G.4)	6
3	O3.3	Identify congruent and similar figures, then determine corresponding parts of similar figures (5.G.3, 5.G.4)	6
3	O3.4	Classify, identify, name, and label points, lines, rays, and angles. (5.G.3, 5.G.4)	6
3	O3.5	Identify reflections, translations, rotations, lines of symmetry, and tesselations (5.MD.3a, 5.MD.3b, 5.MD.4, 5.MD.5, 5.MD.5b)	3
3	O3.6	Classify, identify, compare, name, draw, and label triangles according to angle measurements (5.G.3, 5.G.4)	6
3	O3.7	Solve problems using properties of polygons (e.g., sum of interior angles of a triangle is 180 degrees) (5.G.3, 5.G.4)	6

Term	IO Number	Instructional Objective (CCSS)	LCCSS Element
3	O3.8	Solve an equation or word problem and explain how and why you chose to solve as you did (5.NBT.1, 5.NBT.2, 5.NBT.3, 5.NBT.3b)	1
4	O4.1	Solve whole number problems and sentences involving multiplication and division (5.NBT.5, 5.NBT.6, 5.NBT.7)	2
4	O4.2	Solve problems involving the probability of a simple event and represent this as a fraction, ratio, and a percentage (5.G.2)	8
4	O4.3	Apply fundamental counting principle in a simple problem (e.g., how many different combinations of one-scoop ice cream cones can be made from three flavors and two types of cones?) using a tree diagram (5.G.2)	8
4	O4.9	Solve decimal problems and sentences involving multiplication and division (5.NBT.5, 5.NBT.6, 5.NBT.7)	2

a. IO = instructional objective; LCCSS = local Common Core State Standards; 5.NBT.1 = Item 1 in the Number and Operations in Base 10 subset of the Mathematics section for Grade 5 in the CCSS; 5.OA.1 = Item 1 in the Operations and Algebraic Thinking subset; 5.G.1 = Item 1 in the Geometry subset; 5.MD.3a = Item 3, Point a, in the Measurement and Data subset.

Used with permission.

Table 4.20 Sixth Grade

By the end of Grade 6 Mathematics, the student will . . .		
PS Element	**Local Common Core State Standard**	**Common Core Domain**
1	Read, write, order, compare, identify, locate, and model equivalent forms of decimals, fractions, percents, and ratios	The number system
2	Solve problems involving addition, subtraction, multiplication, division, and estimation and their properties using whole numbers, decimals, fractions, percents, and proportions	The number system

(Continued)

Table 4.20 (Continued)

PS Element	Local Common Core State Standard	Common Core Domain
3	Utilize the appropriate tools, formulas, models, and vocabulary as applied to perimeter, area, volume, weight, length, and angle measures	Geometry
4	Determine and extend sequences, patterns, and functions; evaluate expressions with one variable; and represent functions in a table and coordinate planes	Expressions and equations
5	Analyze all aspects of two- and three-dimensional shapes	Geometry
6	Read, interpret, compare, and create tables and graphs; determine central tendencies and probabilities	Statistics and probability

6M Instructional Objectives (End-of-Term Expectations)[a]

Term	IO Number	Instructional Objective (CCSS)	LCCSS Element
1	O1.1	Idenitify and evaluate place value in whole numbers and decimals to the trillionths (6.NS.1, 6.NS.3)	1
1	O1.2	Write and evaluate numbers using exponential forms (6.NS.1, 6.NS.3)	1
1	O1.3	Evaluate and solve expressions using mathematical properties (6.NS.2, 6.NS.4, 6.NS.5, 6.NS.6, 6.NS.6a, 6.NS.6b, 6.NS.6c, 6.NS.7, 6. NS.7a, 6.NS.7b, 6.NS.7c, 6.NS.7d, 6.NS.8)	2
1	O1.4	Solve expressions using the order of operations (6.NS.1, 6.NS.3)	1
1	O1.5	Form proportions using equal ratios (6.NS.2, 6.NS.4, 6.NS.5, 6.NS.6, 6.NS.6a, 6.NS.6b, 6. NS.6c, 6.NS.7, 6.NS.7a, 6.NS.7b, 6.NS.7c, 6. NS.7d, 6.NS.8)	2

Term	IO Number	Instructional Objective (CCSS)	LCCSS Element
1	O1.6	Convert rates and unit rates (6.NS.2, 6.NS.4, 6. NS.5, 6.NS.6, 6.NS.6a, 6.NS.6b, 6.NS.6c, 6.NS.7, 6.NS.7a, 6.NS.7b, 6.NS.7c, 6.NS.7d, 6.NS.8)	2
1	O1.7	Write and evaluate proportions given a variety of situations (6.NS.2, 6.NS.4, 6.NS.5, 6.NS.6, 6. NS.6a, 6.NS.6b, 6.NS.6c, 6.NS.7, 6.NS.7a, 6. NS.7b, 6.NS.7c, 6.NS.7d, 6.NS.8)	2
2	O2.1	Interpret, express, and apply percents in given situations (6.NS.2, 6.NS.4, 6.NS.5, 6.NS.6, 6. NS.6a, 6.NS.6b, 6.NS.6c, 6.NS.7, 6.NS.7a, 6. NS.7b, 6.NS.7c, 6.NS.7d, 6.NS.8)	2
2	O2.2	Solve one-step equations with all four operations (6.EE.1, 6.EE.2, 6.EE.2a, 6.EE.2b, 6.EE.2c, 6.EE.3, 6.EE.4, 6.EE.5, 6.EE.6)	4
2	O2.3	Read, write, compare, and order integers (6.NS.1, 6.NS.3)	1
2	O2.4	Evaluate integers using all four operations (6. NS.1, 6.NS.3)	1
2	O2.5	Identify and graph points on a coordinate plane (6.EE.1, 6.EE.2, 6.EE.2a, 6.EE.2b, 6.EE.2c, 6.EE.3, 6.EE.4, 6.EE.5, 6.EE.6)	4
2	O2.6	Solve and graph two-step equations using all four operations and positive and negative integers (6.EE.1, 6.EE.2, 6.EE.2a, 6.EE.2b, 6.EE.2c, 6.EE.3, 6.EE.4, 6.EE.5, 6.EE.6)	4
2	O2.7	Read, interpret, compare and create tables and graphs; determine and analyze central tendencies (6.SP.1, 6.SP.4, 6.SP.5, 6.SP.5a, 6.SP.5b, 6.SP.5c)	6
3	O3.1	Identify, classify, compare, and contrast angles, triangles, circles, and quadrilaterals (6.G.2, 6.G.4)	5
3	O3.2	Identify and create transformations of a given shape (6.G.2, 6.G.4)	5
3	O3.3	Use and convert measurements with both customary and metric system (6.G.1, 6.G.3)	3

Term	IO Number	Instructional Objective (CCSS)	LCCSS Element
3	O3.4	Identify and use appropriate formulas to find perimeter, area, circumference, volume, and surface area for given shapes (6.G.1, 6.G.3)	3
3	O3.5	Classify polyhedrons and identify vertices, edges, and faces; identify polyhedrons from a net; and draw top, side, and front views (6.G.2, 6.G.4)	5
4	O4.1	Identify, model, and use proper and improper fractions and mixed numbers (6.NS.2, 6.NS.4, 6. NS.5, 6.NS.6, 6.NS.6a, 6.NS.6b, 6.NS.6c, 6.NS.7, 6.NS.7a, 6.NS.7b, 6.NS.7c, 6.NS.7d, 6.NS.8)	2
4	O4.2	Solve all fraction forms using all four operations (6.NS.2, 6.NS.4, 6.NS.5, 6.NS.6, 6.NS.6a, 6. NS.6b, 6.NS.6c, 6.NS.7, 6.NS.7a, 6.NS.7b, 6. NS.7c, 6.NS.7d, 6.NS.8)	2
4	O4.3	Apply estimation strategies to evaluate reasonable answers in fraction problems (6.NS.2, 6.NS.4, 6. NS.5, 6.NS.6, 6.NS.6a, 6.NS.6b, 6.NS.6c, 6.NS.7, 6.NS.7a, 6.NS.7b, 6.NS.7c, 6.NS.7d, 6.NS.8)	2

a. IO = instructional objective; LCCSS = local Common Core State Standards; 6.NS.1 = Item 1 in the Number System subset of the Mathematics section for Grade 6 in the CCSS; 6.EE.1 = Item 1 in the Expressions and Equations subset; 6.SP.1 = Item 1 in the Statistics and Probability subset; 6.G.2 = Item 2 in the Geometry subset.

Used with permission.

Table 4.21 Seventh Grade

By the end of Grade 7 Mathematics, the student will . . .		
Power Standard Element	**Local Common Core State Standard**	**Common Core Domain**
1	Solve real-life and mathematical problems using numerical and algebraic expressions and equations	Expressions and equations
3	Use properties of operations to generate equivalent expressions	Expressions and equations

Power Standard Element	Local Common Core State Standard	Common Core Domain
3	Analyze proportional relationships and use them to solve real-world and mathematical problems	Ratios and proportional relationships
5	Solve real-life and mathematical problems involving angle measure, area, surface area, and volume	Geometry
6	Apply and extend previous understandings of addition and subtraction to add and subtract rational numbers	The number system
7	Apply and extend previous understandings of multiplication and division and of fractions to multiply and divide rational numbers	The number system
8	Draw and compare inferences about populations	Statistics and probability
9	Investigate chance processes and develop, use, and evaluate probability models	Statistics and probability

7M Instructional Objectives (End-of Term Expectations)[a]

Term	IO Number	Instructional Objective (CCSS)	LCCSS Element
1	O1.1	Describe situations in which opposite quantities combine to make zero (7.NS.1a, 7.NS.1b, 7.NS.1c, 7.NS.1d)	6
1	O1.2	Explain and apply the algorithm of addition and subtraction as it relates to negative numbers (7.NS.1a, 7.NS.1b, 7.NS.1c, 7.NS.1d)	6
1	O1.3	Compute sums and differences using integers (7.NS.1a, 7.NS.1b, 7.NS.1c, 7.NS.1d)	6
1	O1.4	Explain and apply the algorithm of multiplication and division as it relates to negative numbers (7.NS.2a, 7.NS.2b, 7.NS.2c, 7.NS.2d, 7.NS.3)	7

Term	IO Number	Instructional Objective (CCSS)	LCCSS Element
1	O1.5	Compute products and quotients using integers (7.NS.2a, 7.NS.2b, 7.NS.2c, 7.NS.2d, 7.NS.3)	7
1	O1.6	Solve real-world and mathematical problems involving the four operations with rational numbers (7.NS.2a, 7.NS.2b, 7.NS.2c, 7.NS.2d, 7.NS.3)	7
1	O1.7	Calculate measures of central tendency to make inferences about sample populations (7. SP.1, 7.SP.2, 7.SP.3)	8
2	O2.1	Rewrite and explain rational expression in equivalent forms using properties of operations (commutative, associative, distributive, identity) (7.EE.1, 7.EE.2, 7.EE.3)	3
2	O2.2	Interpret word problems to construct and solve expressions that model real-world situations (7. EE.1, 7.EE.2, 7.EE.3)	3
2	O2.3	Interpret word problems to construct and solve equations that model real-world situations (in the form px + q = r) (7.EE.4, 7.EE.4a)	1
3	O3.4	Recall and apply formulas for the perimeter and area of two-dimensional objects (7.G.4, 7.G.5, 7.G.6)	5
3	O3.5	Use angle relationships to write and solve simple equations for an unknown angles in a figure (7.G.4, 7.G.5, 7.G.6)	5
3	O3.6	Identify and apply formulas for the surface area and volume of three-dimensional objects (7.G.4, 7.G.5, 7.G.6)	5
3	O3.7	Compute unit rates measured in like or unlike units (7.RP.1, 7.RP.2, 7.RP.2a, 7.RP.2b, 7.RP.3)	3
3	O3.8	Recognize proportional relationships and identify the constant of proportionality (unit rate) in tables, graphs, equations, diagrams, and verbal descriptions of proportional relationships (7.RP.1, 7.RP.2, 7.RP.2a, 7.RP.2b, 7.RP.3)	3

Term	IO Number	Instructional Objective (CCSS)	LCCSS Element
3	O3.9	Solve multi-step ratio and percent problems (7. RP.1, 7.RP.2, 7.RP.2a, 7.RP.2b, 7.RP.3)	3
3	O3.10	Compute actual lengths and areas from a scale drawing (7.RP.1, 7.RP.2, 7.RP.2a, 7.RP.2b, 7.RP.3)	3
4	O4.1	State the likelihood of an event occurring given the probability (7.SP.5, 7.SP.6, 7.SP.7, 7.SP.7a, 7.SP.7b, 7.SP.8, 7.SP.8a, 7.SP.8b, 7.SP.8c)	9
4	O4.2	Compute the theoretical probability of an event occurring from collected data (7.SP.5, 7.SP.6, 7.SP.7, 7.SP.7a, 7.SP.7b, 7.SP.8, 7.SP.8a, 7. SP.8b, 7.SP.8c)	9
4	O4.3	Develop and compare probabilities to explain possible discrepancies between models (7.SP.5, 7.SP.6, 7.SP.7, 7.SP.7a, 7.SP.7b, 7.SP.8, 7.SP.8a, 7.SP.8b, 7.SP.8c)	9

a. IO = instructional objective; LCCSS = local Common Core State Standards; 7.NS1a = Item 1, Point a, in the Number System subset of the Mathematics section for Grade 7 in the CCSS; 7.SP.1 = Item 1 in the Statistics and Probability subset; 7.EE.1 = Item 1 in the Expressions and Equations subset; 7.G.4 = Item 4 in the Geometry subset; 7.RP.1 = the Ratios and Proportional Relationships subset.

Table 4.22 Eighth Grade

By the end of eighth grade the student will . . .

PS Element	Local Common Core State Standard	Common Core Domain
1	Perform operations and apply properties of radicals and integer exponents	Expressions and equations
2	Interpret the connections between proportional relationships, lines, and linear equations	Expressions and equations

(Continued)

Table 4.22 (Continued)

3	Analyze and solve linear equations and pairs of simultaneous linear equations	Expressions and equations
4	Define, evaluate, and compare functions	Functions
5	Use functions to model relationships between quantities	Functions
6	Recognize and describe congruence and similarity using physical models, transparencies, or geometry software	Geometry
7	Explain and apply the Pythagorean theorem	Geometry
8	Solve real-world and mathematical problems involving volume of cylinders, cones, and spheres.	Geometry
9	Recognize that there are numbers that are not rational and approximate them by rational numbers	The number system
10	Investigate patterns of association in bivariate data	Statistics and probability

8M Instructional Objectives (End-of-Term Expectations)[a]

Term	IO Number	Instructional Objective (CCSS)	LCCSS Element
1	O1.1	Describe and compare rational and irrational numbers (8.NS.1, 8.NS.2)	9
1	O1.2	Evaluate rational and irrational square roots (8.EE.1, 8.EE.2, 8.EE.3, 8.EE.4)	1
1	O1.3	Use rational approximations of irrational numbers to order irrational numbers (8.NS.1, 8.NS.2)	9
1	O1.4	Generate equivalent numerical expressions using properties of integer exponents (8.EE.1, 8.EE.2, 8. EE.3, 8.EE.4)	1
1	O1.5	Express and perform operations with numbers in scientific notation (8.EE.1, 8.EE.2, 8.EE.3, 8.EE.4)	1

Term	IO Number	Instructional Objective (CCSS)	LCCSS Element
2	O2.1	Give examples of linear equations in one variable with one solution, infinitely many solutions, or no solutions (8.EE.7, 8.EE.7a, 8.EE.7b, 8.EE.8, 8. EE.8a, 8.EE.8b, 8.EE.8c)	3
2	O2.2	Solve linear equations using the distributive property and combining like terms (8.EE.7, 8. EE.7a, 8.EE.7b, 8.EE.8, 8.EE.8a, 8.EE.8b, 8.EE.8c)	3
2	O2.3	Construct and interpret scatter plots to describe patterns such as clustering, outliers, positive or negative association, linear association, and nonlinear association (8.SP.1, 8.SP.2, 8.SP.3, 8. SP.4)	10
2	O2.4	Understand that patterns of association can also be seen in bivariate categorical data by displaying frequencies and relative frequencies in a two-way table (8.SP.1, 8.SP.2, 8.SP.3, 8.SP.4)	10
2	O2.5	Establish facts about the angle sum and exterior angle of triangles, about the angles created when parallel lines are cut by a transversal, and the angle-angle criterion for similarity of triangles (8.G.1a, 8.G.1b, 8.G.1c, 8.G.2, 8.G.5)	6
2	O2.6	Demonstrate and describe how the relationship of two-dimensional figures is congruent using transformations (8.G.1a, 8.G.1b, 8.G.1c, 8.G.2, 8.G.5)	6
2	O2.7	Explore the properties of rotations, reflections, and translations to prove congruence (8.G.1a, 8.G.1b, 8.G.1c, 8.G.2, 8.G.5)	6
3	O3.1	Calculate volume of cones, cylinders, and spheres and solve real-world and mathematical problems (8.G.9)	8
3	O3.2	Express functions algebraically, graphically, numerically in tables, or by verbal description (8.F.1, 8.F.2, 8.F.3)	4

Term	IO Number	Instructional Objective (CCSS)	LCCSS Element
3	O3.3	Interpret and define a linear function using y = mx + b (8.F.1, 8.F.2, 8.F.3)	4
3	O3.4	Describe, construct, and graph a function to model a linear relationship between two quantities (8.F.4, 8.F.5)	5
3	O3.5	Interpret slope and intercept in terms of real world problems (8.SP.1, 8.SP.2, 8.SP.3, 8.SP.4)	10
3	O3.6	Define, demonstrate, and apply Pythagorean theorem (8.G.6, 8.G.7)	7
4	O4.1	Graph, compare, and explain slope using unit rates and similar triangles (8.EE.5, 8.EE.6)	2
4	O4.2	Describe and solve systems of linear equations algebraically and graphically (8.EE.7, 8.EE.7a, 8.EE.7b, 8.EE.8, 8.EE.8a, 8.EE.8b, 8.EE.8c)	3

a. IO = instructional objective; LCCSS = local Common Core State Standards; 8.NS.1 = Item 1 in the Number System subset of the Mathematics section for Grade 8 in the CCSS; 8.EE.1 = Item 1 in the Expressions and Equations subset; 8.SP.1 = Item 1 in the Statistics and Probability subset; 8.G.1a = Item 1, Point a, in the Geometry subset; 8.F.1 = Item 1 in the Functions subset.

Table 4.23 Algebra 1

By the end of Algebra 1, the student will . . .

Power Standard Element	Local Common Core State Standard	Common Core Domain
1	Add, subtract, and multiply polynomials	Arithmetic with polynomials and rational expressions
2	Translate words into algebraic symbols	Building functions
3	Determine the probability of one or more independent events	Conditional probability and the rules of probability

Power Standard Element	Local Common Core State Standard	Common Core Domain
4	Create, solve, and graph equations or inequalities with one or two variables	Creating equations
5	Interpret the slope and intercept of linear equations; write linear equations in the context of the data	Interpreting categorical and quantitative data
6	Estimate the slope of a function given its graph; rewrite linear equations into different equivalent forms and explain which fits the given data best	Interpreting functions
7	Graph and express the solutions to linear inequalities; choose the best method to solve quadratic equations from roots, factoring, or the quadratic formula; explain and execute the best method for solving a system of linear equations from substitution, elimination, and multiplication; solve simple rational and radical equations	Reasoning with equations and inequalities

Alg1 Instructional Objectives (End-of-Term Expectations)[a]

Term	IO Number	Instructional Objective (CCSS)	LCCSS Element
1	O1.1	Solve multistep equations and inequalities with one variable; given a situation, create and solve an equation and inequality (9–12.A-CED.1, 9–12.A-CED.2, 9–12.A-CED.3, 9–12.A-CED.4)	4
1	O1.2	Given words, create an expression or equation that models the situation (9–12.F-BF.1)	2
2	O2.1	Graph a linear equation with one or two variables and represent the solution as all points on the line; graph an inequality with one or two variables and represent the solution as all shaded regions; graph quadratic equations (9–12.A-CED.1, 9–12.A-CED.2, 9–12.A-CED.3, 9–12.A-CED.4)	4

Term	IO Number	Instructional Objective (CCSS)	LCCSS Element
2	O2.2	Identify the slope and intercepts of a line given the graph or the linear equation or inequality; write a linear equation given a combination of slope or points in each form (9–12.S-ID.7)	5
2	O2.3	Translate linear equations from one form into another, creating an equivalent equation (9–12.F-IF.1, 9–12.F-IF.6, 9–12.F-IF.8)	6
3	O3.1	Solve systems of equations and inequalities algebraically and graphically; factor polynomial expressions (9–12.A-REI.4, 9–12.A-REI.5, 9–12.A-REI.6, 9–12.A-REI.1, 9–12.A-REI.10, 9–12.A-REI.12, 9–12.A-REI.2, 9–12.A-REI.3)	7
3	O3.2	Add and subtract higher order polynomials; multiply monomials and polynomials using exponent rules and expansion theorems (9–12.A-APR.1)	1
4	O4.1	Solve quadratic equations using factoring or the quadratic formula (9–12.A-REI.4, 9–12.A-REI.5, 9–12.A-REI.6, 9–12.A-REI.1, 9–12.A-REI.10, 9–12.A-REI.12, 9–12.A-REI.2, 9–12.A-REI.3)	7
4	O4.2	Solve simple radical equations; add, subtract, multiply, and divide radicals (9–12.A-REI.4, 9–12.A-REI.5, 9–12.A-REI.6, 9–12.A-REI.1, 9–12.A-REI.10, 9–12.A-REI.12, 9–12.A-REI.2, 9–12.A-REI.3)	7
4	O4.3	Find the probability of simple and compound events; determine when to apply permutations and combinations (9–12.S-CP.2)	3

a. IO = instructional objective; LCCSS = local Common Core State Standards; 9–12.A-CED.1 = Item 1 in the Creating Equations subset of the High School Mathematics section for Algebra in the CCSS; 9–12.F-BF.1 = Item 1 in the Building Functions subset of the High School Mathematics Functions section; 9–12.S-ID.7 = Item 7 in the Interpreting Categorical and Quantitative Data subset of the High School Mathematics Statistics and Probability section; 9–12.F-IF.1 = Item 1 in the Interpreting Functions subset; 9–12.A-REI.4 = Item 4 in the Reasoning With Equations and Inequalities subset; 9–12.A-APR.1 = Item 1 in the Arithmetic With Polynomials and Rational Expressions subset; 9–12.S-CP.2 = Item 2 in the Conditional Probability and the Rules of Probability subset.

Used with permission.

Table 4.24 Algebra 2

By the end of Algebra 2, the student will . . .		
Power Standard Element	**Local Common Core State Standard**	**Common Core Domain**
1	Recognize when a relation is a function and understand function notation; identify the domain in equation form and graphical form	Interpreting functions
2	Recognize a linear equation and its parts; recognize the different forms of lines; be able to graph a line. Write a linear equation from a table of values	Linear, quadratic, and exponential models
3	Construct quadratic and exponential functions given a graph, a description of a relationship, or two input-output pairs (including reading these from a table); create functions by hand and with graphing utilities	Linear, quadratic, and exponential models
4	Express exponential models as logarithms (with bases 10 or e, as well as with other bases) by hand and graphically	Linear, quadratic, and exponential models
5	Interpret the parameters in a linear or exponential function in terms of a context	Linear, quadratic, and exponential models
6	Recognize the complex number *i* such that *i*2 = –1, and every complex number has the form a + b*i*; know how to add, subtract, and multiply complex numbers	Complex numbers
7	Graph complex numbers on the complex plane; use conjugates of a complex number to find moduli and quotients of complex numbers	Complex numbers
8	Solve polynomial equations with complex zeros; apply the Fundamental Theorem of Algebra	Complex numbers
9	Add, subtract, and multiply polynomials using like terms	Arithmetic with polynomials and rational expressions

(Continued)

Table 4.24 (Continued)

Power Standard Element	Local Common Core State Standard	Common Core Domain
10	Find the zeros of a polynomial equation and sketch a rough graph from these zeros; apply the Remainder Theorem	Arithmetic with polynomials and rational expressions
11	Write equations or inequalities in one or two variables and solve for those variables; graph these equations or inequalities; solve the equation for one of the variables	Creating equations
12	Write an expression in a different form by factoring	Seeing structure in expressions
13	Find the zeros, minima, and maxima of a function's graph both by hand and graphically	Interpreting functions
14	Graph translated functions analytically; write translated functions from graphs	Interpreting functions
15	Solve quadratic equations by taking square roots, completing the square, the quadratic formula, and factoring; recognize when the quadratic formula gives complex solutions	Reasoning with equations and inequalities
16	Solve systems of linear equations graphically or with the substitution or elimination method	Reasoning with equations and inequalities
17	Solve systems of equations using matrices	Reasoning with equations and inequalities
18	Use the properties of exponents to interpret expressions for exponential functions	Interpreting functions
19	Solve radical equations involving rational exponents	Reasoning with equations and inequalities
20	Combine two functions into one composite function	Building functions
21	Find the inverse of a function; prove that one function is the inverse of the other	Building functions

Alg2 Instructional Objectives (End-of-Term Expectations)[a]

Term	IO Number	Instructional Objective (CCSS)	LCCSS Element
1	O1.1	Identify a function and its domain (9–12.F-IF.1, 9–12.F-IF.2, 9–12.F-IF.5)	1
1	O1.2	Graph Lines (9–12.F-LE.1, 9–12.F-LE.1a, 9–12.F-LE.1b)	2
1	O1.3	Graph a translated function; write the function from its graph (9–12.F-IF.7b, 9–12.F-IF.7c)	14
1	O1.4	Write and graph linear and absolute value equations and inequalities (9–12.A-CED.1, 9–12.A-CED.2, 9–12.A-CED.4)	11
1	O1.5	Graph and solve one and two variable equations or inequalities (9–12.A-CED.1, 9–12.A-CED.2, 9–12.A-CED.4)	11
2	O2.1	Solve systems of equations algebraically and graphically (9–12.A-REI.5, 9–12.A-REI.6, 9–12.A-REI.7)	16
2	O2.2	Solve systems of equations using matrices (9–12.A-REI.9)	17
3	O3.3	Combine polynomials (9–12.A-APR.1)	9
3	O3.4	Create a quadratic function from data points (9–12.F-LE.2)	3
3	O3.5	Find zeros, mins, and maxs for quadratic functions (9–12.F-IF.4, 9–12.F-IF.7, 9–12.F-IF.7a)	13
3	O3.6	Sketch a rough graph from a polynomial function (9–12.A-APR.2, 9–12.A-APR.3)	10
3	O3.7	Factor quadratic expressions (9–12.A-SSE.2, 9–12.A-SSE.3a)	12
3	O3.8	Solve quadratic equations (9–12.A-REI.4, 9–12.A-REI.4b)	15
3	O3.9	Recognize *i* and complex numbers (9–12.N-CN.1, 9–12.N-CN.2)	6

Term	IO Number	Instructional Objective (CCSS)	LCCSS Element
3	O3.10	Graph complex numbers and compute absolute values; find the conjugate of a complex number and use it to simplify a quotient (9–12.N-CN.3, 9–12.N-CN.4)	7
3	O3.11	Solve higher-order functions for all complex zeros (9–12.N-CN.7, 9–12.N-CN.9)	8
4	O4.1	Simplify radical expressions (9–12.F-IF.8b)	18
4	O4.2	Solve radical equations (9–12.F-IF.8b)	18
4	O4.3	Compute composite functions (9–12.F-BF.1c)	20
4	O4.4	Find and prove inverse functions (9–12.F-BF.4, 9–12.F-BF.4b)	21

a. IO = instructional objective; LCCSS = local Common Core State Standards; 9–12.F-IF.1 = Item 1 in the Interpreting Functions subset of the High School Mathematics Functions section for Algebra in the CCSS; 9–12.F-LE.1 = Item 1 in the Linear, Quadratic, and Exponential Models subset; 9–12.A-CED.1 = Item 1 in the Creating Equations subset of the High School Mathematics section; 9–12.A-REI.5 = Item 5 in the Reasoning With Equations and Inequalities subset; 9–12.A-APR.1 = Item 1 in the Arithmetic With Polynomials and Rational Expressions subset; 9–12.A-SSE.2 = Item 2 in the Seeing Structure in Expressions subset; 9–12.N-CN.1 = Item 1 in the Complex Numbers subset of the High School Mathematics Number and Quantity section; 9–12.F-BF.1c = Item 1, Point c, in the Building Functions subset.

Table 4.25 Geometry

By the end of Geometry, the student will . . .		
Power Standard Element	**Local Common Core State Standard**	**Common Core Domain**
1	Apply theorems about circles; produce the equation of a circle; identify components of the circle; apply properties of inscribed and circumscribed circles	Circles
2	Define key concepts of plane geometry; apply and describe transformations of shapes that carry it onto itself; prove theorems about lines, angles, triangles, and parallelograms	Congruence

Power Standard Element	Local Common Core State Standard	Common Core Domain
3	Apply the distance and slope formulas in the coordinate plane to prove geometric theorems about polygons	Expressing geometric properties with equations
4	Explain surface area and volume formulas and use them to solve problems	Geometric measure and dimension
5	Construct if-then statements	Interpreting categorical and quantitative data
6	Apply theorems about triangle similarity and congruence	Similarity, right triangles, and trigonometry

GEO1 Instructional Objectives (End-of-Term Expectations)[a]

Term	IO Number	Instructional Objective (CCSS)	LCCSS Element
1	O1.1	Apply segment and angle addition postulates; identify angle relationships; solve algebraic equations incorporating angle relationships (9–12.G-CO.1, 9–12.G-CO.10, 9–12.G-CO.11, 9–12.G-CO.3, 9–12.G-CO.5, 9–12.G-CO.8, 9–12.G-CO.9)	2
1	O1.2	Write if-then statements using inductive and deductive reasoning; incorporate into proofs about angles and lines (9–12.S-ID.9)	5
1	O1.3	Produce and solve the distance, midpoint, and slope formulas to prove theorems about lines (9–12.G-GPE.4, 9–12.G-GPE.5, 9–12.G-GPE.7)	3

Term	IO Number	Instructional Objective (CCSS)	LCCSS Element
2	O2.1	Use congruence criteria for triangles to solve problems and to prove relationships in geometric figures (9–12.G-SRT.1, 9–12.G-SRT.1a, 9–12.G-SRT.1b, 9–12.G-SRT.2, 9–12.G-SRT.3, 9–12.G-SRT.4, 9–12.G-SRT.5, 9–12.G-SRT.6, 9–12.G-SRT.7, 9–12.G-SRT.8)	6
2	O2.2	Construct proofs about triangle congruency; apply theorems about points of concurrency; construct proofs about parallelogram properties; classify special quadrilaterals; apply the distance and midpoint formulas to prove figures are triangles or special quadrilaterals (9–12.G-CO.1, 9–12.G-CO.10, 9–12.G-CO.11, 9–12.G-CO.3, 9–12.G-CO.5, 9–12.G-CO.8, 9–12.G-CO.9)	2
3	O3.1	Apply and demonstrate transformations of figures (9–12.G-CO.1, 9–12.G-CO.10, 9–12.G-CO.11, 9–12.G-CO.3, 9–12.G-CO.5, 9–12.G-CO.8, 9–12.G-CO.9)	2
3	O3.2	Prove triangles are similar; apply properties of similar polygons (9–12.G-SRT.1, 9–12.G-SRT.1a, 9–12.G-SRT.1b, 9–12.G-SRT.2, 9–12.G-SRT.3, 9–12.G-SRT.4, 9–12.G-SRT.5, 9–12.G-SRT.6, 9–12.G-SRT.7, 9–12.G-SRT.8)	6
3	O3.3	Use trigonometric ratios and the Pythagorean theorem to solve right triangles in applied problems (9–12.G-SRT.1, 9–12.G-SRT.1a, 9–12.G-SRT.1b, 9–12.G-SRT.2, 9–12.G-SRT.3, 9–12.G-SRT.4, 9–12.G-SRT.5, 9–12.G-SRT.6, 9–12.G-SRT.7, 9–12.G-SRT.8)	6
4	O4.1	Apply theorems about arcs, tangents, secants, and inscribed angles of circles; produce the equation of a circle; identify components of the circle; calculate area and circumference of sectors and arc lengths (9–12.G-C.2, 9–12.G-C.3, 9–12.G-C.4, 9–12.G-C.5)	1

Term	IO Number	Instructional Objective (CCSS)	LCCSS Element
4	O4.2	Calculate the area of polygons; apply properties of interior and exterior angles (9–12.G-CO.1, 9–12.G-CO.10, 9–12.G-CO.11, 9–12.G-CO.3, 9–12.G-CO.5, 9–12.G-CO.8, 9–12.G-CO.9)	2
4	O4.3	Derive and apply surface area and volume of 3-D figures (9–12.G-GMD.1, 9–12.G-GMD.3)	4

a. IO = instructional objective; LCCSS = local Common Core State Standards; 9–12.G-CO.1 = Item 1 in the Congruence subset of the High School Mathematics section for Geometry in the CCSS; 9–12 S-ID.9 = Item 9 in the Interpreting Categorical and Quantitative Data subset of the High School Mathematics Statistics and Probability section; 9–12.G-GPE.4 = Item 4 in the Expressing Geometric Properties with Equations subset; 9–12.G-SRT.1 = Item 1 in the Similarity, Right Triangles, and Trigonometry subset; 9–12.G-C.2 = Item 1 in the Circles subset; 9–12.G.GMD.1 = Item 1 in the Geometric Measurement and Dimension subset.

Used with permission.

Table 4.26 Algebra A

By the end of Algebra A, the student will . . .		
Power Standard Element	**Local Common Core State Standard**	**Common Core Domain**
1	Interpret the structure of expressions with new emphasis on quadratic and exponential expressions	Seeing structure in expressions
2	Extend arithmetic to polynomial functions	Arithmetic with polynomials and rational expressions
3	Create equations that show relationships between numbers	Creating equations
4	Show numeracy with whole numbers and all real number operations	Quantities

(Continued)

Table 4.26 (Continued)

Power Standard Element	Local Common Core State Standard	Common Core Domain
5	Define, identify, and use irrational numbers	The real number system
6	Understand solving equations and inequalities as a reasoning process and interpret solutions within the context of the problem	Reasoning with equations and inequalities
7	Understand the concept of a function and use function notation and interpret function that arise in certain contexts	Interpreting functions
8	Extend knowledge of equations and relationships to function, and build new functions from existing ones	Building functions
9	Construct and compare linear, exponential, and quadratic models (functions) and interpret the parameters within a given context	Linear, quadratic, and exponential models

AlgA Instructional Objectives (End-of-Term Expectations)[a]

Term	IO Number	Instructional Objective (CCSS)	LCCSS Element
1	O1.1	Perform operations on fractions (9–12.N-Q.1, 9–12.N-Q.2, 9–12.N-Q.3)	4
1	O1.2	Perform unit conversions (9–12.N-Q.1, 9–12.N-Q.2, 9–12.N-Q.3)	4
1	O1.3	Apply significant digits to calculations (9–12.N-Q.1, 9–12.N-Q.2, 9–12.N-Q.3)	4
1	O1.4	Simplify expressions by performing order of operations (9–12.A-SSE.1, 9–12.A-SSE.1a, 9–12.A-SSE.1b, 9–12.A-SSE.2, 9–12.A-SSE.3, 9–12.A-SSE.3a, 9–12.A-SSE.3b, 9–12.A-SSE.3c)	1

Term	IO Number	Instructional Objective (CCSS)	LCCSS Element
1	O1.5	Build expressions from a set of written instructions (9–12.A-SSE.1, 9–12.A-SSE.1a, 9–12.A-SSE.1b, 9–12.A-SSE.2, 9–12.A-SSE.3, 9–12.A-SSE.3a, 9–12.A-SSE.3b, 9–12.A-SSE.3c)	1
1	O1.6	Create equations and inequalities in one variable and use them to solve problems (9–12.A-CED.1, 9–12.A-CED.2, 9–12.A-CED.3, 9–12.A-CED.4)	3
2	O2.1	Create equations in two or more variables to represent relationships between quantities (9–12.A-CED.1, 9–12.A-CED.2, 9–12.A-CED.3, 9–12.A-CED.4)	3
2	O2.2	Solve linear equations (9–12.A-REI.4, 9–12.A-REI.4a, 9–12.A-REI.4b, 9–12.A-REI.6, 9–12.A-REI.7, 9–12.A-REI.1, 9–12.A-REI.10, 9–12.A-REI.11, 9–12.A-REI.12, 9–12.A-REI.2, 9–12.A-REI.3)	6
2	O2.3	Solve linear inequalities and interpret the solution (9–12.A-REI.4, 9–12.A-REI.4a, 9–12.A-REI.4b, 9–12.A-REI.6, 9–12.A-REI.7, 9–12.A-REI.1, 9–12.A-REI.10, 9–12.A-REI.11, 9–12.A-REI.12, 9–12.A-REI.2, 9–12.A-REI.3)	6
2	O2.4	Rearrange formulas to highlight a quantity of interest (9–12.A-REI.4, 9–12.A-REI.4a, 9–12.A-REI.4b, 9–12.A-REI.6, 9–12.A-REI.7, 9–12.A-REI.1, 9–12.A-REI.10, 9–12.A-REI.11, 9–12.A-REI.12, 9–12.A-REI.2, 9–12.A-REI.3)	6
2	O2.5	Rewrite expressions using properties of exponents (integers only) (9–12.N-RN.1, 9–12.N-RN.2, 9–12.N-RN.3)	5
2	O2.6	Create a table and graph from an equation (linear) (9–12.A-REI.4, 9–12.A-REI.4a, 9–12.A-REI.4b, 9–12.A-REI.6, 9–12.A-REI.7, 9–12.A-REI.1, 9–12.A-REI.10, 9–12.A-REI.11, 9–12.A-REI.12, 9–12.A-REI.2, 9–12.A-REI.3)	6

Term	IO Number	Instructional Objective (CCSS)	LCCSS Element
3	O3.1	Interpret the following features of a function's graph or table: intercepts (starting value), inc/dec, +/–, rate of change (average rate of change) (linear) (9–12.F-IF.1, 9–12.F-IF.2, 9–12.F-IF.4, 9–12.F-IF.5, 9–12.F-IF.6, 9–12.F-IF.7, 9–12.F-IF.7a, 9–12.F-IF.7e, 9–12.F-IF.8a, 9–12.F-IF.8b, 9–12.F-IF.9)	7
3	O3.2	Create a table and graph from an equation (exponential) (9–12.A-REI.4, 9–12.A-REI.4a, 9–12.A-REI.4b, 9–12.A-REI.6, 9–12.A-REI.7, 9–12.A-REI.1, 9–12.A-REI.10, 9–12.A-REI.11, 9–12.A-REI.12, 9–12.A-REI.2, 9–12.A-REI.3)	6
3	O3.3	Interpret the following features of a function's graph or table: intercepts (starting value), inc/dec, +/–, rate of change (avg. rate of change) (exponential) (9–12.F-IF.1, 9–12.F-IF.2, 9–12.F-IF.4, 9–12.F-IF.5, 9–12.F-IF.6, 9–12.F-IF.7, 9–12.F-IF.7a, 9–12.F-IF.7e, 9–12.F-IF.8a, 9–12.F-IF.8b, 9–12.F-IF.9)	7
3	O3.4	Graph the solution to a linear inequality and give sample solutions (9–12.A-REI.4, 9–12.A-REI.4a, 9–12.A-REI.4b, 9–12.A-REI.6, 9–12.A-REI.7, 9–12.A-REI.1, 9–12.A-REI.10, 9–12.A-REI.11, 9–12.A-REI.12, 9–12.A-REI.2, 9–12.A-REI.3)	6
3	O3.5	Solve systems of linear equations by graphing and algebraically (9–12.A-REI.4, 9–12.A-REI.4a, 9–12.A-REI.4b, 9–12.A-REI.6, 9–12.A-REI.7, 9–12.A-REI.1, 9–12.A-REI.10, 9–12.A-REI.11, 9–12.A-REI.12, 9–12.A-REI.2, 9–12.A-REI.3)	6
4	O4.1	Graph the solution to a system of linear inequalities (usually with context) and give data sets that work and don't work (9–12.A-REI.4, 9–12.A-REI.4a, 9–12.A-REI.4b, 9–12.A-REI.6, 9–12.A-REI.7, 9–12.A-REI.1, 9–12.A-REI.10, 9–12.A-REI.11, 9–12.A-REI.12, 9–12.A-REI.2, 9–12.A-REI.3)	6

Term	IO Number	Instructional Objective (CCSS)	LCCSS Element
4	O4.2	Identify the domain and range for a function, listing any theoretical or contextual restrictions (9–12.F-IF.1, 9–12.F-IF.2, 9–12.F-IF.4, 9–12.F-IF.5, 9–12.F-IF.6, 9–12.F-IF.7, 9–12.F-IF.7a, 9–12.F-IF.7e, 9–12.F-IF.8a, 9–12.F-IF.8b, 9–12.F-IF.9)	7
4	O4.3	Use function notation, evaluate functions for given inputs and function notation within the context of the problem (9–12.F-IF.1, 9–12.F-IF.2, 9–12.F-IF.4, 9–12.F-IF.5, 9–12.F-IF.6, 9–12.F-IF.7, 9–12.F-IF.7a, 9–12.F-IF.7e, 9–12.F-IF.8a, 9–12.F-IF.8b, 9–12.F-IF.9)	7
4	O4.4	Write linear functions as arithmetic sequences and exponential functions as geometric sequences (9–12.F-IF.1, 9–12.F-IF.2, 9–12.F-IF.4, 9–12.F-IF.5, 9–12.F-IF.6, 9–12.F-IF.7, 9–12.F-IF.7a, 9–12.F-IF.7e, 9–12.F-IF.8a, 9–12.F-IF.8b, 9–12.F-IF.9)	7

a. IO = instructional objective; LCCSS = local Common Core State Standards; 9–12.N-Q.1 = Item 1 in the Quantities subset of the High School Mathematics section for Algebra in the CCSS; 9–12.A-SSE.1 = Item 1 in the Seeing Structure in Expressions subset; 9–12.A-CED.1 = Item 1 in the Creating Equations subset; 9–12.A-REI.4 = Item 4 in the Reasoning With Equations and Inequalities subset; 9–12.N-RN.1 = Item 1 in the Real Numbers subset of the High School Mathematics Number and Quantity section; 9–12. F-IF.1 = Item 1 in the Interpreting Functions subset of the High School Mathematics Functions section.

Used with permission.

Table 4.27 Statistics 1

By the end of Statistics 1, the student will . . .		
Power Standard Element	**Local Common Core State Standard**	**Common Core Domain**
1	Understand independence and conditional probability and use them to interpret data; use the rules of probability to compute probabilities of compound events	Conditional probability and the rules of probability

(Continued)

Table 4.27 (Continued)

Power Standard Element	Local Common Core State Standard	Common Core Domain
2	Summarize, represent, and interpret data on a single-count or measurement variable; summarize, represent, and interpret data on two categorical and quantitative variables; interpret linear models	Interpreting categorical and quantitative data
3	Understand and evaluate random processes underlying statistical experiments; make inferences and justify conclusions from sample surveys, experiments, and observational studies	Making inferences and justifying conclusions
4	Calculate expected values and use them to solve problems; use probability to evaluate outcomes of decisions	Using probability to make decisions

STAT1 Instructional Objectives (End-of-Term Expectations)[a]

Term	IO Number	Instructional Objective (CCSS)	LCCSS Element
1	O1.1	Will construct an observation, experiment, and survey, then use statistical analysis to make inferences and conclusions from their findings (9–12.S-IC.1, 9–12.S-IC.3, 9–12.S-IC.5, 9–12.S-IC.6)	3
1	O1.2	Find measures of central tendency and measures of distribution for a data set[s] and summarize the findings (9–12.S-ID.1, 9–12.S-ID.2, 9–12.S-ID.3, 9–12.S-ID.4, 9–12.S-ID.5, 9–12.S-ID.6, 9–12.S-ID.6c, 9–12.S-ID.7, 9–12.S-ID.8)	2
2	O2.1	Use probability formulas to determine probability for simple and compound events (9–12.S-CP.1, 9–12.S-CP.2, 9–12.S-CP.3, 9–12.S-CP.4, 9–12.S-CP.5, 9–12.S-CP.6, 9–12.S-CP.7, 9–12.S-CP.8, 9–12.S-CP.9)	1

Term	IO Number	Instructional Objective (CCSS)	LCCSS Element
2	O2.2	Determine expected values for particular events (9–12.S-MD.1, 9–12.S-MD.2, 9–12.S-MD.4, 9–12.S-MD.5, 9–12.S-MD.5a, 9–12.S-MD.5b, 9–12.S-MD.6, 9–12.S-MD.7)	4
3	O3.1	(9–12.S-MD.1, 9–12.S-MD.2, 9–12.S-MD.4, 9–12.S-MD.5, 9–12.S-MD.5a, 9–12.S-MD.5b, 9–12.S-MD.6, 9–12.S-MD.7)[b]	4
4	O4.6	(9–12.S-MD.1, 9–12.S-MD.2, 9–12.S-MD.4, 9–12.S-MD.5, 9–12.S-MD.5a, 9–12.S-MD.5b, 9–12.S-MD.6, 9–12.S-MD.7)[b]	4

a. IO = instructional objective; LCCSS = local Common Core State Standards Conditional Probability and the Rules of Probability; 9–12.S-IC.1 = Item 1 in the Making Inferences and Justifying Conclusions subset of the High School Mathematics section for Statistics in the CCSS; 9–12.S-ID.1 = Item 1 in the Interpreting Categorical and Quantitative Data subset; 9–12.S-CP.1 = Item 1 in the Conditional Probability and the Rules of Probability subset; 9–12.S-MD.1 = Item 1 in the Conditional Probability and the Rules of Probability.

b. Will use specific language from CCSS

Used with permission.

There it is, a sample of a complete K–12 curriculum in ELA and math, based on and completely aligned to the CCSS. As mentioned earlier, the sampling of various district curricula documents gives a slightly different sound and feeling than from the reading of a complete set of district documents, but I felt the ability to see examples from several districts and several writing styles and approaches to this work would give the reader a better overall feel for the process and the product.

PROCESS SUMMARY

These samples give readers a chance to look at and explore very specific issues they will encounter in this process and see examples of how other educators have addressed those issues. The website will also give the reader a chance to view, comment on, and begin a national conversation about ways to best do this work. Enjoy the journey.

PROCESS CHECKLIST

Make sure you have addressed, or at least considered, each of these tasks and used this in the design of your work:

- ❐ Perform the vertical articulation discussed earlier to ensure a natural progression of learning expectations.
- ❐ As these final documents are developed, there will be differences of opinion. Don't let that derail the process. Remember, thank goodness for Plan, Do, Check, Act—we'll check to see if this works and fix it as needed.
- ❐ Respect the subject matter/grade-level expertise of your teachers—allow them the freedom to experiment.
- ❐ You cannot articulate too much; give teachers plenty of time and structure to share back and forth and make adjustments as needed.
- ❐ Articulation and conversations are great, but there comes a time when it is time to make a choice, play your card, and move on. Try things, get feedback, make improvements, and move on.
- ❐ This is not the venue to discuss course or grade-level organization. If people like or don't like a particular course (i.e., Algebra A, middle school, whatever), this is not the place to decide that issue; develop local CCSS and instructional objectives for the identified courses.

5 The Journey Ahead

CHAPTER EXPECTATIONS

This final chapter takes a bit of a different twist. When dealing with an issue as new as the Common Core State Standards (CCSS), it is difficult to summarize the research, discuss what has worked and hasn't worked, and critique others' efforts. The CCSS are simply so new, we have no place to go but forward, so that's what we'll do. We'll summarize some of the issues presented earlier in the book, and then we'll take a look at the issues real educators see moving forward. We'll end the chapter by sharing what we've learned and giving advice for moving forward.

ACTION STEPS

Here are steps to consider and address in doing this phase of the work:

- Summary of Issues
    - Ensure that the instructional leader fully understands the issues to be considered at the local/national level.
    - Determine whether your local system will politically support this initiative.
- Local Issues
    - Identify and inform the task force of any specific curriculum or political issues that are important at the local level that must be considered in doing this work.
    - Spend the time in the beginning to make sure everyone understands the issues and any expectations around those issues.
    - Ensure that only curriculum issues are addressed; this is a curriculum task force, not a school district reorganization task force or anything else. Stick to the agenda.

- Current Reactions
  - As the instructional leader, familiarize yourself with the reactions and feelings of others who have done this work so that you can address those feelings within your own group.
  - Read the comments in this chapter to ensure that you have some idea of anticipated reactions and things to monitor.

SUMMARY OF ISSUES

State/national issues. The CCSS are "a new face" in public education and the national discourse on teaching and learning, but we really already know a great deal about teaching and learning, so what we must do is apply all the things we know about standards-based curriculum, instruction, and assessment and apply that learning to the CCSS. As Ron Edmonds said so many years ago,

> We can, whenever and wherever we choose, successfully teach all children whose schooling is of interest to us. We already know more than we need to do that. Whether or not we do it, must finally depend on how we feel about the fact that we haven't so far.

We know how to do this work; now let's go do it and use the CCSS as a new tool to guide our work. It is no longer an issue of 50 different sets of standards; we now have our one, national set of standards.

One of the biggest challenges public educators face is the almost automatic response of, "Oh my, *another* initiative is here," a reaction that many in education feel. Having been through so many initiatives, many educators are jaded to almost any initiative and believe the best thing to do is to wait it out—"this too shall pass." Therefore, it is imperative that not only must the national educational leadership hold fast on this course, but also at the local and state level, legislators, teachers, and administrators must show the same tenacity and dedication of leadership in implementing this effort. In the long and the short of it, education simply must come together and define its learning expectations: What *do* we want our students to know and be able to do? If we don't know the answer to that question, we don't have any right to hold students accountable for learning that which we have not defined; it is immoral and unethical to do so.

So let's use the CCSS to come together and define that learning—both the *what* and the *when* of those learning expectations. Like everything else ever created by humankind, the CCSS are not perfect, nor will they ever be perfect, but they are a place to begin and a place to bring public education together on defining expected learning. It's the least we can do to prepare our children for the future in a more competitive, global world, so let's work together to help them ensure that their (and our) future.

Local issues. This book has, hopefully, clearly outlined a process to do the curriculum and assessment work needed to accomplish that goal of operationalizing those national learning expectations; now we need to work together to do that work and clearly define America's learning expectations for its children so that America's teachers can do this essential work at the local classroom level.

This book has also spent time explaining the need for and the components of a curriculum, instruction, and assessment system based on those CCSS. Without a system that (a) defines the expected learning, (b) monitors the implementation of the expected learning activities, (c) measures student progress toward those expected learnings, (d) applies the same criteria for those measurements of student learning, and (e) builds accountability measures for accomplishing that work, there can be no system. Absent a system, there is only the possibility of random acts of innovation and accidental alignment—neither of which can accomplish the work that needs to be done to change public education.

It is imperative that we approach this issue as a system problem. We must develop a local system to ensure that there is a curriculum, instruction, and assessment system in place—it cannot be left to chance. That system must then be monitored and measured, and those working in that system must be held accountable for the faithful implementation of that system. While the CCSS give us the national direction for developing those curriculum expectations, it will be a local responsibility to design, implement, and monitor the entire curriculum, instruction, and assessment system to accomplish the national goals. The federal government has set the standards, now local districts must create the system to achieve those standards. At least the adoption of these CCSS will allow districts across the country to cooperate and learn from each other in that journey to develop that system.

SOME SPECIFIC ISSUES

Staff development. As discussed throughout this book, it is imperative to operationalize the CCSS—that is, put them into practice in the districts, schools, and classrooms of America. That operationalization process will first make sure teachers understand and can work with standards to design instruction and assessments. Additionally, work must be done to familiarize teachers with the CCSS themselves—their expectations, organization, and layout. Any document this long and this complex must be studied, discussed, and understood by those who are expected to implement it.

Just as we would not give students a long, complex piece of literature, mathematics, or science and expect them to read, understand, and synthesize it, we cannot do that to our teachers, either.

By designing specific staff development activities to make sure that learning, understanding, and synthesizing happens, administrative and teacher leadership can ensure that all the classroom teachers who will implement these CCSS are on the same page and expecting the same academic performances between and within classrooms, buildings, districts, and states. We have to abandon that approach to staff development where such complex learning receives brief attention (just like complex learning in the classroom is rushed to cover the entire book) and take the time to ensure that our teachers are fully prepared to do this complex work.

The CCSS are the most important curriculum documents that we have seen in decades, perhaps ever, unless you count the Seven Cardinal Principles of Education (yes, that was satire!). These CCSS define learning expectations at the national level, and will be the basis for the development of a national assessment system. That is huge! For once, let us now take the time to do this entire project correctly. Districts must commit to following the outline of expectations and activities in this book or from somewhere else, and make sure to spend the time and resources to do this thing correctly. But for heaven's sake (as my mom would say), let's take the time to do it right!

Piano. I spent a great deal of my professional career in the south suburbs of Chicago, with lots of diverse racial and ethnic groups. There were lots of first- or second-generation Italian Americans, and they would frequently say, *piano*, which I was always told meant something like, "Take your time, don't get excited, just take it easy and it will work itself out." I now advise all of my partners that *piano* makes a great deal of sense in doing this work–take your time, trust your people, and get it right.

A new curriculum model. Additionally, this book advocates for coming to a national consensus on what a curriculum is and what that suggested curriculum should look like. While some will say it is presumptuous to make such recommendations, I would counter that the failure to come to that consensus on what a curriculum should be is part of what keeps us wandering in the desert of student improvement initiatives.

For too long, curriculum has been this deep, dark secret that is only really understood by the select few who are chosen to study it, design it, and expect others to implement it. The far more simple definition offered by this book allows for easier understanding, implementing, measuring, and universalizing of curriculum expectations across America. The days of the 400-plus page curricula are over; let's present our curriculum expectations in clear, concise, and easily understood documents that clearly define skills to be learned and times in the educational experience when those skills are to be learned.

The curriculum model proposed here is crystal clear in only addressing the skills to be learned and when those skills are to be learned. Those skills must, of course, be based on the CCSS, but those skills are the only things that are to be presented in this proposed curriculum model. The instructional resources, suggested lesson designs, academic vocabulary, assessments, and so on are important to be sure, but those things do not belong in the curriculum itself. Adding these ancillary documents tends to increase the curriculum to unmanageable lengths and make it far more difficult to understand and be used and understood by teachers, students, and parents.

The proposed curriculum model will list what academic performance standard is to be learned and when it is to be learned. The ancillary documents and support that are needed will be located elsewhere. By being ancillary documents, these specific resources and suggested instructional approaches to teaching the skills are an opportunity for a national discussion on ways to best improve student learning. Samples of this electronic curriculum mapping are available at www.partners4results.org/demo. Go to Power Standards Maintenance, select the Curriculum Mapping icon and the course.

A new model for the national curriculum model is also proposed and defined in this book. That is explained fully in Chapter 2, which gives the critical attributes of any curriculum:

- Based on and aligned to the CCSS
- Standards based, not content based
- Be a learnable, not teachable, curriculum
- Nonprescriptive
- Address the *what* and the *when* of student learning
- Encourage creativity and use of alternative learning sources
- Result in common formative assessments

My work and experiences make me believe this new model is what America needs to move forward in doing this work. The work and research of Doug Reeves, Larry Ainsworth, Larry Lezotte, Mike Schmoker, Rick Stiggins, and lots of others show us the efficacy of curriculum alignment as a key strategy to improve student performance, and now education finally has a national set of standards to facilitate the national effort to do this work. This proposed model is not perfect, and just like the alignment work that this curriculum model will inspire, a national conversation and exchange of ideas is needed to improve this model and the documents this model produces. We must work together to build consensus around and understanding of our national learning expectations, and to create the kind of curriculum documents that will facilitate the ultimate goal—improved student performance.

Please join in that conversation and contribute to the solution rather than tear down the proposal. In addition to the traditional print media to exchange ideas, we have created an electronic site where that conversation can be held in real time. In addition to those print media, we believe looking at an electronic, interactive document and sharing your thoughts, concerns, and ideas will help American educators have a more robust, meaningful conversation. You may join in that electronic conversation by going to www.partners4results.org/demo, clicking on K–12 model curriculum, and joining the conversation by reading and posting as you see fit.

Common formative assessments. The common formative assessments are the next step, and these assessments are built by the local educators, based on the local instructional objectives. Most important, these local formative assessments are used to inform instruction; how do we change instructional approaches to improve student learning? This system of common (used and scored on the same scale by all teachers at approximately the same time) formative (used to inform instruction) allows districts to measure student progress toward the mastery of the intended curriculum (CCSS) and to make instructional adjustments based on student need along the way.

By using the naming conventions found in the CCSS throughout this work and at all levels of this work (local CCSS, instructional objectives, assessments, and reports), the skills will become more familiar to everyone. Teachers, students, parents, and everyone can talk about student performance in terms of the academic performance skills outlined in the CCSS.

Electronic assessment issues. The issue of creating custom bubble sheets is still an issue that needs to be addressed. While traditional bubble sheets with their smaller font are acceptable for use with older students, there are issues requiring custom bubble sheets if machine scoring and electronic reporting are to be used, as they almost must be used. To score and report on such massive amounts of data that the common formative assessments will create, in a timely, readable format, requires the use of some kind of electronic scoring and reporting software. Additionally, these custom bubble sheets must be designed so that younger students may use them, requiring larger fonts and machine entering and scoring options.

Also, many teachers feel a need to use more than just bubble sheets to assess student learning. These teachers like the show-your-work model, rubrics, short-answer responses, and other scoring options. To accommodate these specific needs, some custom sample answer sheets were shared, and more can be seen at www.partners4results.org/demo by clicking on Assessment Maintenance and selecting sample bubble sheets. This remains an issue and must be worked on as we move forward, and time and resources must be devoted to this project by technology companies in cooperation with districts and then shared with others to move us forward.

Current Reactions

The long and the short of doing this work, then, is to follow the national research and what we know works and roll up our sleeves and go do it. We can and must do that, but it will be hard work and will call for creating a civil, national dialogue about how to best do that curriculum, instruction, and assessment alignment work and then working together to do the work. As I pondered that daunting task and how to facilitate that process, it came to me that we should probably ask the people who have been struggling with this work for the past several years. Why not ask those people who have been involved in and demonstrated their commitment to doing the curriculum, instruction, and assessment alignment work? Why not ask those who have shown a commitment and a willingness to do this difficult work what their feelings are and what their concerns for future work are?

That's how I decided to end this book—with the thoughts and concerns of *some* of those educators doing this work. That task of surveying those who have done this alignment work presents lots of issues. There is no way I have the time or the resources to identify and survey everyone who has done this alignment work; that would be an entirely separate book and would not be available for publication for a couple of years until I completed all the work in such a massive undertaking.

That delay is not acceptable as we try to put together a process to implement these new CCSS. The CCSS are here and now, and we must begin to move forward as best we know how. As stated throughout this book, we'll move forward by using the processes in this book and the national research, but it is still important to explore the issues as seen by those who have shown a commitment and the willingness to do this work.

I also further concede that the group I am surveying is not a scientific, stratified, random sample; again, the time and the resources prevent that level of sophistication. The people I have surveyed are people I have worked with over the years who have really worked hard and put their heart and soul into doing this work. Does that make this a skewed sample? Absolutely! But again, I feel those who have done the work, where possible, deserve to have a voice in sharing their feelings and concerns as this initiative moves forward.

Also the sample size is not large enough to draw sweeping conclusions designed to set new national policy; these responses and concerns are simply that—concerns and observations intended to inform the reader about general feelings and concerns of local, everyday educators who have tried to do this alignment work and experienced the challenges and issues of doing that work. As these educators who have demonstrated their commitment to curriculum, instruction, and assessment alignment work see the arrival of the CCSS, I think it important to share their thoughts to help all of us better see the potential and the concerns that lie ahead. They have done this work at the state standard level; let's consider what they have learned as we do that same work with the CCSS.

Feedback process. So here's what I did to gather their feelings and concerns. I designed the survey form below. Does it look familiar? It is in a very similar form and format to the feedback sheets I shared in most of my feedback sheets, so if you like the format, there are more forms in Resource B for gathering feedback on all kinds of curriculum and assessment issues. As usual, spaces have been deleted for ease of publishing.

Concerns/Issues–Transitioning to Common Core State Standards (CCSS)

Teacher/Administrator________________________

1 is bad–5 is good!

1. I understand and support curriculum alignment as an important improvement strategy.

1	2	3	4	5
Strongly Disagree		Agree		Strongly Agree

Comments:

2. I understand the academic expectations established in the CCSS.

1	2	3	4	5
Strongly Disagree		Agree		Strongly Agree

Comments:

3. In implementing these CCSS, I am most concerned about the following issues; please attach if more space is needed:

   1. ______________________________

   2. ______________________________

   3. ______________________________

4. If I could say one thing that I wish people would hear about the CCSS, it is this:

5. I really feel my district needs more help/information on the following things:

   Signed (Optional but needed if quote in No. 4 is to be used/attributed to you in the book)

   ______________________ Date______________________

As the reader can see, this is a pretty straightforward survey seeking reactions to several issues: Do you understand and support curriculum alignment? Do you understand the CCSS expectations? Do you have any specific concerns? Is there anything you would like to say? Do you need more help with anything? My surveying has never been incredibly scientific but tries to gather important information designed to foster a better understanding of issues. For those readers demanding more scientific surveying methodologies, I apologize and hope the conclusions and observations I draw from this survey are well-founded in the information and don't offend or anger anyone.

As with all the forms in this book, feel free to use them for your own purposes with your own people. I believe, and my experiences have taught me, it is good to gather feelings and ideas from people as this, or any, work is done. It gives an idea of what is going on out there—not always a scientific explanation, but an idea. The complete form and all responses for this survey are included in Resource A. Below is my summary of those responses.

Responses to the feedback form. In terms of overall responses and attitudes expressed, I was really somewhat pleasantly surprised by the overwhelmingly positive reaction to the CCSS. Almost all the group members were positive about the CCSS, their own understanding of and ability to implement those CCSS, and the work that lies ahead. There is a general concern expressed about the assessment system that will measure student progress and the use of the CCSS while continuing to use state assessments as local measures. Especially from teachers, there is a concern over the time to do the work, and concerns about the staff development were also quite common. Alignment of the standards to the assessments was a concern also expressed frequently.

As one might suspect, the first question was universally supported by the respondents, with 89% responding *5* and the remaining 11% responding *4*. That is probably the kind of response that should be expected from the people who have already spent years doing this kind of work, but it does validate that they see the purpose of their work.

I was somewhat surprised by the answers to the second question, as 47% responded with a *5*, 37% with a *4*, 10% with a *3*, and 5% with a *2*. While the responses are not as positive as responses to the first question, there is definitely an overall confidence in the respondents' knowledge of the CCSS. Frankly, that does not reflect my experiences in working with most districts. In my experiences, the CCSS are usually viewed as an entirely new entity and local understanding is minimal at best. So while the responses are somewhat surprising, I must say they are pleasantly surprising.

People who have been doing this alignment work with state standards have moved forward into the CCSS and are feeling somewhat comfortable with their own knowledge of those CCSS and are willing to admit they need to learn more. That is a good thing, but it causes me to wonder that if these people, who have been doing this work, are not as confident of their knowledge of the CCSS, where does that leave the rest of us who have not been involved in the alignment work? This is a good place for readers to survey their own people and begin to find out local conditions so they may plan accordingly.

In the third question I asked for concerns, so I got concerns. While I have to say the tone of the responses was neither bitter nor angry, the respondents definitely identified their concerns, but for the most part in a low-key, problem-solving way. Maybe that is just my eternally optimistic view, but the readers can read the entire survey (Resource A) and all the responses for themselves and make their own judgments.

Most concerns center on time, assessments, staff development, resources, administrative leadership, and the transition to the CCSS. In my opinion, however, there is an underlying feeling, almost a fear, that this entire process will be used "against us" as education is once again not supported and laden with unrealistic expectations. Again, this is not overtly or angrily stated, but it appears to be an undertone throughout the responses. This could just be my own interpretation of what I read, but I definitely hear that in the responses.

The fourth question asks, "If I could say one thing that I wish people would hear about the CCSS, it is . . ." and again I am struck by the overall positive nature of those responses. Time and again they use words such as *opportunity, refreshing, better, finally have a focus, welcome, love,* and other such incredibly positive words to describe what they would say. While there are concerns expressed in some of the responses, I would not characterize a single response as negative.

Even in those responses that share respondents' frustration with time or whatever, they acknowledge the importance of the work; it is just the time or whatever required that bothers them. Again, an overall positive response to and willingness to move forward with this work is present in all the responses. This, in my opinion, speaks volumes about the character and passion of those doing this work and shows all of us that, if done correctly, we can stir this positive attitude and passion in almost all of our educators. We must be sure to do this work carefully and deliberately to ensure maximum participation and buy-in by as many people as possible. As Larry Lezotte taught us, "It's simple, but not easy."

The fifth and final question solicits where educators feel they need help, and again, the responses are positive and show they have spent time figuring out what they need to do to make this transition to the CCSS. They want help with assessments and directions in how to do this work. The responses to this and all the other questions show an overall positive attitude and willingness to do the work. I understand this is probably related to the skewed sample (those already doing the work), but it does demonstrate that there is a willingness to do the work and that we can build on that willingness if we do this work process correctly.

Additionally, the replies make the point that the actual doing of this curriculum, instruction, and alignment advocated in this book and in the research is what is needed to help us move forward. Respondents are definitely not saying this work cannot or should not be done but that they have concerns and issues with doing the work, which is honest and probably well founded. The responses to the survey and the concerns they express will actually be addressed by doing this alignment work.

Paraphrasing Tom Peters. In working with districts in the change process, I frequently paraphrase Tom Peters's work in the change process; I have told this story so many times, I may have significantly altered it, but my thanks to Tom Peters for sharing it. He tells us that we must see the reform initiative as a football field, with us sitting at the 50-yard line. There are several people down near the goal line ready to score, several more between the five-yard and 20-yard lines who are close to scoring but not quite there, then lots of people milling around between the 20-yard lines, and of course one or two people down on their own goal line with the concrete bunker built, flak jacket on, and machine gun poised and ready. He suggests working with those near the goal line who are ready to score; then you'll have some people on your side who can help those near the 20-yard line score. Pretty soon, those in the middle begin to notice the ruckus at that end of the field and wander down to see what is happening, and you have them on your side as well. The people in the bunker? Leave them alone. Don't waste your time and resources battling them; move your agenda forward and leave those folks in the bunker alone, if you can. You'll never change them, and you'll just waste your time and energy trying. I know this is an oversimplification, and I hope I haven't ruined Peters' story too much in the numerous retellings. Help your leaders move forward and create movement in the right direction.

The concerns they have will be answered by doing the work and creating the curriculum, assessments, and the system to use all of this material. What more can we ask for? Moving forward in a way that research and practice have shown us works, while adjusting and redoing along the journey is, and always has been, the best answer.

FINAL THOUGHTS

The work before us is complex and important, but it is doable, we *can* do it. While the implementation of this process will vary from district to district, the overall approach is flexible enough that it can be modified and adjusted as circumstance and new developments dictate. The CCSS are simply too new to have already worked out the entire process to implement them. This book is intended as a first step in a process that will take us where we need to go.

As we go on that journey, we will learn many things and will be able to change our process as we move forward, but the basic process of creating the local CCSS (Power Standards) and instructional objectives and then using those local CCSS and instructional objectives to drive instruction and assessment are key. We must then apply the continuous improvement cycle of Plan, Do, Check, Act to make sure we improve that initial work.

The development of the common, formative assessments will, again, be a time-consuming learning process for all of us as we work to create those assessments. Then we must ensure that we use those assessment results to inform and improve instruction. I will continue to believe and argue that local assessments directly aligned to local instruction (said local instruction being aligned to the CCSS) are educationally superior to nationally normed assessments.

But as with all of this work, the fact that these are now national standards, the opportunity to share and learn from each other's assessment work is unprecedented. If we are all teaching very similar skills, then our assessments can be used by others as well. When students are learning a skill, the content used to teach and assess that skill does not have to be the same. Students learn to draw inference from grade-level text; the content used to assess that skill is somewhat irrelevant.

National standards create the opportunity for meaningful national conversations. Let's not waste the opportunities we have been given. By identifying skills, rather than content, we enable a national conversation that can help all of us improve what we are doing, if we are smart enough to have those conversations in a civil, helpful way.

The creation of the local curriculum, instruction, and assessment system, complete with monitoring and accountabilities, is the local work that will significantly vary from district to district and contract to contract. There are great resources out there for learning about doing this work and directions for how to do this work.

Do not let the system-building work intimidate you; just like the curriculum, instruction, and assessment alignment work outlined in this book and in other resources, there are resources and research out there that tell us what to do and how to do it. We just have to study those resources and research and then do that work. Don't let the fear of the unknown intimidate you. Do your homework, define your mission, assemble your team, and then go do it. As you do the work, follow the research and the learnings of others to help guide your work, but just do it.

Come on, don't be scared; let's go sailing!

Resource A

Collated Feedback on CCSS Work

Concerns/Issues: Transitioning to Common Core State Standards (CCSS)

Teacher/Administrator ______________________________

1 is bad—5 is good!

1. I understand and support curriculum alignment as an important improvement strategy.

1	2	3	4—II	5—(IIIII) (IIII) (IIII)II
Strongly disagree			Agree	Strongly agree

Comments

- If we can do this and not get torn between ISAT testing and new standards, I think it will work well.
- Most of the schools that are in a failing status are there because of the lack of professional development in the area of curriculum alignment. How do you align the wheels on a car if you know nothing about tires or cars? How do you teach for success if you do not know anything about the content that is supposed to be taught?
- I think it will improve student learning and school collaboration.
- Curriculum alignment helps us to be more efficient in the classroom. Teachers know specifically what content they are responsible for and what students should know and be able to do at the end of the course.

2. I understand the academic expectations established in the CCSS.

1	2—I	3—II	4—(IIII)II	5—(IIII) IIII
Strongly disagree			Agree	Strongly agree

Comments:

- I know the standards but need to know when we start/finish the crossover.
- It's a little overly technical for the middle-school grade level.

3. In implementing these CCSS, I am most concerned about the following issues—please attach if more space is needed.

- Implementation to fidelity—II.
- Transition gaps of students.
- Teachers having time to work on the project, to meet with their own grade levels and other grade levels.
- Using a common language that everyone involved understands.
- Consensus of the administrative team.
- Research based.
- Time to work on vetting the work back out to larger groups of faculty and administrators.
- Careful monitoring of alignment between local curriculum and assessment and what the state will be expecting for exit outcomes.
- Sustainability of a system to utilize human resources during a time of uncertain state budget funding.
- Knowing what the assessment is focused on. Also, how will my school effectively administer an electronic assessment (lack of facilities—impact on academic work in order to test).
- Worried about state assessment not being taken seriously [because] ACT will probably continue to be the ticket into college.
- CCSS are not "less" as advertised.This will slow down teachers when beginning the alignment process.
- Having the materials that are needed. Current textbooks will not be appropriate.
- Having appropriate staff development so that teachers understand the standards, know how and where to access the materials, and understand best practices for instruction.
- Understand the best ways to use formative assessments on a regular basis to keep on track with all students.
- Having appropriate technology to support access to a wider range of materials, applications, and educational options.
- The lack of uniformity of the core curriculum standards . . . states have the flexibility to change a certain percentage of the standards.
- The timeliness of the assessments to ensure that assessments indicate progress of students over a long period of time.
- The possibility that assessments will differ from state to state, which continues the difficulty to really compare how well students are learning among the states.

- There will also be the need for effective professional development to raise the level of expectations by teachers for students and for content knowledge and skill development required within the standards.
- *Time*—in first grade we have to do each assessment 1/1, and oh! it takes so much time away from teaching.
- *Time*—what do we do with 23 other 6-year-olds while we are assessing each student individually?
- *Time*—each student can take up to 30 minutes for *one* assessment.
- How much of this set of standards will be assessed?
- Clearly, it is too much for students to accomplish in our time frame—how to prioritize.
- By the time we align our local standards to the CCSS, will there be so much overlap in the former standards and new ones in high school English that we really won't have much to change, given our limited time to teach these standards? Will this be a waste of time?
- ISAT (Illinois Standards Assessment Testing).
- Higher standards being implemented all at once and not year by year, thereby making it hard for me to up the expectations if the students haven't learned some of the needed background info in lower grades.
- Lack of awareness about the standards in some districts.
- Education departments in each state need to provide and require attendance for administrators and those in charge of instruction when implementing the core standards. Parents need to be part of the equation.
- We are behind academically now because some administrators do not provide prior planning for teachers, do not evaluate teachers as required, and teachers do not plan lessons as lesson plans are not required in many schools.
- Meaningful, authentic assessment of CCSS.
- Teaching to the CCSS.
- Who approved the CCSS and who will revise it?
- Catch up time over the couple of years it will take to get all onboard and so we are not reteaching all concepts—only those in standards (scores on state tests may go down).
- Time needed to develop and modify comparisons of scores can be tricky when comparing classrooms.
- Our state has not adopted the standards.
- Loss of local control in determining curricular issues.
- How progress in meeting the standards will be measured.
- Alignment/planning.

- Implementation.
- Evaluation.
- Measurement.
- Incremental monitoring of progress.
- All staff members understand the need for implementing the CCSS and then everyone making an effort to make the change.
- The time needed for teachers to learn and plan for the change. Can I be a good time steward and help them to use their time wisely?
- Myself being the most knowledgeable on the CCSS and helping to share that knowledge with my staff.
- Time available for professional development.
- The need for specificity in the standards.
- The need for concrete examples of units, assessments, and resources for teachers.
- Connecting math to CCSS.
- Difficulty implementing due to teacher resistance.
- Determining which of the CCSS to focus on because there are so many.
- Explaining to parents why curriculum that they view to be the "correct" curriculum (because that's what they did in school) needs to be changed.

4. If I could say one thing that I wish people would hear about the CCSS, this would be it.

- A good next step in standards alignment.
- This is a process that will continue, as most good plans do. We will revise and tweak as we grow in our understanding.We don't need to rush to complete; it is a continuing process that must be built into our professional development.
- Common core standards serve as a reference or a tool like a North Star to guide curriculum. Consider religion without the Bible or government without the Constitution.Without a common standard we can agree on, we run amuck.
- That this new system of core-curriculum transitioning needs to be viewed as an opportunity to develop clear and consistent learning objectives—in both a horizontal and vertical manner—and to allow a system of accountability that meshes local interests with those of the state and federal levels. We can either complain about what is being done "to us," or we can use our own strong, local voices to continue to grow our own teaching and learning systems to be even stronger and more meaningful than they've ever been before. A spastic and episodic attempt at putting the common core standards

into implementation will result in a chaotic and confusing mishmash of curriculum that is less rigorous, less reliable, and less relevant for students, staff, and parents.

- The unilateral focus on reading and writing is refreshing. This will be incredible leverage for the use of writing and reading strategies across all curricular areas.
- The common core standards provide an opportunity to help move education forward. The challenge is to provide support so that staff is successful in the implementation. Teachers work hard and want to succeed. I do not know of one teacher who goes to work and wants to fail or wants his or her students to fail. It is critical to provide the scaffolding necessary to make the transition so that teachers have the materials, equipment, assessments, and training necessary for success.
- This is an excellent opportunity for school districts to raise the academic expectations for both staff and students. Not only are the standards more clearly defined, students will be required to think at a higher critical level of thinking. Students will become better problem solvers and thinkers while, at the same time, more skilled communicators in both their writing and speaking. The assessments, if developed as is being suggested, will communicate to teachers, students, and parents more effectively the progress which students are making toward each of the standards.
- These assessments might be the newest best idea, and this one might actually *be* that magic bullet we've been looking for since parents put all the responsibility on us and the state let them—*but* I'd like someone to come in and show me how to make all this assessment doable in kindergarten and first grade.
- That they are not a magic bullet any more than any other initiative of the past 100 years. If the CCSS are implemented with fidelity and some narrowing focus they will help students; however, if they are only implemented inconsistently over their entire breadth, not much will change.
- I love the idea of CCSS, but the transition is a bit confusing. I know we are trying for a transition time, which makes sense, but it is going to be a tough sell to have teachers start teaching the new standards while ISATS test the current standards . . . especially when you take into consideration all the talk about having our reviews and salaries tied to test results!
- My concern is the mediocrity that we have in education now. How will we wake some educators up and allow them to realize the importance of their chosen profession and the importance of being well prepared to teach students what they need to know?

- Be open to change; teachers aren't the only people who influence student achievement, and we should build assessment and accountability that respect voices and expertise of all members of the educational community.
- We finally have direction and a focus instead of a "cram it all in and I hope they remember" curriculum.
- The CCSS will require schools and teachers to focus on problem solving, communication, and thinking skills. I believe that there will be less emphasis on knowing content and increased emphasis on the application of content to solve problems.
- The CCSS are a clear set of shared goals and expectations for the knowledge and skills that will help our students succeed.
- These standards are to help our students become more ready and able to compete in the world post-high school, whether it be in college, trade school, or workforce. It is time we change to reflect the changes in our world, today and in the future.
- CCSS will focus our attention and resources on mastery of standards rather than mere coverage of them.
- They really are better. We are all speaking the same language now!
- This a necessary change that has the potential to directly impact education in Illinois.

5. I really feel my district needs more help/information on the following things.

- Assessment example problems from each grade/course.
- Just time and a little direction on next steps to keep everyone focused and moving forward.
- Following scheduled checkpoints on how things are going in regards [to] Power Standards, instructional objectives, and assessments by surveying our staff quarterly to find areas of concern and deal with them before we drift back to everyone doing their own thing.
- We're already signed up with you, Joe. We need nothing else . . . today.
- What the actual focus of the assessments will be. Plain and simple, we will not spend time on standards that are not assessed.
- I feel our district has done a good job training education staff for these Power Standards.
- I think everyone needs to have a department-specific training on the partners4results bubble sheets and how to incorporate the Response to Intervention (RTI) needs that the results of the instructional objectives will fulfill.
- Professionalism, accountability, awareness of standards, training for staff.

- Administrative leadership helping and enforcing time frames and what is to be done.
- We are moving toward the use of project-based learning along with formative assessments and technology to accelerate student learning.
- Implementation.
- Coaching administrators to implement faithfully the CCSS.
- Transitioning to the common core and how to focus on what skills are most important for students to learn.
- Implementation and connection to state assessment . . . effects to IAA?
- How to implement? How to assess?

Resource B

Suggested Forms for Developing Local CCSS (Power Standards) and Instructional Objectives and Feedback Forms

B1: STANDARDS TO LOCAL STANDARDS

1. Read the introductory sections from the Common Core State Standards documents provided and complete those activities.
2. As a group, determine the clusters and domains contained within your grade level/department CCSS and list those.
3. Can these clusters and domains be represented in the elements of the local CCSS you are creating? Can any of these clusters/domains be combined into individual Power Standard elements?
4. Of all the skills contained in the CCSS for your grade level/department, which skills most clearly represent the three criteria of endurance, leverage, and readiness for the next level of learning?
5. Does your list of local CCSS elements represent a learnable versus a teachable number of skills?
6. Write the individual local CCSS elements, making sure to connect each element to at least one CCSS cluster or domain (skill within the standard).
7. Do your local CCSS and all of their elements give your colleagues the focus they need to implement this work?

Adapted from Crawford, 2011.

B2: FOLLOW-UP PROCESS GUIDELINES FOR LOCAL CCSS

Not all of these questions may be answered today by this group. We should begin the discussion and develop a process with dates to ensure this work gets decided and completed. With time and commitment, this will become part of a yearly cycle which will ensure your curriculum is always under review and continually improved. The first year or so will be a bit more difficult as timelines are set and processes for review and revision are established. Please be patient and help by being part of the solution. Share your ideas and help us continually improve.

The *Plan cycle* was completed by the work of this group; now, we must make sure we follow up with the Do, Check, and Act cycles:

Do Cycle

- When will the local CCSS be due?
- To whom?
- In what format? Electronic? On a form?
- What will they look like? Decide now or later.
- Will the task force/faculty see them before final publication? When? Meeting called by whom?
- When will they be published and distributed to staff? By whom? Any follow-up activity by the task force as part of the distribution?

Check Cycle

- When will we gather initial feedback on the local CCSS?
- Who will gather and collate?
- Will we allow midcourse corrections or stick with the initial product for the first year?
- When will we gather end-of-year feedback? Who will do it? How?

Act Cycle

- When will we meet to review the feedback and make improvements and corrections?
- When and how will we release second and subsequent versions?

Adapted from Crawford, 2011.

B3: QUARTERLY INSTRUCTIONAL OBJECTIVES, CRITICAL ATTRIBUTES

1. Are the quarterly instructional objectives written in student- and parent-friendly language?

2. Are the quarterly instructional objectives aligned to the local CCSS?
3. Are all the skills contained in the local CCSS covered (somewhere) in the quarterly instructional objectives?
4. Do all of the quarterly instructional objectives reflect on grade-level standards as defined in the CCSS?
5. Do the quarterly instructional objectives give our colleagues the kind of specific direction needed to guide their instruction?
6. Do the quarterly instructional objectives represent a natural progression of skill acquisition that will maximize student learning?
7. Are the quarterly instructional objectives specific enough to facilitate the development of common, formative assessment items?

Adapted from Crawford, 2011.

B4: FOLLOW-UP PROCESS GUIDELINES: INSTRUCTIONAL OBJECTIVES

Not all of these questions may be answered today by this group. We should begin the discussion and develop a process with dates to ensure this work gets decided and completed. With time and commitment, this will become part of a yearly cycle that allows your curriculum to always be under review and continually improved. The first year or so will be a bit more difficult as timelines are set and processes for review and revision are established. Please be patient and help by being part of the solution. Share your ideas and help us continually improve.

The *Plan cycle* was completed by the work of this group; now we must make sure we follow up with the Do, Check, and Act cycles:

Do Cycle

- When will the instructional objectives be due?
- To whom?
- In what format? Electronic? On a form?
- What will they look like? Numbering system (8LA1, 7M2, and so on)?
- Will the task force see them before final publication? When? Meeting called by whom?
- When will they be published and distributed to staff? By whom? Any follow-up activity by the task force as part of the distribution?

(Continued)

(Continued)

Check Cycle

- When will we gather initial feedback on the local CCSS and instructional objectives?
- Who will gather and collate?
- Will we allow midcourse corrections or stick with the initial product for the first year?
- When will we gather end-of-year feedback? Who will do it? How?

Act Cycle

- When will we meet to review the feedback and make improvements and corrections?
- When and how will we release second and subsequent versions?

Adapted from Crawford, 2011.

B5: INITIAL DISTRIBUTION FEEDBACK

1. I understand the local CCSS and instructional objectives.

1	2	3	4	5
Strongly Disagree	Disagree	Neutral	Agree	Strongly Agree

Comments (use back of page if needed):

2. I understand what I am expected to do with the new local CCSS and instructional objectives.

1	2	3	4	5
Strongly Disagree	Disagree	Neutral	Agree	Strongly Agree

Comments (use back of page if needed):

3. I believe I am capable of teaching the local CCSS and instructional objectives.

1	2	3	4	5
Strongly Disagree	Disagree	Neutral	Agree	Strongly Agree

Comments (use back of page if needed):

4. I believe our students are capable of learning these local CCSS and instructional objectives in the grade level these standards are assigned to.

1	2	3	4	5
Strongly Disagree	Disagree	Neutral	Agree	Strongly Agree

Comments (use back of page if needed):

5. I would be willing to volunteer to work with the local CCSS task force to continue and improve this work.

1	2	3	4	5
Strongly Disagree	Disagree	Neutral	Agree	Strongly Agree

Comments (use back of page if needed):

Grade level ____________________ Building ______________________

Signature (Optional) ____

Adapted from Crawford, 2011.

B6: LOCAL CCSS/INSTRUCTIONAL OBJECTIVES QUARTERLY FEEDBACK

______________Quarter

As you are well aware, we developed and are implementing the Power Standards and instructional objectives this year. As part of our total quality cycle, it is important that we get feedback on how well these are working. We want to make sure we have your reaction to the local CCSS and instructional objectives, and if we need to change the local CCSS or instructional objectives, we need your feedback.

To that end, please take a few moments to answer the questions below as they relate to the local CCSS and instructional objectives you use. Please return this form to your building principal by ________________. Feel free to work with

(Continued)

(Continued)

other members at your grade level/department to discuss or come up with ideas.

1. The local CCSS and instructional objectives for this quarter for my grade level are realistic and reflect what student should know and be able to do.

1	2	3	4	5
Strongly Disagree	Disagree	Neutral	Agree	Strongly Agree

Comments (use back of page if needed):

2. I understand the local CCSS and instructional objectives and am able to build assessments and use those assessments and results accordingly.

1	2	3	4	5
Strongly Disagree	Disagree	Neutral	Agree	Strongly Agree

Comments (use back of page if needed):

3. My students are making acceptable progress toward these local CCSS.

1	2	3	4	5
Strongly Disagree	Disagree	Neutral	Agree	Strongly Agree

Comments (use back of page if needed):

4. I understand the instructional objectives and am able to tie my instruction to them.

1	2	3	4	5
Strongly Disagree	Disagree	Neutral	Agree	Strongly Agree

Comments (use back of page if needed):

5. My instruction is guided by the local CCSS and instructional objectives.

1	2	3	4	5
Strongly Disagree	Disagree	Neutral	Agree	Strongly Agree

Comments (use back of page if needed):

6. I understand the local CCSS and instructional objectives and need no further clarification of them.

1	2	3	4	5
Strongly Disagree	Disagree	Neutral	Agree	Strongly Agree

Comments (use back of page if needed):

Please list below (feel free to use additional sheets) any *specific* changes in wording of the local CCSS or instructional objectives that you would suggest.

Grade level ____________________ Building ______________________

Signature (Optional) ____

Adapted from Crawford, 2011.

B7: QUARTERLY ASSESSMENTS FEEDBACK

1. I understand the first-quarter assessments and what I am to do with them.

1	2	3	4	5
Strongly Disagree	Disagree	Neutral	Agree	Strongly Agree

Comments (use back of page if needed):

(Continued)

(Continued)

2. I understand what I am expected to do with the results of the first-quarter assessments.

1	2	3	4	5
Strongly Disagree	Disagree	Neutral	Agree	Strongly Agree

Comments (use back of page if needed):

3. I believe these first-quarter assessments reflect the skills required in the quarterly instructional objectives.

1	2	3	4	5
Strongly Disagree	Disagree	Neutral	Agree	Strongly Agree

Comments (use back of page if needed):

4. I believe our students are capable of demonstrating proficiency on these first-quarter assessments.

1	2	3	4	5
Strongly Disagree	Disagree	Neutral	Agree	Strongly Agree

Comments (use back of page if needed):

Please suggest any *specific* language changes you would recommend for any of this assessment. Please use the back of the page or additional pages if needed.

Grade level ____________________ Building ____________________

Signature (Optional) ____

Adapted from Crawford, 2011.

B8: END-OF-YEAR FEEDBACK

As you are well aware, we developed and implemented the local CCSS and instructional objectives this year. As part of our total quality cycle, it is important to get feedback on how well these are working. We want to know your reaction to the local CCSS and instructional objectives. To that end, please take a few moments to answer the questions below as they relate to the local CCSS and instructional objectives you use. We will use your input to look at them and decide what, if any, changes are needed. Please return this form to your building principal. Feel free to work with other members at your grade level/department to discuss ideas.

1. The local CCSS and instructional objectives for my grade level are realistic and reflect what student should know and be able to do.

1	2	3	4	5
Strongly Disagree	Disagree	Neutral	Agree	Strongly Agree

Comments (use back of page if needed):

2. The local CCSS and instructional objectives relate to the skills and expectations in the curriculum guide.

1	2	3	4	5
Strongly Disagree	Disagree	Neutral	Agree	Strongly Agree

Comments (use back of page if needed):

3. My students are making acceptable progress toward these local CCSS.

1	2	3	4	5
Strongly Disagree	Disagree	Neutral	Agree	Strongly Agree

Comments (use back of page if needed):

(Continued)

(Continued)

4. I understand the instructional objectives and am able to tie my instruction to them.

1	2	3	4	5
Strongly Disagree	Disagree	Neutral	Agree	Strongly Agree

Comments (use back of page if needed):

5. My instruction is guided by the local CCSS and instructional objectives.

1	2	3	4	5
Strongly Disagree	Disagree	Neutral	Agree	Strongly Agree

Comments (use back of page if needed):

6. I understand the local CCSS and instructional objectives and need no further clarification of them.

1	2	3	4	5
Strongly Disagree	Disagree	Neutral	Agree	Strongly Agree

Comments (use back of page if needed):

Please list below (feel free to use the back of the page if needed) any *specific* changes in wording of the local CCSS or instructional objectives that you would suggest.

Grade level ____________________ Building ______________________

Signature (Optional) ____

Adapted from Crawford, 2011.

B9: CURRICULUM AUDIT: WHAT THE RESEARCH TELLS US

The research and work of Larry Lezotte, Mike Schmoker, Doug Reeves, Rick Stiggins, and many others continually point out the importance of a guaranteed and viable curriculum in improving student performance. The research is crystal clear on the impact of an aligned and viable curriculum as the first step in improving student performance, and gains of 25%–30% are seen by doing this work.

That being said, let's talk about where you and your building/district are in the process of creating a guaranteed (taught in every classroom in the district) and viable (aligned to state standards) curriculum. Please respond to each of the questions below as a kind of reality check on your current efforts and progress toward a guaranteed and viable curriculum.

On a scale of 1 to 5, please rate your current status in each area listed below the scale.

Scale

1 = Not really a strong area—we've talked some about it but that's about it.

2 = We have looked at this issue and have discussed what we should do but have not begun any of the work.

3 = We are in the planning stages but have not really selected our approach or set a budget, timeline, and so forth.

4 = We have begun the process, have a game plan in place, and are moving forward on a timetable.

5 = We have accomplished this goal; our current state reflects national best practice, and we could share our work with others.

1. Our school/district has an actual, published curriculum document in place that is aligned to the state standards and state assessment system and is readily accessible for all.	1	2	3	4	5
2. Our school/district has an actual, published curriculum document that defines and drives all instruction in the school/district and is used by all professional staff to plan instruction.	1	2	3	4	5
3. Our school/district has spent the time and the resources to ensure that our professional staff understands the state standards and is able to use those standards as the basis for designing instruction.	1	2	3	4	5

(Continued)

(Continued)

4. Our school/district has spent the time and the resources to ensure all of our professional staff understands the state assessment system, the skills all of our students must demonstrate, and how they must demonstrate those skills.	1	2	3	4	5
5. Our school/district has a set of aligned common, formative assessments that are used by all professional staff on predetermined dates to measure student progress toward achieving state standards.	1	2	3	4	5
6. Our school/district is able to provide real-time data to our staff to report the results of the common formative assessments in a timely manner so said results can be used in the reteaching loop to address specific, diagnosed weaknesses.	1	2	3	4	5
7. Our school/district has the electronic capability to report to students and parents that same real-time data about student performance on all of our common, aligned assessments.	1	2	3	4	5
8. Our school/district has the electronic capability to enable our administrators to monitor curriculum and instruction and to create and share data charts about current instructional practices with staff for the purpose of improving student performance.	1	2	3	4	5
9. Our school/district has an electronic curriculum map that is interactive and available 24–7 for our staff to share their successes and challenges in curriculum implementation.	1	2	3	4	5
10. The curriculum and instruction system of our school/district formally uses continuous feedback (Plan, Do, Check, Act) to ensure the curriculum is constantly being improved, refined, and made more effective.	1	2	3	4	5

This preassessment is designed to help you see and understand the current state of the curriculum and instruction system in your school/district so that you may better prepare to move forward and improve student performance. In a perfect world, you would be able to rate each area a 5, but that is seldom the current reality.

Adapted from Crawford, 2011.

References and Suggested Readings

Ainsworth, L. (2003a). *Power standards: Identifying the standards that matter the most.* Englewood, CO: Lead + Learn Press.

Ainsworth, L. (2003b). *"Unwrapping" the standards.* Englewood, CO: Lead + Learn Press.

Ainsworth, L., & Viegut, D. (2006). *Common formative assessments: How to connect standards-based instruction and assessment.* Thousand Oaks, CA: Corwin.

Carter, L. (2007). *Total instructional alignment: From standards to student success.* Bloomington, IN: Solution Tree.

Common Core State Standards Initiative. (2010). *Common Core State Standards for Mathematics.* Retrieved from http://www.corestandards.org/assets/CCSSI_Math%20Standards.pdf

Covey, S. (1989). *The 7 habits of highly effective people.* Touchstone, NY: Simon & Schuster.

Covey, S. (1990). *Principle-centered leadership.* New York, NY: Summit Books.

Crawford, J. (2011). *Using power standards to build an aligned curriculum: A process manual.* Thousand Oaks, CA: Corwin.

Darling-Hammond, L. (1997). *The right to learn.* San Francisco, CA: Jossey-Bass.

Deming, W. (1993). *The new economics.* Cambridge: Massachusetts Institute of Technology, Center for Advanced Engineering Study.

English, F. (2010). *Deciding what to teach and test: Developing, aligning, and leading the curriculum.* Thousand Oaks, CA: Corwin.

Gewertz, C. (2011a, March 9). Critics post 'manifesto' opposing shared curriculum. *Education Week.* Retrieved from http://www.edweek.org/ew/articles/2011/05/09/31curriculum.h30.html

Gewertz, C. (2011b, April 28). Gates, Pearson partner to craft common-core curricula. *Education Week.* Retrieved from http://www.edweek.org/ew/articles/2011/04/27/30pearson.h30.html

Hale, J. (2008). *A guide to curriculum mapping, planning, implementing, and sustaining the process.* Thousand Oaks, CA: Corwin.

Hale, J., & Dunlop, R. (2010). *An educational leader's guide to curriculum mapping.* Thousand Oaks, CA: Corwin.

Hattie, J. (2009). *Visible learning: A synthesis of over 800 meta-analyses relating to achievement.* New York, NY: Routledge.

Kachur, D., Stout, J., & Edwards, C. (2010). *Classroom walkthroughs to improve teaching and learning*. Larchmont, NY: Eye on Education.

Leong, M., Stepanek, J., Griffin, L., & Lavelle, L. (2011). *Teaching by design in elementary mathematics, Grades 4–5*. Thousand Oaks, CA: Corwin.

Levine, D. U., & Lezotte, L. W. (1990). *Unusually effective schools: A review and analysis of research and practice*. Madison, WI: The National Center for Effective Schools Research & Development.

Lezotte, L. W. (1992). *Creating the total quality effective school*. Okemos, MI: Effective Schools Products, Ltd.1-800-827-8041.

Lezotte, L. W. (1997). *Learning for all*. Okemos, MI: Effective Schools Products, Ltd. 1-800-827-8041.

Lezotte, L. W., & Cipriano Pepperl, J. (1999). *What the effective schools research says: Safe and orderly environment*. Okemos, MI: Effective Schools Products, Ltd.

Lezotte, L. W., & Jacoby, B. C. (1992). *Sustainable school reform: The district context for school improvement*. Okemos, MI: Effective Schools Products, Ltd. 1-800-827-8041.

Lezotte, L. W., & McKee, K. (2006). *Stepping up: Leading the charge to improve our schools*. Okemos, MI: Effective Schools Products, Ltd. 1-800-827-8041.

Lezotte, L. W. et al. (1986–present). Various topics in Effective Schools Research Abstracts. Available from Effective Schools Products, Ltd., Okemos, MI (1-800-827-8041).

Makas, E. (2011). *From mandate to achievement: 5 steps to a curriculum system that works*. Thousand Oaks, CA: Corwin.

Psencik, K. (2009). *Accelerating student and staff learning: Purposeful curriculum collaboration*. Thousand Oaks, CA: Corwin.

Reeves, D. B. (1996–1998). *Making standards work: How to implement standards-based assessments in the classroom, school, and district*. Denver, CO: Center for Performance Assessment.

Reeves, D. B. (2000). *Accountability in action: A blueprint for learning organizations*. Denver, CO: Advanced Learning Press.

Reeves, D. B. (2001). *101 questions & answers about standards, assessment, and accountability*. Denver, CO: Advanced Learning Press.

Reeves, D. B. (2002). *Leader's guide to standards*. San Francisco, CA: Jossey-Bass.

Reeves, D. B. (2004). *Accountability for learning*. Alexandria, VA: Association for Supervision and Curriculum Development.

Reeves, D. B. (2004). *101 more Q&A about standards, assessment, and accountability*. Denver, CO: Advanced Learning Press.

Schmoker, M. (1996). *Results: The key to continuous school improvement*. Alexandria, VA: Association for Supervision and Curriculum Development.

Schmoker, M. (2006). *Results now: How we can achieve unprecedented improvements in teaching and learning*. Alexandria, VA: Association for Supervision and Curriculum Development.

Schmoker, M. (2010). *The results fieldbook: Practical strategies from dramatically improved schools*. Alexandria, VA: Association for Supervision and Curriculum Development.

Schmoker, M. (2011). *Focus: Elevating the essentials to radically improve student learning*. Alexandria, VA: Association for Supervision and Curriculum Development.

Solomon, P. G. (2009). *The curriculum bridge: From standards to actual practice*. Thousand Oaks, CA: Corwin.

Stepanek, J., Leong, M., Griffin, L., & Lavelle, L. (2011). *Teaching by design in elementary math, Grades 4–5*. Thousand Oaks, CA: Corwin.

Stepanek, J., Leong, M., Griffin, L., & Lavelle, L. (2011). *Teaching by design in elementary math, Grades 2–3*. Thousand Oaks, CA: Corwin.

Squires, D. A. (2009). *Curriculum alignment: research-based strategies for increasing student achievement*. Thousand Oaks, CA: Corwin.

Tedlow, R. S. (2005, December 12). The education of Andy Grove. *Fortune, 152,* 12.

Tuchman Glass, K. (2005). *Curriculum design for writing instruction: Creating standards-based lesson plans and rubrics*. Thousand Oaks, CA: Corwin.

Tuchman Glass, K. (2007). *Curriculum mapping: A step-by-step guide for creating curriculum year overviews*. Thousand Oaks, CA: Corwin.

Wiggins, G., & McTighe, J. (2005). *Understanding by design* (2nd ed.). Alexandria, VA: Association for Supervision and Curriculum Development.

Index